Hitler and Nazi Germany
The Seduction of a Nation

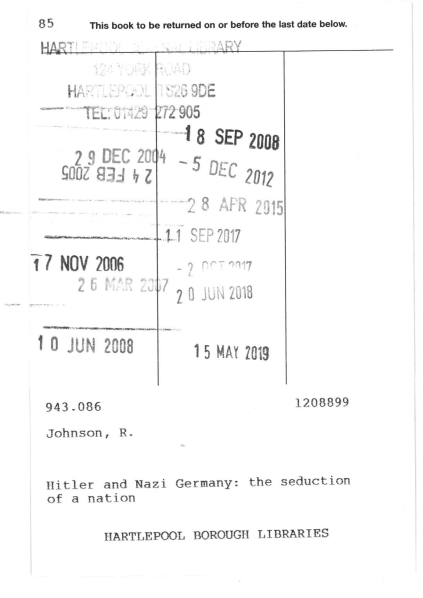

D0785910

Studymates

British History 1870–1918
Business Organisation
The Changing Nature of Warfare 1792–1918
English Reformation
European History 1870–1918
European Reformation
Genetics
Getting Started in Radio
Hitler and Nazi Germany (3rd edition)
Burr's Land Law
Lenin, Stalin and Communist Russia
Macroeconomics
Organic Chemistry
Poems To Live By
Practical Drama & Theatre Arts
Revolutionary Conflicts
Social Anthropology
Social Statistics
Speaking Better French
Speaking English
Studying Chaucer
Studying History
Studying Literature
Studying Poetry
The New Science Teacher's Handbook
Troubleshoot Your Problems
Understanding Forces
Understanding Maths
Using Information Technology
War Poets 1914–18
Writing an Academic Essay
Writing Your Master's Thesis

Many other titles in preparation

Studymates

Hitler and Nazi Germany

The Seduction of a Nation

3rd edition

Dr Robert Johnson

with a foreword by Professor Jeremy Black

'Those who forget the past are condemned to repeat it.'

(The inscription on the memorial at Belsen Concentration Camp)

First published in 2004 by Studymates Limited, PO Box 2, Bishops Lydeard, Somerset TA4 3YE, United Kingdom

Telephone: (01823) 432002
Fax: (01823) 430097
Website: http://www.studymates.co.uk

Typeset by PDQ Typesetting, Newcastle-under-Lyme
Printed and bound in Great Britain by The Baskerville Press Ltd.

Contents

List of Illustrations

Picture credits and acknowledgements

Peter Padfield, Himmler (London, 1990); Centre for the Study of Cartoons and Caricature, University of Kent, Canterbury; the Imperial War Museum, London; German Poster Museum, Essen; Popperfoto; Ullstein Bilderdienst, Berlin; Süddeutscher Verlag, Munich; Hultan Getty; AKG, London; the Bettmann Archive; Zeitgerchichtliches Bildarchiv; Museum für Deutsche Geschichte. The author would also like to acknowledge the following for the extracts in this book: Exeter University Press; Oldham Press Ltd; Weidenfeld and Nicolson Ltd; Palgrave-Macmillan Ltd; Penguin Books Ltd; Hodder and Stoughton; marxists.org/glossary/people/e/pix/ebert.jpg. This book is dedicated to Emilie.

Foreword

This is a vigorous, clear and judicious account of one of the seminal periods in recent history. Within the constraints of the available space, Robert Johnson has produced a comprehensive and thorough account that will be of great value for history students. It is worthy of attention, not least because it is clear that Hitler was not some aberration in European history, but the product of strong tendencies, some of which, alas, are still with us. Thus this book serves both as a valuable introductory historical account and a timely warning for the modern world.

Professor Jeremy Black
University of Exeter

Introduction

This new edition is not only revised and updated with all the recent historiography of the last five years, but has been substantially restructured to incorporate more on the Weimar Republic, the Holocaust and Nazi social policies. Thanks to you, the readers, this book reflects areas of current interest and great historical importance in a succinct form: many have helped shape the format and the contents by their kind and helpful suggestions.

There continue to be many pressures for students to contend with, especially in the first year of university, at AS/A2 level, or prior to examinations. History is an academic subject that demands an analytical approach to historical problems and a command of a wide range of factual material, and, more importantly, access to a broad historiography. Students are expected to be well-read, and familiar with all the historical arguments and approaches. With a subject like Hitler and the Third Reich, there is a relevance to courses beyond history, but the problem is the same: how do you gather all the important information, process all the data, and become aware of the arguments of other historians in a short space of time? That's where this guide comes in.

The aim of this Studymate is to provide you, the reader, with rapid access to the key themes, vital details, and historical debates on Hitler and Nazi Germany. It can be used as a study or revision guide, or as a starting point for courses that are run in more depth. The emphasis of this book is towards a concise and streamlined framework, that is detailed enough to provide you with all the important material. It is designed to be your guide for essays, seminars and formal classes. It is also interactive: there are small confirmatory activities and tasks to complete at the end of each chapter. As the chapters are short, you will find that you are able to work through the book quickly.

I do hope that you find this new edition useful, stimulating and accessible, and I wish you the best of luck in your studies.

Rob Johnson@studymates.co.uk

Hitler, History and the Historians

One-minute overview – Hitler's background is obscure and has been the subject of much speculation. In his early life he had attempted to become an artist in Vienna, but was turned down by the art college he applied to. He spent months drifting through the capital of the multi-racial Austro-Hungarian Empire and absorbed some political ideas. He interpreted world history as a struggle between races and regarded ethnic Germans as superior to Eastern Europeans. He felt it was no accident that the Germanic Austrians had colonised the Slav peoples of central Europe and the Balkans. Regarding himself as essentially 'German', he enlisted in the Kaiser's forces in 1914. After his experiences in the First World War, his solutions to Germany's problems became radical, racist and militaristic. For a time he was an army spy, but he soon joined a band of right-wing extremists. The early Nazi party aimed to seize power by a coup d'état (armed takeover) but in 1923 their first attempt failed. Hitler was imprisoned, during which he wrote his autobiography Mein Kampf.

From these inauspicious beginnings, Hitler went on to secure power just ten years later and mobilised the German people en masse, hurling them into history's most destructive conflict. In his name, millions of men, women and children were bombed, shot, gassed and tortured. Unsurprisingly, Hitler has become the most notorious figure in world historiography. There are literally thousands of books, articles and websites on Hitler and Nazi Germany. What is the cause of this obsession? Was Hitler mad, or perhaps 'evil'? Why was he able to secure power with so much popular support, and what does this tell us about the state of mind of the German people in the 1930s?

In this chapter you will learn:
- ▶ *The significance of Hitler in history.*
- ▶ *Hitler's early life.*
- ▶ *The Weimar Republic and the early history of the Nazi Party.*

...ificance of Hitler in history

...... is great interest in the study of Hitler and Nazi Germany

Adolf Hitler continues to exert a powerful influence on Western historiography (the writing of history). For good or ill, many academic institutions include a course on the Nazi dictator. Thousands of books, journals and web pages

Figure 1. Hitler in a frenzy during a public speech.

contribute to the great mass of detail on Hitler's life and deeds. In Germany, there is some disquiet about this fascination with Nazism, particularly as there have been over fifty years of successful democracy in that country. Those who argue that there was something intrinsically 'wrong' with the Germans must now acknowledge that, in the broad scheme of history, German people were no different from other Europeans. This is especially true when it comes to manifestations of racism. Anti-Semitism was, sadly, not an issue confined to Germany in the 1930s and 1940s, for France and Russia had their own episodes of violent persecution. Indeed, racialist categorisations could be found in all the European empires which dominated the globe in the first half of the twentieth century.

The gravity of Hitler's crimes makes him the focus of intense study

The chief reason why Hitler and Nazi Germany is the focus of so much attention is that the Nazis were able to mobilise millions of people from a modern European state, launch them into the most destructive war in world history and commit hideous crimes against humanity in the death camps. In short, Hitler is notorious because he presided over mass mobilisation and mass murder.

It was not Hitler, but what he represented, that explains support for the Nazi regime

Hitler compels a fascination because, when exposed to analysis, he appears to have been such an unlikely leader. Ian Kershaw notes that both the left and the right wings underestimated him. Too much emphasis has been laid on his ability as a public orator to explain his 'effect' on the German people, although those close to him have testified to a certain magnetism. This attraction was not based on a traditional loyalty, even though some worshipped him, but rather more on his 'other worldly' quality – something approaching a supernatural appeal. Even

Hitler's closest associates regarded him as a 'distant' individual. No doubt his cosmic vision seemed to elevate people's hopes for a brighter future at a time of acute economic and political distress, but loyalty to the legitimate government is a far more effective means of explaining support for Hitler. This helps us to understand why so many Germans continued to back the regime to the very end.

> ## COMMENT
> *It is all too easy to explain Nazism as Hitler-ism, that is, to focus on an individual and his actions, but much of Hitler's so-called 'charisma' was attributed to him by his followers because of his objectives and Germany's apparently 'desperate' situation.*

The Germans were not simply the willing agents of Nazism

Among the more absurd ideas about Hitler's Germany is that the majority of people 'willingly' embraced every facet, however extreme, of Nazi ideology. The fact is that people did not. The majority endured the Nazi regime, and, in a completely human and understandable way, they adapted their lives to avoid trouble with the government, or continued with their jobs 'to make ends meet'. The focus on 'ordinary Germans' has intensified in the last decade but generalisations have proved remarkably difficult. What is clear is that large numbers of Germans believed the Nazis could provide a solution to the short-term problems of the Depression. Many were attracted by the radicalism of the party and the Nazis' intolerance of the country's difficulties. Hitler offered a solution that was simple and decisive. Nevertheless, despite the broad, cross-class appeal of the early years, the fact is that more people opposed the Nazis than supported them. It is simply the case that, as the Third Reich became established, people got better at concealing their views.

German reactions to Nazism were human ones

The war changed the sway of opinion in Germany. Goebbels, the Propaganda Minister, noted in his infamous diaries that the German people had fallen into a 'light depression' when the war broke out. The rapid victories of 1940 brought a sense of relief, as there had been widespread fear of a repeat of the slaughter that had characterised the First World War. However, a gap appeared between the

Figure 2. Josef Goebbels – the Nazi propagandist – rallies the public in the 1920s.

attitudes on the Home Front and amongst the personnel in the operational theatres. Surrounded by death and destruction, and directed by distant authorities to punish 'sub-human' enemies, sections of the German army killed civilians and prisoners. It is noticeable how the Red Army of the Soviet Union also encouraged its personnel to punish and murder, in contrast to the Western governments who regarded atrocities by troops as illegal. However, as Christopher Browning has shown in *Ordinary Men* (2001), not every German soldier obeyed the command to kill non-combatants. Some refused, and sympathetic commanders did not punish them, but military discipline was sufficient to ensure obedience in many more cases. However, in the death camps, the enigma surrounding the attitude of the Nazi personnel has yet to be fully unravelled. If testimonies are to be believed at face value, there is a strong suggestion that both inmates and staff blocked out the reality of what was happening and entered a twilight world. The numbness of shock also characterised the civilians who were bombed out, were raped by Red Army troops, or witnessed the horror of the dismembered dead.

Could it happen again?

In the last decades of the twentieth century, Germany has established democracy and enjoyed economic prosperity. There is almost universal loathing of the Nazi period, and the neo-Nazis are a noisy, offensive and irrelevant minority. Germany

Figure 3. Hitler as Wagnerian hero.

was reunified in 1990 without the resurgence of militant nationalism that marked the 1930s. Moreover benign traditions in Germany have survived, from wine festivals to impassioned performances of Wagner, despite the attempts by the Nazis to incorporate all these events within their own rituals. In fact, the remarkable thing is that Nazism has not survived as a world ideology in the same way that, say, communism or militant Islam did. Nevertheless, part of the fascination with the study of Nazism is the fear that it could happen again. After all, the Weimar Republic was a progressive democracy not unlike our own. Yet Kershaw notes that the return of the style of politics of the 1930s – with its justification of racism and imperialist aggression – is very unlikely. What is more likely is the transformation of Western liberal democracy as it adjusts to the threats of international terrorism, the proliferation of weapons of mass destruction and rivalry for scarce resources. However, ideologues and extremists – whether Islamic fundamentalists or eco-warriors – will probably also challenge and threaten democracy in the next few decades.

There is still merit in studying the phenomenon of Nazism

Some academics are troubled by sensationalist documentaries on the Nazis, and the almost lurid obsession with every aspect of Hitler's life, including the intimate. Whilst historians welcome the airing of opinion, the welter of debate, and the fresh analysis derived from new and original research, there is disquiet about 'the trivialisation of Nazism in the mass media', as Kershaw puts it. The German Ambassador to Britain lamented the continued emphasis on Hitler in academia and the media, and a group of intellectuals gathered in 2002 to call for a broadening of British historical studies beyond 'Hitler and the Henrys'. In the final analysis it is clear we have benefited from our studies of this subject. Awareness of the folly of dogmatic ideology, of racism, of imperial wars and of genocide is greater now than ever before. Although peace movements continue to condemn war, democratic governments have shown resolve in resisting modern forms of fascism and fundamentalism. In this respect, the history of Hitler and Nazi Germany has something to teach us. Moreover, in the end, the free world defeated Hitler: his twisted world-view was, as Churchill put it: 'purged and . . .blasted from the surface of the earth'. For that, we should be ever grateful to the generation of the 1940s.

Hitler's early life

Hitler's early life is obscure

The main source on Hitler's early life is his autobiography, *Mein Kampf* (*My Struggle*). However, historians disagree on its accuracy, so there seems to be some doubt on how, or when, Hitler developed his ideas. He was born at Braunau am Inn, right on the border between Austria and Germany. His strict father, Alois, was a customs official who regulated business between two German-speaking countries.

Figure 4. Hitler in the First World War.

Hitler was mediocre at school, and left home for Vienna in 1907 when his parents died. Vienna was the capital of the multi-racial Austrian Empire, and Hitler appears to have drifted through the poor districts of the city having been rejected in his application to the Academy of Fine Arts. It is likely he grew bitter about his poverty, and always considered himself an artist. It is also possible that he developed a loathing of Jews, and picked up political ideas in cafe debates.

Germany and Austria-Hungary pursued aggressive policies, 1899–1914

Germany and Austria-Hungary shared a common desire to maintain their imperial prestige against rival states in the early twentieth century. Both empires were also afraid of nationalist movements. Austria's rulers hoped to preserve the monarchy and its power, despite the growing nationalist assertiveness of the Hungarians, Croats, Serbs and Czechs. Germany's elites were less concerned with their own racial minorities, but looked anxiously over the border at Russian nationalism. Nevertheless, their greatest worry was the rising support for left-wing organisations within the Reich. Both Germany and Austria shared a deep distrust of France and Russia, two powers that had signed a military alliance to contain Germanic ambitions in 1893. The Kaiser of Germany grew more aggressive and unpredictable, and, by 1912, he was secretly advocating a 'great fight' to destroy the power of France, Russia and their partner, Great Britain. The Kaiser also advocated the colonisation of Eastern Europe as *Lebensraum* 'living space' for the surplus urban population of Germany.

The elites feared the masses of Germany

The German historians of the 1960s and 1970s suggested that the Kaiser's bullish diplomacy before the First World War could be explained by his deep-seated fear of the German masses. Democracy was certainly a sham for, although there were political parties, they had no influence over matters of state. Worse, the Kaiser privately designated a third of his own population *Reichsfeinde* – enemies of the state – because they held views he despised. To solve his domestic problem, the Kaiser welcomed a war as a means of unifying his country with nationalism.

The rise of the far right could be traced to this period

It is noticeable that, despite the growth of moderate democratic parties, such as the Social Democratic Party (SPD) in the *Reichstag* (lower house of parliament), there was also an increase in support for far right movements, especially amongst the middle classes. It was a phenomenon that inspired Karl Bracher to suggest that the roots of National Socialism (Nazism) could be traced back to pre-First World War antecedents. Certainly it is striking how the Agrarian League or the Navy League members favoured aggressive, nationalist, expansionist and anti-Semitic beliefs, but none of them exactly represented the cross-class appeal of the programme of Nazism that was to appear in the early 1920s.

Hitler's reaction to the First World War and defeat

The outbreak of the First World War was, to Hitler, a blessing. He rejected the multi-racial Austrian army and enlisted in the German forces. He admired the army's sense of purpose and discipline and he observed with pride the way the war had mobilised millions for a national cause. Hitler acted as a 'runner' in the trenches, delivering messages under fire for which he was decorated twice, receiving the Iron Cross, Germany's highest award for bravery. He felt that others, especially civilians at home, should have shown more courage and endurance during the war, and believed that this would have saved Germany from defeat. When the war ended, Hitler was recovering in Passewalk hospital from a gas attack. He was bitterly disappointed by the defeat. He believed that enemies of Germany had undermined the country's will to win and that the soldiers had been 'stabbed in the back'. He felt that these people were dangerous and had to be neutralised.

Hitler's wartime experiences were formative

Hitler's war experiences should not be underestimated. Alan Bullock and Ian Kershaw, who have written biographies of Hitler, suggest that Hitler's military service explains many of his ideas. Psychologists have suggested many theories, but none have the same substantial evidence of the biographers. The war, and the consequences of Germany's defeat in 1918 seemed to clarify Hitler's beliefs. Many German units were relatively unscathed by the fighting of 1918, and almost all were still situated on French soil following their victory against the Russians in 1917.

Figure 5. Hitler in Bavarian dress, 1924.

Hitler was unaware that German troops facing the main Allied effort had collapsed, and his bitterness was intense.

The Revolution of 1918 and the internal collapse of Germany

In Germany, food riots indicated that the civilian population had been pushed to the limit of endurance with shortages caused by the Allied naval blockade. The German sailors of the *Kriegsmarine* refused to set sail for a last-ditch attack on the Royal Navy and mutinied. The Kaiser abdicated.

The Weimar Republic and the early history of the Nazi Party 1919–23

This section is organised as follows:

▶ The Weimar Republic – constitutional weaknesses.
▶ The Putschist years.
▶ The Treaty of Versailles.
▶ The Ruhr crisis and hyperinflation.
▶ The formation of the Nazi Party.
▶ The Munich Putsch.

The Weimar Republic – constitutional weaknesses

When the old Kaiser abdicated, the powers of the Imperial Chancellor were handed to Freidrich Ebert, a moderate politician of the old *Reichstag*. To forestall

any move by German communists, a democratic republic was proclaimed. A fatal split had developed between the moderate left, represented by Ebert and the Social Democratic Party, and the extreme left, under Karl Liebknecht. Ebert quickly secured the loyalty of the old civil service and of the German army in a deal brokered by General Groener. Historians of the Weimar Republic have looked for the seeds of later decline in this early period and two

Figure 6. Karl Liebknecht, the points are immediately apparent:
Spartakist leader, killed in 1919.

1.   The army had no true loyalty to the Weimar Republic as they saw the SPD as the lesser of two evils (the other being the communists).

2. The division of the left would mean a fundamental inc
    face of a common, right-wing threat.

Edgar Feuchtwanger points out that this view needs to b
since the circumstances in which Hitler later gained power were s
those in 1918–1919. However, Feuchtwanger is critical of Ebert's failure to
properly control the army.

There are doubts about the loyalties of the people to the early Weimar Republic

The constitution of the Weimar Republic was very democratic and this fact alone
proves the Germans were quite capable of engaging in moderate politics. This, in
turn, means any idea that Hitler's rise to power was 'inevitable' is also wrong.
When the first elections were held for a Constituent Assembly in 1919, the

moderate SPD gained a majority of the seats and
they dominated the General Congress of Workers
and Soldiers Councils (which represented grass
roots opinion). However, the SPD were dependent
on other parties to form a government and to sustain
support for the republic. In addition, recent research
has shown that the councils, especially outside of the
great cities, were made up of middle class delegates.
The demobilised soldiers, the *Freikorps* (Free
Corps), were also strongly represented. These facts
mean that sympathy for democracy may have been
doubtful, at least early on.

Figure 7. Gustav Stresemann,
Foreign Minister and Chancellor
of the Weimar Republic.

The provisions of the constitution were its strengths

▶ The system was one of proportional representation, so that all groups could be
  heard, including minorities.

▶ The vulnerable in society were protected by the state. These included: those
  unable to work through illness or old age; men and women were granted a right
  to work; insurance was to be provided to all those incapacitated by illness or
  accident; the unemployed were to be supported.

▶ All citizens were equal before the law. The President was not above the law.

▶ There was freedom of speech and freedom of conscience (religious worship).

There was universal suffrage.

There were weaknesses in the constitution

▶ Delegates owed their loyalty to the party (which selected them), not to their constituents (voters).

▶ Some parties were committed to the destruction of democracy.

▶ Article 48 gave the President unlimited powers of Emergency Decree.

▶ Weak and short-lived governments were common because the parties had to compromise, but they found this close co-operation difficult in a crisis.

▶ There was a great deal of faith in 'strong' leaders and figures of authority, especially in times of crisis.

Revolution!
▶ Street fighting
▶ Abdication of the Head of State
▶ Economic hardship caused by the war

Restoration of order
▶ Democratic politicians strike a deal with the army
▶ Free Corps paramilitarites crush the Far Left

Challenges for the 1920s
▶ Constitutional flaws – too much power in the hands of the executive
▶ Political elites unenthusiastic about democracy
▶ Terms of defeat imposed by the Allies at Versailles
▶ Extremist groups and parties still at large

Figure 8. The Weimar Republic in crisis.

The Putschist years

The threats from the extreme left
Amidst unrest and street fighting of the November 1918 Revolution, a republican government was established at Weimar, but almost immediately it faced a communist coup d'état attempt by a party called the Spartakists. Their leaders,

Rosa Luxemburg and Karl Liebknecht, were killed as
formations of demobilised soldiers known as *Freikorps*
(Free Corps) continued to fight for their country, as
they saw it, against 'foreign idealists'. The success of
the *Freikorps*, both inside Germany and, a few months
later, in the Baltic Republics of Estonia and Lithuania,
convinced Hitler of the value of such groups in
Germany's future. These paramilitaries, he reasoned,
could save Germany against its internal foes. The
Freikorps were so successful in fact that the Weimar
government felt unable to ban them, particularly when

Figure 9. Rosa Luxemburg,
communist intellectual.

the communist threat continued to hover over the Republic. In April 1919,
communists declared Munich a Soviet Republic, and, after three weeks, the
Freikorps joined regular army units in crushing the Reds. These events coincided
with a bloody civil war in Russia in which Bolsheviks (communists) were trying to
secure power. What made the Russian situation so alarming was the Bolshevik
call for a 'world revolution': they wanted German communists to rise up and join
them and there was some contact between the Bolsheviks and the German USPD
(communist) party. However, the threat subsided when the Bolsheviks were
defeated by the Polish outside Warsaw in 1920.

Kapp's Putsch was a right wing attempt to seize power
Dr Kapp, a *Freikorps* leader, felt emboldened by the defeat of the communists to
replace the moderate socialists of the Weimar Republic. The trigger for his Putsch

(attempt to take power) was the decision to
accept the Allied demand for a reduction in the
size of the regular army. When Ebert asked if
the army, under General von Seekt, would
support the government against Kapp's right
wing coup, there was reluctance to act.
Crucially, therefore, the army was unreliable
when it came to fighting the far right.
Nevertheless, the trade unions across Germany
refused to support Kapp's illegal declarations
of power and went on a general strike. Germany
came to a standstill. Even conservatives,
sympathetic to the right, thought Kapp's

Figure 10. Friedrich Ebert,
first President of Germany in 1919.

actions were foolhardy. Dr Kapp fled, lacking

Figure 11. *Freikorps*, 1919.

any popular support. However, the army was immediately deployed against communists in the Ruhr, the so-called Red Guards, who tried to turn the general strike into a full-scale assault on the republic. These events indicate just how weak the Weimar government was, and how dependent it had become on the fragile loyalties of the army and the trade unions. It has been suggested that Weimar was 'a republic without republicans', but this may be an exaggeration. The fact is, despite the crises it faced, the Weimar Republic survived.

The Treaty of Versailles

There are problems in interpretation over the Treaty of Versailles
Many are convinced that the Treaty of Versailles, the peace settlement for Germany after the First World War, was unduly harsh, and, as a result, Hitler was inspired to launch a second European war in 1939. However, there are fundamental problems with this simplistic analysis. It assumes that Hitler's rise to power was either inevitable or closely connected to the terms of the Treaty. In fact it was not. Hitler spent the years 1919–30 criticising the Treaty of Versailles with negligible effect on the German population. Those who supported him were largely concerned with domestic matters. Moreover, many of the treaty terms had already been revised before Hitler came to power.

German democracy was tarnished
Nevertheless, the *perception* of the German people in 1919 was that Versailles was too harsh. The strong reaction against the peace terms when they were announced on 7 May 1919 was understandable when the Germans had expected victory just 12 months before. The terms were lenient compared with those presented by Germany to the Russians at Brest Litovsk, and the ones they had *planned* to present to the West, if they had won. Moreover, the infamous 'war guilt clause', the section that stated Germany had been responsible for causing the war, does now seem to have been justified: Germany had planned the First World War at least two years before its outbreak. What *is* controversial is that the democratic government of Weimar had to bear the punishment for a crime committed by the old Kaiser

and his military elite. Since the Weimar politicians accepted the terms of the Treaty of Versailles, Germany was left with what Richard Grunberger called: 'the ugly birthmark of defeat'.

The terms of the Treaty of Versailles

► Germany was stripped of her overseas colonies, namely Togoland, Kamerun, German South West Africa, German East Africa, German New Guinea and her Pacific islands. Although German nationalists complained, the colonies were of little economic value to Germany and its possessions were on a small scale compared to Britain and France.

► Germany lost Alsace-Lorraine, but these provinces had been stolen from France at the end of the Franco-Prussian War (1870–71) so they were being restored. By contrast, France was not tempted to annex the Rhineland and the Allies insisted only on a demilitarised zone.

► The Germans had to accept a temporary army of occupation on the Rhine. The British contingent left in 1926 and the French in 1930.

► The rich coal mining Saar basin was administered by the new League of Nations, but it was to be allowed to rejoin Germany if its people so wished.

► Very small territories were offered to Belgium (Eupen and Malmedy), and Memmel was given to Lithuania.

► Given the destructive record of the German armed forces, it was not surprising that the Allies insisted on their reduction (100,000 troops, no airforce and a coastal defence flotilla).

The only controversial elements concerned the territories of the east and war reparations.

► Germany was forbidden to unify with Austria in order to reduce the scale of her political and military influence in Central Europe.

► Germany was denied the 'self-determination' of its peoples when the 'Polish Corridor' was created. The strip of land was given to Poland in order to provide it with access to the sea and thus a viable economic future.

► The war reparations were to be the least effective aspect of the Treaty of Versailles, and the most damaging to the reputation of the Weimar Republic. The French were eager to ensure that, with their own industrial sector devastated by the war, the Germans did not recover more quickly than themselves.

The German public were angry

Germany had lost 1.8 million men, ended the war on foreign soil, and were forced
to pay for reparations. It had lost its colonies and some German territory.
Germans regarded the Treaty of Versailles as the 'Diktat' (dictated peace), when
every expectation had been that the November Armistice was the prelude to
negotiations. The Nazis later claimed the treaty had been part of a grand anti-
German conspiracy which the anti-patriotic elements, the 'November
Criminals', had eagerly connived in.

The Ruhr crisis and hyperinflation

The figure of how much Germany would have to pay in reparations repayments to
the Allies was announced in 1921. However, the Weimar Republic defaulted on its
instalment of 1922, and as a result the French army (and some Belgian units) invaded
Germany and occupied the Ruhr basin between January and September 1923. The
Ruhr was the industrial heartland of the Republic, and the French seemed to believe
that the Germans would simply continue to work whilst the profits would go directly
to France. However, when the German workforce refused to co-operate, the French
brought in their own workers and began to extract what they could. The French were
criticised for their 'aggression'. The effect of this was to create a reluctance to enforce
the terms of the Treaty of Versailles. The will to act evaporated in a wave of pacifism in
the 1930s. According to Anthony Lentin, it was in fact this failure to *enforce* the treaty
that was far more important than the terms of the treaty itself.

Weimar seemed to be powerless

The passive nature of the Weimar government's resistance, and their capitulation,
infuriated German nationalists. In fact, there were episodes of violence between
German people in the Ruhr and the French, but the Weimar government did not
defend the area. In addition, the government's attempt to deal with the loss of its
primary industrial region, and therefore a large slice of its revenue, was to print
more currency. This option was chosen partly because it was feared that an
increase in taxation would provoke the German public into revolutionary action.
The problem was that inflation had been steadily increasing in Germany from the
war years (resulting in a fall in value of each *Reichsmark*). However, whereas in
the war years, the government had issued bonds to raise capital, that facility no
longer existed in peacetime. Without gold reserves to sell off, only good German
industrial performance backed the currency, and the French occupation took this
out of the government's hands. This led to hyperinflation, and the value of the
German *Reichsmark* collapsed.

One *Reichsmark* in 1913 would need 450 in 1923 to have the same spending power. Savings in banks evaporated. German citizens had to pay thousands, even millions of *Reichsmarks*, simply for a loaf of bread. A kilo of potatoes cost 1.24 million marks. Workers who were paid in the mornings discovered their wages could be rendered practically worthless by the time they reached the shops in the evenings. Desperate, the government attempted to negotiate for the withdrawal of the French, and introduced the *Rentenmark*, a temporary currency, on 20 November 1923. This had the immediate effect of revaluing the mark. In the long term, many Germans lost faith in the financial security of the German state. Some had lost savings, but, as always, it was the poorest who suffered the most. The hyperinflation was, however, short-lived.

Far left **KPD**	**Form of government:** communism, but taking guidance from Moscow **Preferred economic system:** state ownership of all production, exchange and distribution **Foreign policy:** defend USSR against fascism
Socialist left Some members of the **SPD**	**Form of government:** democracy **Preferred economic system:** state ownership of the economy with welfare support for the poor **Foreign policy:** peace
Moderate left **SPD**	**Form of government:** democracy **Preferred economic system:** regulated capitalism with welfare support for the poor **Foreign policy:** peace
Centre **Centre Party**	**Form of government:** democracy **Preferred economic system:** limited regulation of capitalism with welfare support for the poor **Foreign policy:** peace
Moderate right **DVP**	**Form of government:** (initially monarchist) democracy **Preferred economic system:** unfettered capitalism **Foreign policy:** revision of the Treaty of Versailles by diplomacy
Nationalist right **DNVP** and **BVP**	**Form of government:** tolerates democracy, but prefers strong leadership **Preferred economic system:** unfettered capitalism **Foreign policy:** robust defence of national interests
Far right **NSDAP**	**Form of government:** strong leadership, racial state that excludes foreigners **Preferred economic system:** regulated capitalism **Foreign policy:** complete revision of Versailles settlement; war if necessary

Figure 12. The spectrum of the political parties.

The formation of the Nazi Party

Hitler joined the German Workers' Party in 1919
The German Workers' Party (*Deutsche Arbeiter Partei*) was founded on 9 January 1919 by Anton Drexler, a railway engineer, and was led by a committee, chaired by a journalist, Karl Harrar. The early party was anti-Semitic and nationalist, but stood out from many other groups of this type by its appeal to a mass audience. Hitler's initial contact with this group was subversive. As a specially selected army spy, he was ordered to observe this organisation for fear that it was a left-wing 'workers' movement. However, Hitler quickly realised that its title was misleading. He was attracted to it primarily by its nationalism, but also its appeal to all Germans. He left the army and joined as its 55th member, rapidly impressing the other members with his oratory style, a mixture of angry outbursts and dramatic gesturing.

Hitler drew up the party programme
Hitler rose rapidly in the movement, and he was promoted to chief of propaganda. However, Hitler was impatient with the endless dialogue of party meetings and longed for action. He assisted Drexler and Gottfried Feder in drawing up a party programme which was issued in February 1920. The party programme stressed a commitment to the restoration of Germany's pre-war borders and a new definition of citizenship based on ethnicity as a German. There was a general attack on big business and on the communists, whilst the rights of the workers and lower middle classes were promoted. Hitler's ideas were clearly evident, and the party was renamed the National Socialist German Workers' Party or NSDAP (*Nationalsozialistische Deutsche Arbeiterpartei*) in 1920 from which the shortened version, 'Nazi', was derived.

Bavaria became a haven for the right wing
In 1921, the Weimar government had emerged from the maelstrom of revolution, and after initial misgivings, the army agreed not to interfere in the Republic's politics in return for immunity from reform by the socialist dominated parliament (*Reichstag*). However, in Bavaria, there was little sympathy for the left-wing government and an historic aspiration for autonomy. When the Weimar government banned the *Freikorps* and other extremist, right-wing parties, following a coup d'état attempt by Dr Kapp (1920), the conservative elements of Bavaria refused to do the same. As a result, right-wing parties flocked to Munich, confident of the protection afforded them by the Bavarian leader, Gustav von Kahr.

Hitler became leader of the party

Hitler meanwhile, challenged the committee leadership of the NSDAP, and threatened to resign, unless his demands for changes were met. In the delay, he left. Deprived of their chief propagandist, the party complied with Hitler's demands and he was appointed, not as chairman, but as Führer (leader). This position gave him undisputed control of the party and its direction. By 1922, Hitler was well known enough to have been appointed leader of a coalition of right-wing parties known as the *Kampfbund* (Fighting League). He maintained contact with the German army's commander in Bavaria, General von Lossow, through Captain Ernst Roehm, and established cordial relations with General von Ludendorff, the famous commander of the German Imperial army. Hitler hoped that such a celebrity as Ludendorff would soon bring greater attention to his party on a nationwide basis.

Squads of fighters protected the meetings

The movement was a magnet to some former soldiers and officers, and many of them filled the ranks of the paramilitary squads that protected the meetings from communists. Rising from 3,300 in the middle of 1921, the paramilitaries were known as the SA (*Sturmabteilung*) or Storm Troops, a name given to the formations that had achieved significant battlefield success in 1918).

Figure 13. The 'Old Fighters' of the Munich Putsch retrace their steps in 1934.

The Munich Putsch

The background: The French invaded the Ruhr industrial region

Hitler's opportunity to seize power seemed to arrive in 1923 when the French invaded the Ruhr. The Weimar government failed to resist the invaders and meekly negotiated their withdrawal. For Hitler, such solutions were evidence of the weakness of democracy. He arranged through Captain Roehm, his army contact, that the *Reichswehr* (army) would not intervene against a right-wing coup d'état. He acquired the support of von Kahr, and other members of the Bavarian government, that they would not stand in his way. He briefed von Ludendorff that he was to accompany him into a nationalist government. The moment of seizing power would resemble Mussolini's 'March on Rome', which had occurred the year before (1922). The plan was to seize the Munich government and then advance to Berlin.

Hitler failed to secure the support of the army as he had expected

The Putsch on the 8 November 1923 went wrong. Hitler succeeded in arriving dramatically at a meeting called by von Kahr; firing a pistol into the air with the announcement that the National Revolution had begun. As his party marched on the *Residenz* (Munich provincial government), it was clear that the army had not joined his revolt and that von Kahr had changed his mind about defying the national government in Berlin. Hitler and his comrades faced a hail of bullets, and 14 Nazis were shot down. The Nazis later revered a Swastika flag (the *Blut Fahne*), which allegedly was dipped in the blood of their Putschist comrades, at their subsequent party parades, and every year they staged a reconstruction of the Putsch with the 'old fighters', but the rituals couldn't disguise the fact that the Putsch was a miserable failure.

Hitler was arrested and imprisoned

Hitler was arrested, and tried for treason in 1924. However, he knew that the trial judge was sympathetic to his cause, and, in his defence, Hitler claimed to have been acting for selfless motives of national interest, 'as Germans who wanted the best for their people and their fatherland'. He played to the press in order to achieve maximum publicity. Although he was sentenced to five years, the most lenient sentence available, he only served five months. During his imprisonment at Lansberg, he dictated his autobiography and 'political testament' known as *Mein Kampf*.

The Weimar Republic had survived the Putschist years

Although the Weimar Republic had been rocked by several crises, it had survived each one. Those who believe that the Weimar Republic was inherently weak in 1933 when Hitler took power should acknowledge just how resilient democracy had been in the face of far greater threats between 1919 and 1923. The Weimar Constitution appeared to give considerable powers to the president, especially Article 48, the power of emergency decree, but the moderate parties were able to co-operate sufficiently to preserve democracy. The army was lukewarm about supporting the new republic, but it had not backed Hitler in 1923 and supported democracy against the far left in 1919–21. The Spartakists had tried to overthrow Weimar and remained committed to the destruction of democracy, but they were contained and eventually participated in the democratic process. Hyperinflation and reparations also threatened to reduce Germany to poverty, but German industry began to make a slow recovery. Thus the Weimar Republic appeared to be weak but had proved remarkably successful at surviving the threats.

Tutorial

Progress questions

1. What was Hitler's reaction to the defeat of Germany in 1918?

2. How was the Weimar Republic able to survive revolutionary threats between 1919 and 1923?

3. How did Hitler become leader of the Nazi Party?

4. What aspects of the Weimar Republic and its policies alienated sections of the German population? For example, what angered the right wing?

Discussion point

Why is it that the Weimar Republic and German democracy after 1945 are studied less than Hitler and the Nazi period? What are the disadvantages of this situation?

Practical assignment

Hitler's Beerhall Putsch. Write two or three paragraphs to explain the reason for, and failure of, Hitler's Beerhall Putsch in 1923. Check back through this chapter to make sure that the details are correct. Why did Hitler believe his actions, which were treasonable against his own country, were justified?

Study tips

1. The most typical questions about this period are concerned with the strengths and weaknesses of the Nazis and the Weimar Republic. It is a good idea to be familiar with the various factors by drawing up a list of strengths and weaknesses. When assessing the success or failure of the Weimar Republic, bear in mind that you can judge 'survival' as a success. In other questions about success, try to think what the aims were and whether these aims were achieved wholly or in part.

2. Draw a timeline of events from 1918 to 1923, labelling the incidents in Hitler's early career.

3.   Begin a biographical dossier on the Nazi personalities you come across. If you keep a list in alphabetical order, you will build up a list of who's who as you progress through this book.

4.   Keep a file for 'Hitler's setbacks' and start with the Putsch. This will help you to build up a picture of his failures and ensure that you don't fall into the trap of assuming, as some do, that everything went Hitler's way in his struggle for power.

Why, despite so many critical problems, did the Weimar Republic last so long?	How was Hitler, an extremist with barbaric ideas, able to come to power at all?
Was the Weimar Republic doomed from the outset?	What was it that was appealing about Nazism? Why did so many people vote for Hitler?
Was there a 'Golden Age' for the Weimar Republic?	Was Hitler responsible for his assumption of power (this is known as 'agency'), or were there other factors that propelled him into power?
What were the strengths and weaknesses of the Weimar Republic?	How did the Nazis control society?
What was the nature of the Nazi regime, and why did it persecute so many of its own citizens?	How successful was the Nazi economic programme from 1933 to 1945?

Figure 14. Key questions for historians who study this period.

Hitler's Ideas

One-minute overview – Hitler's autobiography Mein Kampf is also the basis of his political ideas and central to his beliefs was his racial interpretation of the world. All other Nazi philosophies can only be understood with reference to this interpretation, and historians have sometimes failed to analyse Hitler's decisions by not acknowledging this factor sufficiently. Hitler interpreted history as a process whereby races struggled for supremacy. He equated nations with ethnic groups and looked upon the nations of Europe as particularly successful racial types because of their nineteenth-century empire building. However, he believed that for some time, dated either from the French Revolution or the end of the First World War, forces of the left had been undermining the wholesome and traditional values of the right, and consequently of German society. Democracy was a weakening phenomenon in Hitler's eyes since liberals had permitted the spread of degenerate ideas and practices. Most dangerous of all, in Hitler's view, was the elevation of the Jews. They, he argued, were engaged in a conspiracy to interbreed with the higher races of the world, the highest of which were the Aryan Germans. Therefore Hitler saw his mission as the preservation of the German race, and, by extension, of world civilisation.

In this chapter you will learn:
▶ Hitler's racial theory.
▶ Hitler's views on nationalism.
▶ Hitler on national recovery, democracy and socialism.
▶ Hitler's attitude towards physical and mental illness.
▶ Hitler on leadership.
▶ Historical controversies surrounding Hitler's ideas and the origins of Nazism.

Hitler's racial theory

The world 'locked in a struggle for survival'

Hitler's ideas developed at a time when theories about racial characteristics were being used to explain the rise and fall of empires, and the rule of Europeans over other peoples of the world. Darwin's theory about the struggle of animal species (Charles Darwin, *The Origin of Species*) was used in a human context, and races

Figure 15. Charismatic leader?
Hitler surrounded by adoring Nazis.

were thought to be locked in a struggle for survival known as Social Darwinism. As Europeans tried to come to terms with their rapid colonial expansion, some turned to racial interpretations. But Hitler was influenced directly by the ideas of three thinkers.

Gobineau feared racial degeneration

The Count de Gobineau produced a pessimistic view of the world in the 1850s. This minor aristocrat felt that the ordered, cultured world of the nineteenth century was threatened by the ill-educated masses, who would revolt and plunge the world into anarchy. As a linguist, de Gobineau became aware of a connection between language and race. He divided the world into three groups: Black, Yellow and Aryan. To the Aryans he ascribed the greatest cultural achievements, and felt mankind would tolerate a degree of racial interbreeding for its enhancement, but he feared that this process could also lead to degeneracy and predicted that this would occur in 5,000 years' time.

Wagner believed in a super race

The second influential character for Hitler was the composer and philosopher, Richard Wagner. Wagner was a Romantic, part of a philosophical movement that rejected modernism (represented by the industrial world) in favour of a rural, pre-industrial and spiritual idyll. Wagner also viewed the world in racial terms and hated Jews as 'outsiders' in Germany. After meeting de Gobineau, he believed the inevitable degeneration of mankind could be reversed by the breeding of a super race (*Herrenvolk*). This application of Darwinian science was a commonly-held idea in the nineteenth century, but Wagner was especially important to Hitler. Hitler adored Wagner's fantasy operas which emphasised the ability of individual heroes to change destiny.

Chamberlain applied a 'scientific' analysis to race

Houston Chamberlain was the third influence on Hitler. Chamberlain married Wagner's daughter and had been decorated during the war for anti-British

Figure 16. Nazi election poster: Germany Awake!

propaganda, but he was influential because of his book, *Foundations of the Nineteenth Century* (1899), in which he argued that racial mixing in the Austrian Empire had eroded Germanic culture. He felt that the fall of the Empire was inevitable, just as the Roman Empire had fallen, because of the diluting effect of racial interbreeding. Chamberlain's language was emotional, but was backed with an empirical and moderate approach which he had developed from his career as a plant biologist. Chamberlain concluded that the Jews were the greatest threat to the German race, a view shared by Hitler's schoolteacher, who in turn, passed on the ideas to Hitler himself.

Hitler regarded the Jews of Europe as parasites

Hitler inherited the idea that nations were essentially racial groupings. The supreme group were the Aryans, and the Germanic peoples in particular (Austrian and German, but also to some extent Scandinavians and English), since they had produced the greatest leaders and artists in history; such as Beethoven, Goethe, Schiller, Hegel, and Bismarck. Other races in the world were weaker and produced fewer, if any, 'great men'. At the bottom of the scale for Hitler were Slavs and gypsies from Eastern Europe, and below these were the Jews. Hitler believed that the Jews were in fact so degenerate as to be sub-human (*Untermenschen*). Their blood was so corrupted, he thought, that if contained and only allowed to breed with themselves, they would soon die out. Conscious of this, they spread themselves amongst the Aryans and interbred with them, eroding the brilliance of the Aryans and ensuring their own survival, like a parasite.

Hitler thought Germany was 'infected'

Hitler wrote that this was the cause of Germany's ills. It had allowed itself to become 'infected': 'Blood mixture and the resultant drop in racial level is the sole cause of the dying out of old cultures; for men do not perish as the result of lost wars, but by the loss of that force of resistance which is contained only in pure blood. All those who are not of good race in this world are chaff. And all occurrences in world history are only expressions of the races' instinct for self-preservation' (*Mein Kampf*).

Hitler feared a Jewish world conspiracy

Hitler believed the Jews would use any method to achieve their aim of racial mixing. The First World War, Hitler believed, had been designed to kill off

Germany's best – a Jewish plot. Communism was designed to enslave Aryans by enforcing common ownership, thereby stifling the Aryans' gift for creativity. Equally, capitalism was designed to enslave Aryans by harsh terms of employment, the burden of debt and the misery of poverty. Hitler felt that if the Jews succeeded, then ultimately the blood of all mankind would be corrupted. Then it would be only a matter of time before de Gobineau's prediction was realised, and man would die out. Hitler was convinced he was destined, like a Wagnerian hero, to save the human race.

Hitler blamed all Germany's misfortunes on the Jews

Hitler looked back to an age when Germany was a robust, militaristic, patriotic and agrarian-based society. Naturally he ignored all the errors of his forebears and the defeats and occupations such as the Napoleonic rule of the early nineteenth century (and the extent of collaboration by German states). Instead, Hitler applied a racial perspective and saw Jews behind every misfortune that had befallen Germany. He regarded Jews as personifying all the negative features of his world view. Hence they had brought democracy to sap the Germans' ability to resist, or their ability to see the Jewish threat. Communism and capitalism were both little more than 'front organisations' for the Jews, designed to enslave the Germans in a materialist world order, or to promise perpetual chaos in revolution. Hitler's solution to this 'problem' was to combat this undermining influence by abolishing democracy and attacking the Marxist-Jewish threat. He would create a powerful state, made up of healthy ethnic Germans, whose army and internal forces of order would destroy any threat.

Hitler hinted at a 'biological' war of racial survival

Hitler's reactions to the appalling casualties of the 1914–18 war can be detected in his racial interpretation of this event. Hitler believed that the Jews had started the First World War to kill off as many of the bravest and strongest Aryans as possible, then sapped the 'will to fight' of the civilians by spreading pacifist propaganda. Hitler believed the Jews did this so that they could weaken the resistance of the Aryan Germans and interbreed with them. Only by interbreeding with higher racial orders, Hitler thought, could this most degenerate race ever survive. If Jews could be kept apart from Germans, then their degeneracy would ultimately mean they would die out. Hence, a new view of the causes of the Holocaust perhaps presents itself. The policy of ghettoisation was the first stage in letting the Jews die out, whilst tapping them for war labour. The final solution was designed to speed

up this process of removing the biological threat, even if the war had to be brought
to an end.

Hitler thought the Jews had been behind the 1918–19 German Revolution

The Jews were considered to have been behind the Bolshevik revolution in Russia
(1917), which had destroyed the traditional state institutions, advocated the
acceptance of defeat, preached internationalism instead of patriotism, and led to
years of civil war and anarchy in Russia. News of atrocities against innocent
people committed by the Bolsheviks reached Germany throughout 1918 and
when German communists tried to seize power in 1919, there was panic. It came
as no surprise to Hitler that five of the seven leaders of the Spartakists were Jews.
Hitler was also convinced that Jews in big businesses and in the communist
movement were working together in a secret plan to kill Germans and weaken
their resolve. Hitler continued to warn of another communist revolution
throughout his career.

Hitler's views on nationalism

Hitler was bitter about the defeat of his country

The defeat of Germany in 1918 led to a battery of penalties imposed by the Allies
in the Treaty of Versailles. The German people had been led to believe that the
Fourteen Points' peace programme, drawn up by American President Woodrow
Wilson, would be used to ensure a fair settlement for Germany. Hitler was
shocked when the new, post-war, German government was invited to the peace
conference only to sign the Treaty, and not to discuss it. Hitler regarded these
'traitors' as 'despicable and depraved'. Germany lost some of its own lands when
other nationalities had the right to self-determination (the choice of which
country they wished to live in). Germany was expected to pay war reparations for
the damage that had resulted from the war. They also had to accept in legal terms,
that Germany had been the sole cause of the war. Immediately after the war
though, this seemed to be a humiliation. Hitler felt particularly strongly about the
Treaty of Versailles, and his criticism of it featured in many of his speeches. The
continuation of war reparations kept alive the memory of this damage to prestige.
Hitler called for the restoration of Germany's national pride. This view was
shared by millions of Germans and was the most popular of his ideas.

Hitler was more than simply patriotic

Figure 17. Hitler saluting the SA, 1934.

Hitler was not just a patriot. He wanted Germany to assert its supremacy over its neighbours. He aimed to return the lands lost under the terms of the Treaty of Versailles, and unite Austrian Germans in one ethnic, German state. He demanded a national zeal from his followers and could use non-compliance with his plans as evidence of a lack of patriotic feeling. This was a useful tool of coercion, but Hitler was genuinely nationalistic himself. Hitler's use of nationalism makes it seem that his aims were quite limited – perhaps only the revision of the Treaty of Versailles – but the racial dimension of his ideas and the opportunities that he grasped in the 1930s, indicate that he had far-reaching ambitions.

Hitler was concerned about the effect of population growth

The rapid growth of the German population from the late nineteenth century alarmed Hitler who believed that it was only a matter of time before the size of the population outstripped the food supply available. Germany would soon need more agricultural land, and Hitler looked eastwards to the grain producing areas of the Ukraine, and the vast plains of Eastern Europe. Small pockets of ethnic Germans, from migrations during the middle ages, convinced Hitler that Germans should reject the materialist values of Western Europe and take up their historic migration to the east, or *Drang nach Osten*. The clearance of indigenous peoples and colonisation of the eastern European territories would provide the Germans with *Lebensraum* (living space).

Hitler saw differences between city and country people

The fastest growing populations were in urban areas, and Hitler believed that urban dwellers lacked the daily physical exercise of country folk. Farmers seemed to represent a healthy, outdoor lifestyle, and rural Germans tended to be more traditional in their beliefs. They understood, Hitler reasoned, the importance of a life which was dependent on what grew in the soil. City people seemed less concerned with the community, more selfish, less in touch with the vagaries of nature. City people did not understand, or care about, the quality of the land and

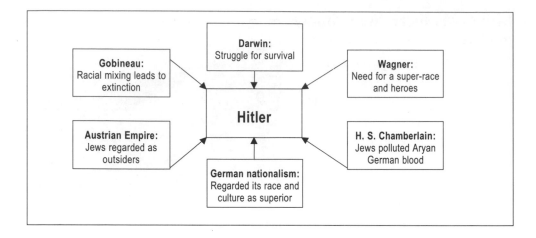

Figure 18. Hitler's ideas.

Figure 19. The Arcadian Idyll: Hitler believed rural life was superior.

they lacked a spiritual faith. Whereas rural areas were devoutly religious, city dwellers were surrounded by materialism, prostitution and immorality. Hitler's solution was to resettle many Germans in new lands in the east. He aimed to construct rural communities with an appreciation of nature, and an ample supply of food. Failure to combat over-population would lead to famine, civil war, and chaos.

National recovery, democracy and socialism

Hitler wanted national recovery

The losses of the First World War, in manpower and material, would need to be made good as a first step in Germany's recovery. Hitler believed that Germany's destiny was to expropriate the raw materials of countries with lower racial groups. Hitler felt that the racially superior Germans should be entitled to the best lifestyle. The economic depression in agriculture and industry between 1928 and 1933 convinced Hitler that Germany's enemies were seeking to crush the country and weaken resistance to their ideas. Hitler regarded the economy as a biological organism to be fed and nurtured, but wanted it to serve the German nation, not the other way around.

The war had demonstrated to Hitler how an economy should be geared to a war footing, producing all the country needed to supply its soldiers. Shortages of vital materials had undermined the war effort in 1914–18 and he was determined that it should not happen again.

Figure 20. German troops of the First World War.

Hitler believed democracy was weak

Hitler regarded democracy as a weak form of government which served the interests of a small, feeble-minded group at the expense of the German people. The democratic politicians, he argued, lacked the willpower to fight communism and lacked the knowledge or conviction to combat the racial threat. Democrats, he reasoned, were too eager to let obstacles (such as trade unions) get in the way of building a strong German state. Hitler also loathed the financial speculators who made money in stock markets without doing any physical work. Hitler saw these groups in stark contrast to the soldiers who had dug trenches, fought and died in the war. Hitler's view was that in the life or death struggle of trench warfare, social class barriers were brought down. The aristocratic officer ate the same food as his men. He fought alongside them, and died with them too. Hitler wanted to recreate this sense of comradeship (*Kameradenschaft*) in society. He wanted provision for the old, and the education of German children on an equal footing. He wanted people to develop a sense of community (*Volksgemeinschaft*), and he wanted to rid Germany of capitalist profiteers.

Hitler opposed 'equality'

Hitler hated the communist, and socialist, international approach. Their concept of destroying the classes, by killing or enslaving their class enemies, horrified Hitler. Hitler wanted a Germany made up only of ethnic Germans, not a multi-racial society. He wanted all Germans united, but still retain respect for tradition and authority. He did not want the egalitarian idea of socialism because he believed strongly in the hierarchy of strong leadership. Hitler later called his party 'National Socialist' to make clear the distinction from the usual definition of socialism.

Hitler's views on physical and mental illness

Weak, physically or mentally-impaired people were regarded as people who lacked a determination or will, or the capacity, to participate in Hitler's new Germany. Mental or physical illness was evidence, to Hitler, of the consequences of racial interbreeding. He regarded such individuals as burdens on society, and a war could be won more easily, he reasoned, without these burdens. It is not surprising therefore that Hitler considered the removal of the mentally and physically impaired from German society imperative and this resulted in a programme of euthanasia.

Hitler's ideas on leadership

Although Hitler never served in the military high command, he respected the army's strict hierarchy where individuals obeyed their leaders without question in a crisis. Throughout his life, Hitler placed enormous emphasis on obedience and loyalty to him. In the face of danger, disagreement might cause delay, with fatal results. Discipline ensured that all members of a group worked towards a common goal, regardless of casualties. Hitler felt that wars and crises brought natural leaders to the fore. However, historians have speculated about Hitler's belief in Social Darwinism in his leadership. He saw history as a record of struggles between races. The weakest died out, the strongest and the fittest breeds survived. Leaders too, faced the challenge of this natural competition and Hans Mommsen has argued that, whilst Hitler himself was a weak leader, his subordinates did struggle for supremacy with each other, producing a 'polycratic' regime (rule of many groups), rather than a straightforward dictatorship. Alan Bullock and Karl Bracher have disagreed, and see Hitler as the central figure in Germany's leadership, with many skills and responsibility for the direction of Nazism.

Figure 21. Hitler as orator.

Hitler's ideas – a summary

Hitler's vision of a new Germany was the result of his deep convictions about race and German history. He frequently spoke of Germany's destiny and he was utterly convinced that Germany faced a cataclysmic future. His ideas were based on an interpretation of biological science and history, which were pessimistic, but idealised the solution. His messages were simplistic, but were clouded in an emotional delivery. His solutions would involve the destruction of others, and he never made any secret of the fact. Yet such was the humiliation, pain, and desperation of many Germans that they were prepared to support Hitler. However, it would be fair to say that the majority failed to appreciate the full extent of Hitler's plans, and felt that his aims were limited to Germany's recovery.

Historical controversies on Hitler's ideas and the origins of Nazism

German historians after the Second World War found difficulty in explaining Hitler and his ideology of Nazism. Either Hitler had been completely outside the continuity of German history, a freak occurrence, or he had been a product of historical processes, and it was these same processes that had brought him into power. Historians were therefore eager to know where Nazism had come from. There was also a desire to know where responsibility lay for the rise of Nazism, either with Hitler, or with the broad mass of the German population. There are two identifiable interpretations: the Marxist historians and the liberal historians.

The Marxist interpretation

The collaboration of the capitalists in an anti-proletarian conspiracy was the essence of the Marxist interpretation of Nazism. The search by big businessmen for a populist, but essentially anti-working class, organisation was the explanation for the existence and growth of the Nazis propounded by F. L. Neumann and R. Brady. They argued that capitalism, when in crisis, produced a mass middle-class movement to crush the proletariat. But there is little evidence for this. Many capitalists had made profits from the war, and the early party programme condemned war profiteers and the capitalists who threatened the commercial survival of the small shopkeeper. Perhaps it could be argued that although the Nazi party existed, the capitalists showed little interest until they faced a crisis later in the 1920s. This is difficult to resolve with the fact that the radicalism of the NSDAP actually deterred capitalists supporting the Nazis.

The Liberal interpretation: the historic weaknesses of democracy

Historically, democracy had been flawed in Germany. After the Unification of Germany in 1871, the Prussian Chancellor, Bismarck, had reserved considerable power for himself and the Emperor at the expense of the elected *Reichstag*. Historians such as Rohan Butler and W. Shirer have pointed to an unhealthy and excessive respect for authority in Germany dating as far back as the 1848 revolutions. The failure of liberalism to establish itself for more than a few months in those revolts led to a greater faith in strong leadership and in nationalism. This particular historiographical approach is attractive to those historians who sought to show that Hitler's seizure of power could be explained by weaknesses in the system.

Weaknesses in German democracy were short term

Volker Berghahn has argued that in fact the Weimar Republic's constitution was one of the most democratic in Europe, and that the idea of a tradition of tolerance for right-wing regimes is flawed. More convincing is the view, supported by Ernst Nolte and Gerhard Ritter, that specific social and economic pressures led to a weakening of Weimar and the faith of Germans in the regime as a whole. The trauma of the First World War, with the shock of defeat and the widespread sense of loss, may explain the emergence of the Nazis too. They were, perhaps, a product of the anger and anguish that many Germans shared in the years following the Armistice.

There were widespread feelings of anger and humiliation

Frau Luise Solmitz, a Nazi sympathiser, referred to 'distress' that affected all sections of society. Many others testified to the 'shame' of Versailles. Other grievances identified by Richard Grunberger, such as the revolution of 1918, or the fact that the Weimar government signed the Treaty of Versailles, created a climate which favoured extremist politics. The French invasion of the Ruhr in 1923, and the hyperinflation of the same year, Grunberger believes, damaged the reputation of the Weimar Republic irrevocably in the eyes of the *Mittelstand* (middle classes).

The Intentionalist and Functionalist debate

The Intentionalist and Functionalist approaches are two opposing avenues for explaining Nazism and Hitler's importance in influencing events.

Intentionalist historians put the emphasis on the individual in history

Intentionalist historians tend to regard Hitler as the central and most important figure in Nazism. Without him, there would have been no Nazi party and his decisions need to be studied in order to trace the development of the movement. These historians believe that Hitler 'intended' certain outcomes and largely these were achieved. Some historians, labelled 'programmists' (such as E. Jäckel), believe that Hitler was in fact following an agenda, and his intention was to fulfil every aspect of a planned programme. These historians, taken together, regard Hitler as bearing the sole responsibility for the path the Third Reich later took and their views are sometimes referred to as 'Hitlerism'. An example of Intentionalist argument would be that, had Hitler not been a strong and manipulative character, then the party would never have survived the split after the Munich Putsch. They would argue that Hitler held the party together.

The Functionalist or Structuralist historians regard Hitler as 'weak'

The Functionalist historians view Hitler as a weak individual who was propelled into power more by circumstance than by his abilities. The supporters of Hitler were far more important. Their collective grievances, such as anger at the Treaty of Versailles, coincided with Hitler's aims and ensured his growth in popularity. Functionalists believe that the roles of Hitler's subordinates, and the rivalry between them for Hitler's approval, set up a dynamic of its own. Hitler was not so

Figure 22. Crowds cheering Hitler.

much in control as the prisoner of extremist supporters and exceptional events. An example of this historical approach can be found in the explanation of how Hitler became leader of the party.

Hitler's strengths and abilities are at the centre of the controversy

Alan Bullock believed that Hitler possessed certain skills and gifts in propaganda and oratory, which seemed to secure him the leadership of the early party. This view would not have found favour with Functionalist Hans Mommsen, who believed that Hitler was weak. In a small party, Hitler's effect would undoubtedly have been great and therefore disproportionate to his ability. The resolution of this argument is difficult. Nevertheless, Hitler secured his support by a combination of inflammatory speaking, his clever manipulation of feelings of German patriotism, and his hectoring demands, all of which tend to refute 'weakness'.

> *COMMENT:*
> *Alan Bullock wrote: 'The fact that his career ended in failure, and that his defeat was pre-eminently due to his own mistakes, does not by itself detract from Hitler's claim to greatness. The flaw lies much deeper…the lack of anything to justify the suffering he caused rather than his own monstrous and ungovernable will…makes Hitler so repellent and so barren.'*

A verdict on the debate

Despite the disagreement of historians over the Intentionalists and Functionalists / Structuralists approaches to Nazism, there can be little doubt that Hitler's ideas played a central role in Nazism, and that *Mein Kampf* is one of the most important records we have of Hitler's beliefs. It is remarkable how much of Hitler's *Mein Kampf* was put into practice, but there is still some doubt as to whether Hitler was following some sort of agenda or programme. In other words, whilst Hitler's ideas were laid out in *Mein Kampf* that does not mean that it was inevitable that they would be executed in practice and there was no timescale for their implementation.

The historical controversies surrounding *Mein Kampf*

Hugh Trevor-Roper believed Hitler wanted expansionism

Hugh Trevor-Roper has argued that Hitler's ideas were consistently transferred from *Mein Kampf* into policy, but that we have become too distracted by the Holocaust. Hitler's aim was to create *Lebensraum* in Eastern Europe. The expropriation of the east was therefore clearly indicated in *Mein Kampf*, whilst the final solution was a long-term, or unplanned by-product of this programme.

The German historians' views: Hitler wanted world domination

Hillgruber's interpretation (1963) offered a different approach, and stated that Hitler had been following a three-part plan called the *Stufenplan*. This was the desire to dominate first Europe, then Britain, and finally the USA. Hillgruber identified this programme from the 1928 edition. However, Klaus Hildebrand (1973) thought that Hitler wanted nothing more than world domination. Perhaps Hitler sought to do this in racial terms, which would have explained the vagueness and lack of specific detail in how it would be achieved. But this raises another point, that Hitler was an opportunist, and was never tied to any specific agenda. To take one example, one could refer to the plethora of contingency plans he had drawn up by military staff officers prior to the outbreak of the Second World War.

Tim Mason argued Hitler wanted to revise the Treaty of Versailles

Tim Mason believes that Hitler planned only to revise the Treaty of Versailles, and to solve Germany's economic problems. These drove Hitler on, and led to war. However, it is striking how often Hitler referred to Germany's future in apocalyptic terms, and the racial struggle for survival was the theme Hitler used in launching the Four Year Plan in 1936. 'This crisis cannot and will not fail to occur', he stated, 'the essence and goal of Bolshevism is the elimination of those social strata that have hitherto provided the leadership and their replacement by world-wide Jewry.'

Hitler seemed to have intended to exterminate the Jews

There is a remarkable continuity between his ideas in 1924 and the years 1933–1945. This would suggest that when Hitler wrote (or dictated) *Mein Kampf*, he had already made up his mind how his theories worked and what would be required to implement his ideal. Intentionalists, such as Lucy Dawidowicz, have argued that this was evidence of Hitler's intent to annihilate the Jews, and that he was really only waiting for the opportunity. Hitler refers, for example to the creation of the *Ostmark* (Eastern region), which suggests that he had already decided in 1924 to replace Poland with a region that would be run by Germany and would enslave the Jews, just as he actually did in 1944.

There are doubts about Hitler's intentions

It was not inevitable that Hitler would come to power, nor was he likely to be in 1924 since he was in prison as a traitor. He was, perhaps, just another extremist. Kershaw is unconvinced by Dawidowicz's Intentionalism. Whilst foreign policy aggression was promoted, Hitler was less clear on the Holocaust. One would have expected him to be far more specific, just as he was on citizenship, propaganda and so on, especially as anti-Semitism was such a strong theme. This has led to speculation (not by Kershaw) that anti-Semitism was just another tool of social coercion. However, although this is true of the 1925 and 1928 editions of *Mein Kampf*, it is not applicable to the 1943 edition, which is amended to include a phrase that if Jews had been gassed in the First World War, then many Germans would have been saved.

Were Hitler's ideas the result of a wartime trauma?

Figure 23. Klara and Alois, Hitler's parents.

More recently, Lucy Dawidowicz and others have argued that as early as Hitler's recuperation at Passewalk hospital, after he had been gassed by the British in the First World War, Hitler had decided on the 'Final Solution'. This was the moment that the grand design entered Hitler's mind. There has even been speculation that whilst in a delirious state, Hitler imagined his doctor, a Jew, to have raped or assaulted his

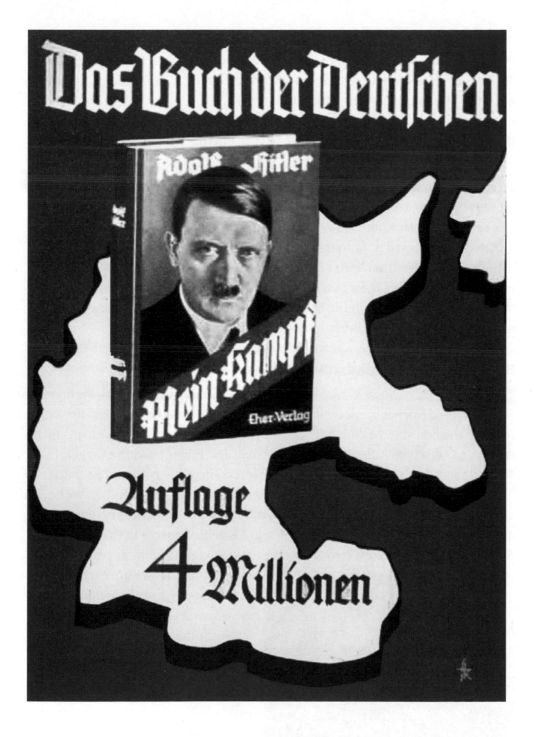

Figure 24. Advert for *Mein Kampf* (*My Struggle*).

mother, and swore the most terrible revenge. This is pure speculation and no evidence for such an event has been produced. Nevertheless, Dawidowicz confidently states: 'Hitler openly espoused the policy of annihilation . . . later to become the blueprint for his policies.'

Was the struggle with the Jews just a vague idea in Hitler's mind?

The trouble with these theories are that they are impossible to substantiate, and are based on conjecture, not empiricism. Historians are divided on the issue: Klaus Hildebrand has stated that Hitler did plan from the beginning to exterminate the Jews, and Hans Mommsen, who regarded Hitler as a weak dictator, was accused of failing to make this obvious connection. However, Mommsen believed that 'cumulative radicalisation', the effect of each agency in Hitler's regime trying their best to please the Führer and be more enthusiastic than their rivals, had led to the Holocaust and therefore it was not pre-planned, even if it had existed as a fairly remote idea in Hitler's mind.

Hitler's autobiography: a verdict

The first volume of *Mein Kampf* is Hitler's autobiography up to 1924. Perhaps the reason why so few people actually read *Mein Kampf* was the necessity to wade through the first volume which is hardly coherent or inspiring. Some aspects of this are reliable, but little can be corroborated, and Hitler liked to exaggerate. Nevertheless, Hitler felt his book was an expression of the National Socialist 'will'. Hitler frequently referred to this phenomenon, which seems to have been a combination of his personal determination to take power, his angry diatribes against elements he could not stomach, and his achievements to that date. *Mein Kampf* seems to indicate a strong determination to implement his plans, since so many of his views were carried through (such as propaganda), but eyewitnesses to his working methods suggest otherwise.

Mein Kampf thus presents us with a challenging problem, but from it, we can:

▶ learn about some aspects of Nazism

Figure 25. Hitler in Landsberg Prison where he wrote *Mein Kampf*.

The Nazis' Rise to Power, 1924–33

One-minute overview – Hitler refounded the party on his release from Lansberg Prison and took up a parliamentary approach in order to destroy democracy from within. This may have been the result of a number of factors. First, the revolutionary or 'Putschist' period of Weimar was over because the Republic seemed to have survived the attempts to overthrow it. Second, Hitler had no choice but to adopt a parliamentary path as his attempts to take power by force had failed. Third, the Nazis did better than expected in local elections in Bavaria and this seemed to offer a direct route to power. However, Hitler did not become a democrat and never ruled out the use of extra-parliamentary methods to get into power. The Nazis benefited from economic collapse in Germany following an agricultural and industrial depression. Germans began to vote for the Nazis, and other extremist parties, in unprecedented numbers. The traditional elites (aristocrats, leading politicians and the army) saw benefits in using the mass support of the Nazis for their own ends, and, reluctantly, having tried all other options, they agreed to let Hitler form a government which they thought they could control. Mass support for the Nazis has led to speculation by historians that there had to be something unusual, even enigmatic, about Nazism for large numbers of people from a modern society to vote for an extremist party. Others have tried to find an explanation in the exceptionally dire economic circumstances that Germans found themselves in.

In this chapter you will learn:
- ▶ *Why the Nazis adopted a parliamentary path to power.*
- ▶ *The Golden Years of the Weimar Republic.*
- ▶ *Why more people voted for the Nazis than before.*
- ▶ *How Hitler intrigued with the elites to become Chancellor.*

The Nazis adopted a parliamentary path to power

Hitler's reasons for adopting a parliamentary path to power can be divided into two parts.

- ▶ speculate about an agenda
- ▶ observe that Hitler felt there were some iron laws in history
- ▶ begin to gain an understanding of Hitler's racial interpretation of the world, and how important that was to Nazism as a whole, perhaps the most important point of all.

Tutorial

Progress questions

1. To whom did Hitler owe his ideas about the Jews?

2. How popular were Hitler's ideas on the restoration of national pride?

3. Explain Hitler's idea that leadership was based on Social Darwinism.

4. What was the Marxist explanation for the origins of Nazism?

5. Explain the meaning of the terms Functionalist and Intentionalist.

Discussion points

1. To what extent was *Mein Kampf* a blueprint for a war against the Jews?

2. '*Mein Kampf* is so incoherent that it is doubtful whether we can refer to a "Nazi ideology" at all'. Is this verdict justified?

3. Using the historical controversy sections, make out a list of historians and divide them into two groups – or those who would regard the emergence of the Nazis as an exceptional and unique event, and those who would regard Hitler as part of the continuity of German history. Having done this, consider different views on the subject: What evidence is there that Hitler was a 'gifted' leader, or was he just an extremist who benefited from a coincidence of events?

4. Which is the more convincing line of argument: Intentionalism or Functionalism?

Practical assignment

Summarising Hitler's beliefs. Study the diagrams on 'Hitler's ideas' (Figure 18) and 'Weimar in crisis' (Figure 8). Take each box and make your own notes to explain each element. For example, can you explain why Hitler felt that the Jews were involved in a conspiracy against Germany? Once you have made your notes, try to explain to a partner the reasons why Hitler believed that he was answering his nation's call.

Document question

Study the following extracts and answer the questions which follow.

A. Extracts from The German Workers' Party programme, 24 February 1920.

3. We demand land and property (colonies) to provide food for our nation and settlement areas for our population surplus.

4. Only a fellow German can have the right of citizenship. A fellow German can only be so if he is of German parentage, irrespective of religion. Therefore no Jew can be considered to be a fellow German.

7. ...If it should prove impossible to feed the whole population of the state, foreign nationals (with no right of citizenship) should be repatriated.

8. Any further immigration of non-Germans must be prevented.

24. We demand freedom of religion in the Reich so long as they do not endanger the position of the state or adversely affect the moral standards of the German race.

25. ... We demand the setting up of a strong central administration for the Reich.

(Source: J. Noakes and G. Pridham, *Nazism* Vol. I, Exeter, pp.14–15.)

B. Extract from Hitler's speech at his trial, 26 February 1924.

From the very first I have aimed at something more than becoming a Minister. I have resolved to be the destroyer of Marxism.

What did we want on the evening of the 8 November? ... We wanted to create in Germany... order in the state, throw out the drones, take up the fight against international stock exchange slavery, against our whole economy being cornered by trusts, against the politicising of the trade unions, and above all, ... the duty of bearing arms, military service. And now I ask you: Is what we wanted high treason?

The Court of History... will judge us as Germans who wanted the best for their people and their fatherland, who wished to fight and to die.

(Source: J. Noakes and G. Pridham, *Nazism* Vol. I, Exeter, pp.34–5.)

C. Extract from *Mein Kampf*

What we must fight for is to safeguard the existence and reproduction of race and our people, the sustenance of our children and the purity of our blood, the freedom and independence of the fatherland, so that our people may mature for the fulfilment of the mission allotted to it by the creator of the universe.

(1969 edn. transl. Ralph Mannheim, p.95)

1. Explain Hitler's reference to purity of blood in source A.

2. Compare sources B and C. How far do they indicate that Nazism was a patriotic movement which may have appealed to a wider audience than simply their own members?

3. Using these sources and your own knowledge, how far were the themes expressed here likely to appeal to a mass audience in Germany?

Study tips

1. Take a large sheet of paper lengthways and write down the headings of Hitler's ideas at the top of the page. Under each heading, list the main features as a series of bullet points.

2. Remember that understanding Hitler's ideas is the most crucial part in trying to understand the history of Germany in this period.

3. Notice how the historians disagree. Each interpretation must be supported by evidence if it is to be convincing. Get into the habit of supporting each statement that you make with a clear, succinct explanation, and judicious and sound evidence. In essays, try to build a case using this formula. Avoid writing a simple narrative account of what happened and focus on the arguments instead.

a.   factors over which he had no control
b.   lessons learnt from the failure of the Putsch.

Factors outside Hitler's control

The post-Putschist years required a new strategy
Hitler learnt from the Munich Putsch that an armed insurrection was unlikely to succeed without the co-operation of the army. Ernst Roehm, leader of the SA and a serving captain, had managed to persuade conservative elements not to ban the Nazis before, but the inability to secure support at the crucial moment had resulted in the failure of the coup attempt. The revolutionary atmosphere of 1923 had also died away. The economy, bolstered by American loans in the so-called Dawes Plan, was stable. The Weimar government appeared to have 'weathered the storm', and so a coup d'état attempt seemed inappropriate after 1924.

Hitler changed to a parliamentary path
Whilst Hitler was in prison at Lansberg, the party collapsed. Leaders quarrelled, factions developed, and people deserted the movement. These factors seemed to indicate Hitler's importance in the party. Without his presence, the NSDAP was hopelessly divided. Against this background, Hitler realised that only by working to get popular backing, could the party get into power. He pointed out that this did not mean that they had to embrace democracy, only to use it as a means to secure power. He stated: '. . . It will be necessary to pursue a new policy. Instead of working to achieve power by armed conspiracy, we shall have to hold our noses and enter the Reichstag . . . If outvoting them takes longer than outshooting them, at least the results will be guaranteed by their own Constitution'.

Lessons learnt from the failure of the Putsch

These included:

1.   Retraining the SA.
2.   Regional organisation.
3.   The formation of the SS and other groups.

Retraining the SA

Hitler reorganised the party
Hitler reorganised the party on the 27 February 1925 and overcame divisions by

Figure 26. Captain Pfeffer,
leader of the SA, with Hitler in 1928.

appealing to the members' loyalty to him personally. A faction who wanted to see socialist principles retained within the movement called themselves the Working Group, but Hitler defeated them at a party conference at Bamberg in February 1926. Hitler demanded that all party members obey him without question in the manner of natural leadership (*Führerprinzip*). The SA was also refounded and abandoned its 'military' training in favour of fist-fighting skills. They were to continue to protect meetings, but also attack communist meetings whilst advertising Nazi values of courage, discipline and determination.

Hitler circumvented the law

The SA tactics were illegal, but Hitler was able to claim that they were only responding to communist threats or attacks. Hitler liked to argue that the SA were taking action when the unpatriotic Weimar government would tolerate communist traitors. Unlike the old Free Corps, the SA were part of a political party which gave them a degree of immunity from prosecution. After their experiences of 1919, when communists had tried to seize power, the Weimar politicians believed that the communists were a greater threat and this may explain their inaction against the SA.

Regional organisation

Hitler also divided the party into areas so as to maximise their effect in elections. Regions (*Gaue*) were controlled by a *Gauleiter*. Districts (*Kreis*) and branches (*Orten*) had their own leaders too. When Hitler took power, he transferred this party hierarchy directly into the state. The NSDAP quickly established offices and SA sections across the country, but there were cadres in the northern provinces who were deeply suspicious of the party headquarters in the south.

The formation of the SS and other groups

Hitler also established the SS (*Schutz Staffel*), a bodyguard selected from the SA on the basis of their loyalty and racial appearance. The Hitler Youth (*Hitler Jugend*) acted as a focus for radical young men, and the Nazi Teachers Association began to infiltrate schools. The party expanded from 27,000 in 1925 to 72,000 in 1927. Nevertheless, the Nazis remained a minority, extremist movement and in the 1928 Reichstag elections, the NSDAP polled only 2.6% and only 12 seats. These results have led historians to speculate that, without the economic depression of the 1930s, the Nazis may have remained an unimportant fringe organisation.

The Golden Years of the Weimar Republic

The Weimar Republic entered a period of stability called the 'Golden Years'

The Weimar Republic had survived the Putschist years, the invasion of the Ruhr and the financial chaos of the hyperinflation. In 1923, Gustav Stresemann became Chancellor and, under his able direction as Foreign Minister (an appointment he dominated until 1929), he brought about reconciliation with the wartime Allies.

In 1925, Friedrich Ebert died and the aged Field Marshal Paul von Hindenburg was elected as President. These two men were to give the Weimar Republic a degree of respectability. In fact, both men represented a moderate nationalist line and their election tells us a great deal about German politics in this period. Above all, compared with the crises that followed, these leaders seemed to reflect a 'golden age' for the Weimar Republic. Nevertheless, some historians have questioned whether the stability was real or just an illusion.

Figure 27. Gustav Stresemann.

Weimar's financial stability was based on foreign support

It was Hans Luther, the Finance Minister, who introduced the *Rentenmark* in 1923 to bring hyperinflation to an end. The new currency was supposed to be based on the performance of industry and agriculture, but in fact the German currency was dependent on foreign exchange. In 1924, the Dawes Plan was concluded with the United States. The Americans agreed to loan the Germans money to give their currency solvency but also to pay off their reparations to the Allies. Germany appeared to prosper under this new arrangement: industrial

Figure 28. SA Fighting: The last years of the Weimar Republic were marred by political violence.

- ▶ speculate about an agenda
- ▶ observe that Hitler felt there were some iron laws in history
- ▶ begin to gain an understanding of Hitler's racial interpretation of the world, and how important that was to Nazism as a whole, perhaps the most important point of all.

Tutorial

Progress questions

1. To whom did Hitler owe his ideas about the Jews?

2. How popular were Hitler's ideas on the restoration of national pride?

3. Explain Hitler's idea that leadership was based on Social Darwinism.

4. What was the Marxist explanation for the origins of Nazism?

5. Explain the meaning of the terms Functionalist and Intentionalist.

Discussion points

1. To what extent was *Mein Kampf* a blueprint for a war against the Jews?

2. '*Mein Kampf* is so incoherent that it is doubtful whether we can refer to a "Nazi ideology" at all'. Is this verdict justified?

3. Using the historical controversy sections, make out a list of historians and divide them into two groups – or those who would regard the emergence of the Nazis as an exceptional and unique event, and those who would regard Hitler as part of the continuity of German history. Having done this, consider different views on the subject: What evidence is there that Hitler was a 'gifted' leader, or was he just an extremist who benefited from a coincidence of events?

4. Which is the more convincing line of argument: Intentionalism or Functionalism?

Practical assignment

Summarising Hitler's beliefs. Study the diagrams on 'Hitler's ideas' (Figure 18) and 'Weimar in crisis' (Figure 8). Take each box and make your own notes to explain each element. For example, can you explain why Hitler felt that the Jews were involved in a conspiracy against Germany? Once you have made your notes, try to explain to a partner the reasons why Hitler believed that he was answering his nation's call.

Document question

Study the following extracts and answer the questions which follow.

A. Extracts from The German Workers' Party programme, 24 February 1920.

3. We demand land and property (colonies) to provide food for our nation and settlement areas for our population surplus.

4. Only a fellow German can have the right of citizenship. A fellow German can only be so if he is of German parentage, irrespective of religion. Therefore no Jew can be considered to be a fellow German.

7. ...If it should prove impossible to feed the whole population of the state, foreign nationals (with no right of citizenship) should be repatriated.

8. Any further immigration of non-Germans must be prevented.

24. We demand freedom of religion in the Reich so long as they do not endanger the position of the state or adversely affect the moral standards of the German race.

25. ...We demand the setting up of a strong central administration for the Reich.

(Source: J. Noakes and G. Pridham, *Nazism* Vol. I, Exeter, pp.14–15.)

B. Extract from Hitler's speech at his trial, 26 February 1924.

From the very first I have aimed at something more than becoming a Minister. I have resolved to be the destroyer of Marxism.

What did we want on the evening of the 8 November? ...We wanted to create in Germany... order in the state, throw out the drones, take up the fight against international stock exchange slavery, against our whole economy being cornered by trusts, against the politicising of the trade unions, and above all, ...the duty of bearing arms, military service. And now I ask you: Is what we wanted high treason?

The Court of History...will judge us as Germans who wanted the best for their people and their fatherland, who wished to fight and to die.

(Source: J. Noakes and G. Pridham, *Nazism* Vol. I, Exeter, pp.34–5.)

C. Extract from *Mein Kampf*

What we must fight for is to safeguard the existence and reproduction of our race and our people, the sustenance of our children and the purity of our blood, the freedom and independence of the fatherland, so that our people may mature for the fulfilment of the mission allotted to it by the creator of the universe.

(1969 edn. transl. Ralph Mannheim, p.95.)

1. Explain Hitler's reference to purity of blood in source A.

2. Compare sources B and C. How far do they indicate that Nazism was a patriotic movement which may have appealed to a wider audience than simply their own members?

3. Using these sources and your own knowledge, how far were the themes expressed here likely to appeal to a mass audience in Germany?

Study tips

1. Take a large sheet of paper lengthways and write down the headings of Hitler's ideas at the top of the page. Under each heading, list the main features as a series of bullet points.

2. Remember that understanding Hitler's ideas is the most crucial part in trying to understand the history of Germany in this period.

3. Notice how the historians disagree. Each interpretation must be supported by evidence if it is to be convincing. Get into the habit of supporting each statement that you make with a clear, succinct explanation, and judicious and sound evidence. In essays, try to build a case using this formula. Avoid writing a simple narrative account of what happened and focus on the arguments instead.

3

The Nazis' Rise to Power, 1924–33

One-minute overview – Hitler refounded the party on his release from Lansberg Prison and took up a parliamentary approach in order to destroy democracy from within. This may have been the result of a number of factors. First, the revolutionary or 'Putschist' period of Weimar was over because the Republic seemed to have survived the attempts to overthrow it. Second, Hitler had no choice but to adopt a parliamentary path as his attempts to take power by force had failed. Third, the Nazis did better than expected in local elections in Bavaria and this seemed to offer a direct route to power. However, Hitler did not become a democrat and never ruled out the use of extra-parliamentary methods to get into power. The Nazis benefited from economic collapse in Germany following an agricultural and industrial depression. Germans began to vote for the Nazis, and other extremist parties, in unprecedented numbers. The traditional elites (aristocrats, leading politicians and the army) saw benefits in using the mass support of the Nazis for their own ends, and, reluctantly, having tried all other options, they agreed to let Hitler form a government which they thought they could control. Mass support for the Nazis has led to speculation by historians that there had to be something unusual, even enigmatic, about Nazism for large numbers of people from a modern society to vote for an extremist party. Others have tried to find an explanation in the exceptionally dire economic circumstances that Germans found themselves in.

In this chapter you will learn:
▶ Why the Nazis adopted a parliamentary path to power.
▶ The Golden Years of the Weimar Republic.
▶ Why more people voted for the Nazis than before.
▶ How Hitler intrigued with the elites to become Chancellor.

The Nazis adopted a parliamentary path to power

Hitler's reasons for adopting a parliamentary path to power can be divided into two parts.

a.   factors over which he had no control
b.   lessons learnt from the failure of the Putsch.

Factors outside Hitler's control

The post-Putschist years required a new strategy
Hitler learnt from the Munich Putsch that an armed insurrection was unlikely to
succeed without the co-operation of the army. Ernst Roehm, leader of the SA and
a serving captain, had managed to persuade conservative elements not to ban the
Nazis before, but the inability to secure support at the crucial moment had
resulted in the failure of the coup attempt. The revolutionary atmosphere of 1923
had also died away. The economy, bolstered by American loans in the so-called
Dawes Plan, was stable. The Weimar government appeared to have 'weathered the
storm', and so a coup d'état attempt seemed inappropriate after 1924.

Hitler changed to a parliamentary path
Whilst Hitler was in prison at Lansberg, the party collapsed. Leaders quarrelled,
factions developed, and people deserted the movement. These factors seemed to
indicate Hitler's importance in the party. Without his presence, the NSDAP was
hopelessly divided. Against this background, Hitler realised that only by working
to get popular backing, could the party get into power. He pointed out that this did
not mean that they had to embrace democracy, only to use it as a means to secure
power. He stated: '. . . It will be necessary to pursue a new policy. Instead of
working to achieve power by armed conspiracy, we shall have to hold our noses
and enter the Reichstag . . . If outvoting them takes longer than outshooting them,
at least the results will be guaranteed by their own Constitution'.

Lessons learnt from the failure of the Putsch

These included:

1.   Retraining the SA.
2.   Regional organisation.
3.   The formation of the SS and other groups.

Retraining the SA

Hitler reorganised the party
Hitler reorganised the party on the 27 February 1925 and overcame divisions by

Figure 26. Captain Pfeffer,
leader of the SA, with Hitler in 1928.

appealing to the members' loyalty to him personally. A faction who wanted to see socialist principles retained within the movement called themselves the Working Group, but Hitler defeated them at a party conference at Bamberg in February 1926. Hitler demanded that all party members obey him without question in the manner of natural leadership (*Führerprinzip*). The SA was also refounded and abandoned its 'military' training in favour of fist-fighting skills. They were to continue to protect meetings, but also attack communist meetings whilst advertising Nazi values of courage, discipline and determination.

Hitler circumvented the law

The SA tactics were illegal, but Hitler was able to claim that they were only responding to communist threats or attacks. Hitler liked to argue that the SA were taking action when the unpatriotic Weimar government would tolerate communist traitors. Unlike the old Free Corps, the SA were part of a political party which gave them a degree of immunity from prosecution. After their experiences of 1919, when communists had tried to seize power, the Weimar politicians believed that the communists were a greater threat and this may explain their inaction against the SA.

Regional organisation

Hitler also divided the party into areas so as to maximise their effect in elections. Regions (*Gaue*) were controlled by a *Gauleiter*. Districts (*Kreis*) and branches (*Orten*) had their own leaders too. When Hitler took power, he transferred this party hierarchy directly into the state. The NSDAP quickly established offices and SA sections across the country, but there were cadres in the northern provinces who were deeply suspicious of the party headquarters in the south.

The formation of the SS and other groups

Hitler also established the SS (*Schutz Staffel*), a bodyguard selected from the SA on the basis of their loyalty and racial appearance. The Hitler Youth (*Hitler Jugend*) acted as a focus for radical young men, and the Nazi Teachers Association began to infiltrate schools. The party expanded from 27,000 in 1925 to 72,000 in 1927. Nevertheless, the Nazis remained a minority, extremist movement and in the 1928 Reichstag elections, the NSDAP polled only 2.6% and only 12 seats. These results have led historians to speculate that, without the economic depression of the 1930s, the Nazis may have remained an unimportant fringe organisation.

The Golden Years of the Weimar Republic

The Weimar Republic entered a period of stability called the 'Golden Years'

The Weimar Republic had survived the Putschist years, the invasion of the Ruhr and the financial chaos of the hyperinflation. In 1923, Gustav Stresemann became Chancellor and, under his able direction as Foreign Minister (an appointment he dominated until 1929), he brought about reconciliation with the wartime Allies.

In 1925, Friedrich Ebert died and the aged Field Marshal Paul von Hindenburg was elected as President. These two men were to give the Weimar Republic a degree of respectability. In fact, both men represented a moderate nationalist line and their election tells us a great deal about German politics in this period. Above all, compared with the crises that followed, these leaders seemed to reflect a 'golden age' for the Weimar Republic. Nevertheless, some historians have questioned whether the stability was real or just an illusion.

Figure 27. Gustav Stresemann.

Weimar's financial stability was based on foreign support

It was Hans Luther, the Finance Minister, who introduced the *Rentenmark* in 1923 to bring hyperinflation to an end. The new currency was supposed to be based on the performance of industry and agriculture, but in fact the German currency was dependent on foreign exchange. In 1924, the Dawes Plan was concluded with the United States. The Americans agreed to loan the Germans money to give their currency solvency but also to pay off their reparations to the Allies. Germany appeared to prosper under this new arrangement: industrial

Figure 28. SA Fighting: The last years of the Weimar Republic were marred by political violence.

giants like I. G. Farben and United Steelworks emerged in 1926 and production in 1927 finally reached its pre-First World War levels. However, there is a mistaken belief that Stresemann and the Weimar governments should be credited with this achievement rather than the wartime Allies. After the threat of Communist revolutions in Germany, the Allies saw merit in assisting in Germany's recovery (just as they did again in 1945).

The conservatives still influenced domestic politics

The election of Hindenburg and the economic recovery meant that the German nationalists were more prepared to support the Weimar Republic. Industrialists and the army were more satisfied with the Republic's policies too. General von Seekt, an outspoken champion of the right, resigned when the government refused to countenance his plan to invade Poland and recover the Polish Corridor (lost under the terms of the Treaty of Versailles) in October 1926. Despite the good electoral performance of the SPD, the moderate right also did well, and the old aristocratic elites seemed to retain their influence in politics.

The Weimar Republic adopted a policy of 'fulfilment' in foreign policy

Any attempt to obstruct the Allies over the Treaty of Versailles was likely to lead to war, that point was clear from the French invasion of the Ruhr in 1923. However, Germany refused to enforce the charges of war crimes against the Kaiser and his military leaders, they deliberately delayed the disbandment of the *Freikorps* legions and there was a general reluctance to see through the disarmament process. In April 1922, under the terms of the Treaty of Rapallo, Germany and the Soviet Union signed bilateral trade and investment agreements and also secretly arranged that the German army would be able to locate and train units inside Russian territory. The possibility of the Germans and Russians moving closer together convinced the Western Allies that Germany must be supported. Thus when Stresemann offered to guarantee the Western borders of Germany against any further changes, the Allies were eager to agree and the result was the Locarno Pact (1925). The following year, the British forces of occupation left Germany and in 1927 the Inter-Allied Control Commission (the body charged with implementing the terms of the Treaty of Versailles) also left.

There are doubts over the sincerity of German foreign policy objectives

The fruits of 'fulfilment' policy were the final removal of all Allied forces in August 1929, the reduction of reparations under the Young Plan (1929), and finally the Moratorium of 1930 (which effectively suspended reparations for good). Stresemann was awarded the Nobel Peace Prize and Germany was admitted to the League of Nations in the same year. Liberal historians in the West once argued that Stresemann was a 'good European', eager to reintegrate Germany in the family of nations, but this view has been challenged. Marxist historians of the Soviet Union used to believe that Stresemann was simply a bourgeois politician eager to set up a capitalist front in Germany with foreign backing so as to defeat the German revolutionary proletariat and confront the Soviet Union. Given the German co-operation with the Soviets in 1922, this latter view seems invalid, but it is clear from Stresemann's own memoirs that he was keen to back German interests and revise the Treaty of Versailles. He refused to guarantee the eastern border of Germany, hoping, like many nationalists, to reduce or remove the Polish Corridor. Stresemann also knew that Versailles was deeply unpopular with the German people. Brüning, the Chancellor of 1930–32, later tried to exploit this nationalist sentiment.

Was the period 1924–29 really the 'golden era' of the Weimar Republic?

The Weimar Republic lacked any track record of success in dealing with a crisis, and many key agencies in Germany felt little loyalty to the system at all. The army's support was half-hearted. The civil service and those in education were generally hostile. The political parties were bitterly divided, even though the political system within which they operated was dependent on consensus and co-operation. The German economy was also unstable. The currency was propped up by foreign loans, and there was a growing imbalance of trade: more was being imported than exported each year. This meant that Germany was sinking deeper into debt even before the Depression (1.3 billion *Reichsmarks* between 1924 and 1930).

COMMENT:
Events like the breakdown of the Weimar Republic are rarely mono-causal, but it is inadequate to simply attribute its fall to 'a variety of factors'. It is far more important to identify and weigh up the relative importance of those elements.

Apparent strengths	Clear weaknesses
Strong executive powers for the President and the Chancellor	A collection of military and right-wing personnel influential in politics
Economic recovery after the First World War	Economy dependent on American loans and performance of German industry
Rehabilitation in the League of Nations	Widespread discontent about the territorial losses after the Treaty of Versailles and war reparations payments
Extremist groups marginal in German politics	The continued existence of extremists disrupted German political life
Flourishing cultural life and widespread participation in democracy (high voter turnout)	Considerable hostility to democracy amongst the civil service and political elites

Figure 29. The problems of the Weimar Republic.

The Nazi breakthrough in the elections 1928–1930

This section will be divided into two parts.

a.   Why more people voted for the Nazis than before.
b.   The historical controversy which explains how the Nazis came to power.

Why more people voted for the Nazis than before

There were several factors that explain the surge in support for the Nazis:

(i)   The Agricultural Depression.
(ii) The Depression caused by the Wall Street Crash.
(iii) The polarisation of politics in Germany.

The Agricultural Depression
Farmers in the late 1920s were angry because over-production of food had lowered prices by up to 30%, and rents were on the rise. They were annoyed with the Weimar government which had raised the pay of its civil servants and which seemed unwilling to control those financiers who speculated in land prices. The Nazis realised that their anti-government message was popular in the countryside. In the rural north of Germany, the Nazis won considerable support. The Nazis also stressed that they were firm supporters of those who tilled the soil, because country folk were keen to preserve German traditions, seemed healthier and braver, and were more patriotic than city dwellers.

Figure 30. Election poster urging all German industrial workers to vote for Hitler.

The Depression caused by the Wall Street Crash

There seems little doubt that the economic crisis of 1929 played a key role in the rise of the Nazis. The collapse in the value of shares on the American Stock Exchange on Wall Street, caused a stagnation in the flow of trade around the world. As a result, investors lost confidence in the banking system, and a panic led to the withdrawal of American financial support for Germany. Demands were made for the repayment of short-term, high-interest loans. The German government lacked any finances to spend their way out of the crisis: their foreign capital assets fell from 5 billion *Reichsmarks* in 1928 to 700 million in 1930. As Germany struggled to pay its loans, it joined other countries in reducing imports. As a result, both food

Figure 31. Wall Street Crash: Wall Street, home of the New York Stock Exchange, full of panicked investors after the market crashed in 1929.

prices and demand for raw materials collapsed. Consumer demand fell away as people concentrated on the essentials. Industries started to go bankrupt, and workers were made redundant. The number of unemployed rose from 2 million in 1929, to 5 million in 1932, reaching a peak of 6 million in 1933. When banks like Credit-Anstahlt also started to collapse, many people were left destitute.

The polarisation of politics

▶ *There was a growth in extremist parties.*

The far Left and far Right pointed to the failure of democracy to provide any solution to the collapse. Moderate parties found their supporters bitter, and eager for new solutions. The Weimar government appeared to be powerless, and, short of money, Brüning (Chancellor, 1932) cut the allowance of the unemployed. The Nazis tuned in to the discontent and claimed to offer radical, fresh solutions. They refused to co-operate with other right-wing parties, and demanded a complete change in the system. Germans voted in unprecedented numbers for the NSDAP. By 1930, at the height of the crisis, and amid massive levels of unemployment, the Nazis polled 6.4 million votes. But overall, 39.6% of the electorate supported non-democratic parties, and the Nazis tended to do well at the expense of the traditional right-wing groups.

▶ *The extreme left wing also did well: fostering violence.*

On the left the communists (KPD) gained 14% of the vote, but this gave the

Nazis the opportunity to argue that the communists were a growing threat to Germany. In 1932, the Nazis became the largest single party in the *Reichstag* (National Assembly) and in 1933 they polled 43.9% of the vote. On the streets there was political chaos. Several people died in street fighting each week during the election campaigns. The Nazis argued that only they could restore order to Germany's streets, even though they had started the fighting. The effect was to discredit the Weimar Republic's ability to keep order.

The historical controversy which explains support for the Nazis

The influence of the Depression

It would be misleading to think that the Wall Street Crash alone caused the collapse of democratic government in the Weimar Republic. Even before the Depression, Germany's unemployment was rising (1.8 million in 1928). Many Germans had lost savings in the hyperinflation of 1923, and Stresemann (Foreign Minister, 1923–29), had stated in 1929 that 'Germany is dancing on a volcano' because of public anger at the financial chaos in the country. In fact the unemployment figures do not include casual, part-time, or unregistered people. Middle-class people were affected just as much as the poorer in society, but many of the small-scale shopkeepers had already been under pressure from bigger industries. The rural workers may have had the benefit of cheaper food, but unemployment meant that they were unable to pay their rents and they were often evicted. The Depression after 1929 worsened the situation.

Nazi exploitation of the Depression

The Nazis are often regarded as having exploited the grievances that existed in Germany between 1929 and 1933, but all party programmes did this. If the aim of the Nazi party was simply to get into power, then we must remember that this was the aim of other political parties, which is the nature of a democracy. What was undemocratic about the Nazi takeover was its method. Their electoral achievement was built on people's misery in the Depression, and they themselves added to the political chaos by inciting violence. Many people saw the Nazis as patriots who wanted to rebuild the country. Most people were unaware of, or unwilling to believe, what the Nazis intended to do with their enemies.

The intrigue with the elites, 1932–33

Hitler intrigued with the elites to obtain power, but the elites had motives for wanting to use the popularity of the Nazis for their own ends. Their calculations were that:

▶ they hoped to keep power
▶ they had become disillusioned with democracy
▶ they thought communism was a greater threat than Nazism.

This section is divided into two areas:

a. Hitler's intrigues with the elites
b. the crisis of 1932–33.

Hitler's intrigues with the elites

Hitler appealed to the more wealthy echelons of society, as well as to the unemployed and working classes who had been hit hard by the economic crisis of 1929–33. These appeals can be summarised as:

(i) the middle classes
(ii) the business world
(iii) the army.

The appeal to the middle classes

Hitler realised that he would need the co-operation of the elites in Germany if he was going to take power. This had been one of the lessons of the Putsch (see Chapter 2). However, Hitler also realised that popular support was not enough either. He nevertheless began to try to win over middle-class voters. He appealed to their patriotism and tried to play down the party's radical image. He excused the SA's street violence as a struggle against communism on behalf of all patriotic Germans. His message about the economic recovery of Germany was well received by those badly affected by the economic depression, especially the lower middle class.

The appeal to the business world

Alfred Hugenburg helped Hitler to develop a respectable image in the business world. At a speech to the Dusseldorf Industry Club in 1932, Hitler spoke of his

Figure 32. Hitler's earnestness appealed to many voters.

desire to see an economic recovery. He did not mention the Jews. He hinted at rearmament, envisaging a 'sound national body politic armed to strike'. He also spoke of the need to develop a 'great internal market', but the industrialists did not realise that Hitler meant an internal market that went beyond the existing frontiers of Germany. Hitler believed in the acquisition of *Lebensraum* and the colonisation of eastern Europe. It is difficult to tell if the industrialists voted for Hitler for anything more than his promises to regenerate the economy, but Hitler argued that political stability had to be achieved before recovery was possible.

The appeal to the army

Figure 33. Hitler salutes the party faithful at Nuremberg.

The Nazis also tried to win over support in the army. Young army officers were receptive to Hitler's calls for the restoration of national pride. Senior officers were more suspicious. In particular they were afraid that the radicals in the SA would remove the senior officers since they were mainly aristocrats. Some disdainfully regarded Hitler as an uncouth former corporal, who was really no more than a rabble rouser. Yet senior members of the Weimar Republic, with military backgrounds, believed they could make use of the Nazis and their popular following.

The crisis of 1932–33

There were several phases in the collapse of the Weimar Republic and the appointment of Hitler as Chancellor. These were:

(i)   The presidential elections of 1932.
(ii)   The fall of Brüning.
(iii) The Chancellorship of von Papen.
(iv)   The search for a solution.
(v)   The Chancellorship of von Schleicher.

The presidential elections of 1932

Encouraged by the growing support in the countryside and in the towns, as the Depression began to bite, Hitler stood for the presidential elections held on the 13 March 1932. The level of support for the Nazis can be gauged by the results.

Hindenburg (a conservative and highly respected war leader)	50%
Hitler (NSDAP)	30%
Düsterburg (nationalist)	7%
Thälmann (communist)	13%

The SA planned a coup d'état
Hindenburg had failed to win an overall majority, so a second election was scheduled. During the second campaign, Severing, the Socialist Minister of the Interior in Prussia, ordered the police to raid SA headquarters, a decision prompted by SA violence on the streets. The police discovered plans, drawn up by the SA, to overthrow the Weimar Republic in a coup d'état if Hitler did not win the second election. This was treason against the state, so he reported it to the national government's Interior Minister, General Groener. Groener, as a military officer, had a strong sense of duty and he knew the SA should be banned for this conspiracy.

von Schleicher advised against a ban of the SA
However, his political advisor, General von Schleicher, was keen to use the SA as a force that could be enrolled into the army, and perhaps fight the communists in the event of a revolution. The SA would make good soldiers, he reasoned, as they were fit, disciplined and brave. Schleicher even tried to persuade Groener that if he banned the SA, he would be seen to be working for the left wing. But Groener was undeterred and the SA were banned after the second presidential election on 13 April 1932. The election resulted in Hindenburg's victory over Hitler, 53% to 37%, with the communists down to 10%.

The fall of Brüning

Brüning made enemies of the working classes
Schleicher was furious that his advice over the SA had not been followed, and he engineered Groener's fall (13 May 1932). Brüning, the Chancellor, was also in trouble. He had tried to make cuts in all areas of Germany's economic life in an attempt to get the Allies to give up their demands for reparations repayments. He

Figure 34. Brüning: Chancellor
of Germany, 1932.

hoped that he could also challenge British and French policy elsewhere in Europe, and rally the country behind him in patriotic defiance. But Brüning cut the dole benefits when unemployment was rising. Unemployment was nearing 6 million in 1932, and this move made him extremely unpopular with the electorate.

Brüning also made enemies in the upper classes
Brüning also planned to seize the estates of Prussian aristocrats and resettle the urban unemployed. Since the Prussian aristocracy was Hindenburg's own social class, the President was easily persuaded to remove Brüning (30 May 1932). Hindenburg selected Franz von Papen, a Catholic ex-army officer who had served in the same regiment as Hindenburg's son in the First World War. Schleicher was instrumental in obtaining Nazi support for von Papen's chancellorship, in return for an end to the ban on the SA (16 June 1932). It was also agreed that there would have to be an election.

The Chancellorship of von Papen

Papen calculated on nationalist support
Papen aimed to remove Weimar democracy as soon as possible. He wanted a dictatorship of traditional, conservative aristocrats. But to seize power he would need the support of the army and the majority of the people. He would also need to silence the opposition. Papen first dissolved the SPD-Catholic coalition government in Prussia. He took over the government himself and removed all those who opposed him, including civil servants in the administration. Prussia, the largest federal state in Germany, was in his hands and these changes were possible because he was able to use the power of emergency decree with the President's approval. To get military support was relatively easy too since the President was also Commander in Chief of the army. But gaining popular support was to be more difficult. Papen had few seats in the *Reichstag* and little popular backing in previous elections. He believed that if the Nazis could be

harnessed, all their enthusiastic supporters could be made to support a right-wing bloc. In the July 1932 election, amid much violence, the Nazis won 37% of the vote and became the largest single party in the *Reichstag*.

Hitler tried to become Chancellor
Hitler demanded to become Chancellor. He had, he felt, won the election. But without an overall majority, and with all the parties in the *Reichstag* failing to co-operate, Hindenburg was forced to rule by emergency decree – article 48 of the Constitution. As the President also had the power to select a Chancellor, he chose to keep von Papen, despite the fact that the nationalists had the smallest number of seats in the *Reichstag* and the least votes. Hitler therefore tried to persuade the President directly in a meeting held on 13 August 1932. Hindenburg refused, but appealed to Hitler's patriotism not to harm his country by taking any revolutionary action. Hindenburg and von Papen were aware that, with three million SA men, and as many communists, the tiny German army (100,000) would be unable to crush a revolution or prevent a civil war. Hitler agreed to merely oppose the government legally, but in private confided to Otto Meisner, the State Secretary of the President's Chancellory, that he would 'overthrow the Reich President'. This suggests Hitler was considering a coup d'état, but it isn't clear under what circumstances this would happen.

The search for a solution to the crisis, July to November 1932

Hindenburg had several qualities
Hindenburg has often been portrayed as a senile and ineffective figure. In fact, it appears that he was the only person in power still holding out against the Nazis. He was a very traditionalist individual. When he was first made President, it is alleged that he took a copy of the Constitution and underlined his powers in blue pencil and those of others in red, just as an officer would mark up a map for battle. He had a deep sense of duty and patriotism. He may have wanted to keep Hitler out of office because, as President, he had sworn to defend the Weimar constitution. He was only by-passed when he died (2 August 1934).

Figure 35. Hitler meets von Hindenburg in 1933. Despite the mock cordiality, neither trusted the other.

Figure 36. Evoking the memory of the First World War: Hitler as 'front line soldier'.

Hitler was refused office by Hindenburg
Hitler's failure to become President deeply affected the Nazi party which had expected to see their leader in power. Goebbels noted in his diary, 'Who knows if their units [the SA] will hold together?'. Papen still contemplated a coup of his own, but would need the army's co-operation to crush the communists and the Nazis. Schleicher, newly appointed as Minister of Defence, told Papen that the army would not support this plan, especially as many junior officers were already pro-Nazi. Papen decided to call another election, more confident that the Nazis had lost heart. Goebbels, the Nazi's chief propagandist, took up a radical line against Papen and portrayed his 'Cabinet of the Barons' as 'reactionary'. But Hitler toned down this theme, concerned lest the middle classes were put off. The November 1932 election did not see a significant increase in support for Papen, but the Nazis also lost support (37% down to 33%). Party funds were running out, but Hitler still refused to join Papen's Cabinet.

The Chancellorship of von Schleicher

Schleicher aimed to split the Nazis
Although Hindenburg still wanted Papen as Chancellor, Schleicher intervened and warned him that the army would not support Papen's coup. Instead Schleicher proposed a new form of government that could appeal to national sentiments, but deal vigorously with social and economic problems. He hoped to split the Nazis, by drawing the radical SA away from the rest of the party. He also hoped to attract left-wing support. Gregor Strasser resigned from the Nazi party, but Hitler prevented a flood by making it an issue of loyalty to him personally.

Figure 37. Kurt von Schleicher.

Papen tried to use Hitler's support to return to power
Hindenburg had approved Schleicher's plan and appointed him Chancellor. Papen, resentful at being side-lined, met Hitler on 4 January 1933 and agreed to work with the Nazis to get rid of Schleicher. Hitler made his conditions for co-operating as follows:

▶ Hitler would become Chancellor.
▶ Jews and communists would be removed from positions of leadership.
▶ The Nazis would restore order.

Whilst Papen tried to persuade Hindenburg to accept Hitler's terms, the Nazis won a by-election (15 January 1933) which seemed to indicate that they were not a spent force.

The East Prussian scandal threatened to discredit the President
Crucially, Hitler also learned of an enquiry that was about to take place concerning misuse of government money. It was alleged that public funds were being used to back up aristocrats and prevent their bankruptcy. This was important because Schleicher intended to settle people on the estates of bankrupt aristocrats (just as Brüning had considered). Hitler discovered that Oskar von Hindenburg, the President's son, was involved, and in a secret meeting, Hitler agreed to crush the enquiry if he was made Chancellor. It seems likely that Oskar persuaded his father to let Hitler in. But equally, there were other reasons for a change of Chancellor. A secret army report, for example, revealed that they could not contain the Nazis and communists.

Hitler was appointed Chancellor
Papen was still trying to convince the President that Hitler could be tamed and used. Schleicher was demanding emergency powers to set up a military dictatorship. Hindenburg refused, so Schleicher resigned, leaving the President perplexed. He really wanted Papen as Chancellor, but he had tried him and the other candidates and they had all failed. The Nazis were the largest party in the *Reichstag*. Finally, he agreed to Papen's request, and, as a last resort, he let Hitler and two other Nazis join a nationalist cabinet (30 January 1933). If he had refused the Nazis again, it is likely that there would have a been a civil war, or at least, that was their calculation.

Tutorial

Progress questions

1. Why were the Germans more prepared to listen to Hitler's messages in 1932 than in 1924?

2. Hitler was the last choice of Chancellor. Who was most responsible for his appointment? von Schleicher? Hindenburg? von Papen? or Hitler himself?

3. What arguments did the Nazis use to persuade the voters and the elites to accept them as the national leadership in the final months of 1932–33?

4. What was the role of the SA and the SS in this period?

Discussion questions

1. The Nazis are often regarded as a sinister organisation because they collaborated with the ruling elites to get into power. Nevertheless, could it not be argued that alliance with any party likely to assist them in getting into power was legitimate? What made their assumption of power illegal?

2. What were the Nazis' ultimate aims as regards the conservative elites of Germany? To what extent were the elites gullible, calculating, or driven by desperation?

Practical assignment

Read the documents below and answer the questions which follow.

A. Hitler defending three army officers accused of subversion in a court at Leipzig, September 1930.

'The National Socialist movement will try to achieve its aim with constitutional means in this state. The constitution prescribes only the methods, not the aim. In this constitutional way we shall try to gain decisive majorities in the legislative bodies so that the moment we succeed we can give the state the form that corresponds to our ideas'.

B. Otto Meissner's personal account of a meeting between Hitler and the President, 13 August 1933

'The discussion [between Hitler and Hindenburg] was followed by a short conversation in the corridor between the Reich Chancellor and me, and Herr Hitler and his companions, in which Herr Hitler expressed the view that future developments would lead to the solution suggested by him and to the overthrow of the Reich president.'

1. Explain what Hitler meant by: 'The constitution prescribes only the methods, not the aim' in source A.

2. The documents appear to be contradictory, but are they in any sense complementary and consistent with Hitler's plans and methods?

3. Using these sources and your wider knowledge, to what extent were Hitler's predictions fulfilled when he took power in 1933?

Study tips

1. Complete a chronology of events between 1930 and 1933 on a timeline. Annotate summaries of the key events in boxes, and link these summaries to the timeline with arrows.

2. Under headings for each of the Chancellors, assess the strengths and weaknesses of their policies during the Depression.

3. Examine each group in society (army, workers, farmers, churches, middle classes) and try to determine their expectations. Record them in a diagram.

4. Tick off how many of these demands were met by the Nazis by 1933.

5. Make a list of the changes Hitler made to the direction of the party after the Putsch, and update this list as you progress through the book to find more examples of his opportunism.

6. Divide a page in two. List legal methods of trying to take power on one side, and illegal methods on the other. For example, SA violence was illegal. The legality or otherwise of Hitler's rise to power is a question favoured by examiners.

The Nazi Seizure of Power, 1933

One-minute overview – *Hitler had not been elected, he was selected to become Chancellor. Hitler undoubtedly enjoyed some popular support – his party was the largest in the Reichstag, but the key factor is how the elites thought they could make use of Hitler and his popular backing for their own ends. The elites miscalculated and underestimated him. As Chancellor, Hitler banned his opponents, struck deals with party leaders who would compromise, and obtained new powers to deal with an alleged communist revolution. This gave the takeover an air of legality. However, his methods were not within the spirit of the Constitution, and political violence, which he frequently encouraged, was illegal. The Nazis moved quickly against the agencies that sought to control them and the new government began to pass decrees that would by-pass the president's powers. When the old President died, Hitler was undisputed leader of Germany.*

In this chapter you will learn:
▶ *How the Nazis destroyed democracy by 'legal' means.*
▶ *The consolidation of power.*
▶ *The historical controversies on the Nazi seizure of power and the failure of the Weimar Republic.*

How the Nazis destroyed democracy by legal means

This can be explained as follows:

a. the *Reichstag* Fire
b. the Enabling Law
c. the removal of opposition.

The *Reichstag* Fire

Hitler's position was initially weak

When Hitler became Chancellor on 30 January 1933, he was merely one of three Nazis in office. Despite the euphoria of his supporters, Hitler had little power to act because of the *Reichstag* and the President, to whom he was responsible. Papen was so confident that the Nazis could be harnessed that he told Hindenburg, 'in two months we shall have pushed Hitler so far into a corner that his pips will squeak'. Hitler demanded that Goering be placed in charge of the police in Prussia, and Frick controlled the rest in Germany. Although other nationalists had all the other posts, Hitler had ensured the co-operation of all the forces of internal security. One of his first moves was to reduce press freedom and deny freedom of assembly (4 February).

Personnel	
Brüning	Centre, but tried to win support by foreign policies. The economic crisis ended his career.
von Papen	Lack of popular support. Lost election of November 1932.
von Schleicher	Military leader and political advisor who became Defence Minister in 1932. Proposed a combination of left and ring wing to escape crisis.

Options proposed	
von Papen	Aristocratic military dictatorship.
Schleicher	Military dictatorship disguised as national government.
Civil war	NSDAP and communists might defeat small army.
Communist Revolution!	
Hitler	Destruction of Constitution, but unknown quantity.

Figure 38. Hindenburg's choices for a Chancellor.

The Nazis made use of the police and their own paramilitaries
Goering set about replacing police chiefs with Nazis. The SA and the SS became auxiliary police (special or supporting police), and they unleashed a wave of terror – now legal since they were part of the state – upon their left-wing

opponents. The SA rounded up their enemies and bullied them in camps which concentrated them in one place. Only later did the SS take over the running of all the concentration camps. The radical zeal of the

Figure 39. The SA setting up an early concentration camp.

SA was difficult to contain, and many complaints reached Hitler, but he was planning a final coup.

Hitler proclaimed a left-wing threat
Hitler had to portray the left as if they were a greater threat to the regime than the SA. The communists had always advocated a revolution and when the *Reichstag* building caught fire on the night of the 27 February 1933, Hitler blamed the communists, and argued that this was their signal for the revolution. Hindenburg agreed to pass an emergency decree which allowed enemies of the state to be imprisoned without trial. The SA and police swept 25,000 people into gaol. Frick took over the control of all the states in Germany in order to 'restore law and order', even though it was the SA who were causing most of the disturbances. Frick appointed Nazis in regional posts and made all of them answerable directly to Berlin. Germany's federal system was thus abruptly ended.

The Enabling Law

The March 1933 election
The elections Hitler had called for (5 March 1933) went ahead because Hitler wanted the Nazi takeover to appear legal. However, it is impossible to be sure how accurate the results were, due to an increasing intimidation of the voters. The percentage of the vote increased to 43.9%, but remember this was less than half of all voting Germans.

Figure 40. Hitler at the *Reichstag*.

Whilst the Nazis were the biggest party in the *Reichstag* (288 seats out of 647), they did not have a two-thirds majority which they would need to change the Constitution. However, the communists had been arrested, and some socialists were removed because of their earlier associations with the communists.

The Catholics supported Hitler for their own survival
Hitler persuaded the older nationalist parties to support him (as an anti-Marxist leader), and only the Catholic Centre Party remained to be allied because the SPD would never align itself with Hitler. Dr Kaas, the leader of the Catholic Centre Party, obtained Hitler's assurances that the Catholic church and its youth organisations would be allowed to remain intact in a Nazi state, and, fearful of the consequences of opposing the Nazis, Dr Kaas agreed to support Hitler in the forthcoming Enabling Bill. The Enabling Bill would allow Hitler to assume all the powers of the state, except those of the President, and therefore Hitler could make all his own laws.

Procedural amendments ensured support for the Enabling Bill
However, Frick changed the details of the legislation before it was presented on the 21 March 1933, in order to give Hitler complete power and total freedom of action. This was done in secrecy so that the other parties who agreed to support Hitler were now unwittingly supporting a proposal to which they had not agreed. Reassuring the traditional elites (landed aristocracy, senior military officers and the upper classes) that the 'old order' was about to be restored (and their powers), the Nazis obtained enough support to pass their Enabling Law. To make sure, Goering had declared any absentee would count as a 'yes' vote (for the Law). Communists' seats therefore automatically counted as 'yes' votes, and the SA and SS men who lined the entrance to the temporary *Reichstag* prevented some SPD deputies from getting inside to vote. Even when they were inside, SPD members were threatened and intimidated. The Nazis won their vote by 441 to 94.

The removal of opposition

Immediate action followed against the trade unions
The Enabling Law rendered other political parties unnecessary, and by June the Nationalists had merged into the Nazis. Jews were removed from parties and the civil service (7 April) and on 1 April 1933 there was a boycott of Jewish shops and businesses. Hitler also moved swiftly against the trade unions. Leaders were swept up in a wave of arrests. Hitler announced the unions could have May Day (1

May) as a holiday, something for which they had campaigned for many years, but on the next day he abolished trade unions, seized their assets and destroyed their offices. There were public information rallies, and Hitler announced the formation of the German Labour Front to replace the unions.

Figure 41. Nazi celebrations on Hitler's appointment as Chancellor, 30 January 1933.

Other groups were banned
On 22 June the SPD was banned. The Catholic Centre Party, facing imminent abolition, secured a final deal to protect Catholic schools and the right to preach in Catholic churches, before agreeing to its dissolution on 5 July 1933. On 14 July the NSDAP banned all other parties and Germany became a one-party state. German democracy had been destroyed, and all the major agencies of opposition, except the Presidency, had been removed.

The consolidation of power

There were two phases in the consolidation of power:

(i)   the *Gleichschaltung* (co-ordination)
(ii) the Night of the Long Knives, 1934.

Gleichschaltung (co-ordination)

The co-ordination of power was a process that took place over one year
The Nazis had taken power, but they were not secure in that power until they could be sure that every agency that could oppose them had been neutralised. The action they had taken by the end of 1933 was as follows:

▶ political parties had been banned
▶ left-wing opponents were imprisoned
▶ trade unions had been replaced by the (Nazi) German Labour Front
▶ the Catholic church had negotiated its neutrality
▶ the Protestant church leaders accepted that the Nazis were the legal authority in Germany.

Figure 42. The *Sturmabteilungen* (SA).

The SA came into conflict with the old conservative right
Nevertheless, there was still the President and the army to deal with. The President had been outflanked by the creation of emergency powers for Hitler with the Enabling Law. The army was the real target for Hitler's ambition. There remained one other threat, and that was the more socialist elements within his own party. The SA leadership reflected the views of many of the SA men. They were eager to settle a few scores with employers and other members of the bourgeoisie (middle class). They really wanted to see German society made into an egalitarian, state-owned system which benefited the SA themselves primarily, but also the poorer sections of the state. They wanted to see an end to the privileges of the super-rich, the landed aristocracy, the titled leaders of the army, and the big businessmen. They were, however, fiercely loyal to Hitler. They put loyalty above all else.

The Night of the Long Knives (30 June 1934)

The SA aimed for a social revolution
Hitler did not share the sentiments of the SA. He had no sympathy for socialism, and regarded the priorities as the reconstruction of Germany, the regeneration of its economy, and the preparation of the German people for war. Hitler called the seizure of power 'the national revolution', because he liked to claim that the nation had spoken and propelled the Nazis into power. SA leaders began to talk about a 'second revolution' which would purge German society of the middle class and the rich whom the SA felt they were the real enemies of Germany. The army began to show concern that the SA might seize power themselves and force the army's high command to resign, replacing them with a rebellious citizen's army. They were encouraged in this belief by the SS leadership who regarded the SA as rivals.

The purge of the SA leadership followed
Under the fictitious guise of stamping out a planned revolution, Hitler and the party leaders, using SS personnel, with trucks and weapons supplied by the army, launched dawn raids on the SA leadership on the 30 June 1934. This event was called the Night of the Long Knives because each member of the SS

Figure 43. Ernst Roehm, the SA leader 'liquidated' by the SS in 1934.

carried a long dagger. Many SA men were arrested and approximately 170 were killed. In the butchery, some old scores were settled. Gregor Strasser was assassinated. Ernst Roehm, the overall leader of the SA and one of Hitler's most loyal lieutenants, was shot shortly after his imprisonment by SS killers, as was General von Schleicher, the former Chancellor.

Hitler became Führer

The purge of the SA leadership was immediately legalised by the Reich Cabinet, and presented as timely intervention to prevent a civil war. Blomberg, the defence minister, thanked Hitler on the army's behalf. The real beneficiaries of the action though were the SS and their leader, Heinrich Himmler. When the old President died on 2 August 1934, the Nazis had already prepared their announcement that Hitler was to be known as the Führer (leader), a new appointment that combined the old posts of Chancellor and President in one. On 20 August the army swore an oath of allegiance to Hitler personally, as well as to Germany. The last agency that could oppose Hitler had therefore been neutralised.

Fear of civil war
Unknown reactions if Nazis were denied power: SA had plans for a coup d'état

Mass support
Pressure on elites to grant a place in government

Hitler selected as Chancellor

Alternative leaders
Unsuitable for reactionary aims

Elites wanted a safe pair of hands
Hitler seemed to have rejected radicalism

Figure 44. Hitler's selection as Chancellor.

The historical controversy on the Nazi seizure of power, and the failure of the Weimar Republic

The errors of the Weimar Republic

Explaining the lack of support for democracy is problematic
It could be argued that the German people stopped supporting the democratic

system of Weimar rather than voting positively for the Nazis, since the Nazis were able to 'tune in' to existing grievances in different sections of the population and exploit them. However, there are flaws with this view. Even at their most popular, Goebbels admitted that barely 48% of the country had voted in favour of the Nazis. Even so, more voters supported anti-democratic parties in the November 1932 and March 1933 elections, which suggests that the electorate had lost faith in democracy. The Weimar governments certainly committed errors, but extraordinary events, such as the economic depression also ensured the alienation of large sections of the population.

The distress of the economic crisis was very influential
There can be little doubt that 'distress' affected all sections of society. Unemployment figures (see page 51) actually record only the registered unemployed, so that amongst casual labourers the numbers unemployed are not recorded and the effect of the economic crisis was devastating for those already on or below the poverty line. The Weimar Republic also experienced a polarisation in its politics as a result of the joint agricultural and industrial depressions. High unemployment, which followed the stagnation of trade, was worsened by a failure of the democratic parties to co-operate in the teeth of a crisis. This polarisation spawned a wave of political violence, giving the impression that the Weimar system was unable to cope with crises. A succession of Chancellors added to the air of chaos.

The elites abandoned democracy and considered a dictatorship their only option
The elites in Germany, and the leaders of the Weimar Republic in its final months, all lost faith in the continuation of democracy. Papen, Schleicher, and even Brüning, aimed to crush the left and impose some form of dictatorship. The President was keen to uphold his duty, but after the Enabling Law of March 1933, found his powers curtailed. J. Noakes and G. Pridham imply that Oskar von Hindenburg persuaded the President to accept Hitler to avoid exposure of his corruption in the East Prussian aid project. The support of aristocrats and some leading capitalists, such as Alfred Hugenburg, seems to fit in with the Marxist interpretation of Nazism, but the threat of violence, the prospect of civil war and the ambiguous position of the army do not tally with a Marxist model. In November 1932, there seems to be evidence that some voters switched their allegiance away from Hitler, and began to vote for the nationalists again.

The Nazis' achievements

Who voted Nazi?
It could be argued that it was not so much Weimar's errors, but Hitler's achievements that secured power for the Nazis. Thomas Childers examined who voted for the Nazis in an attempt to analyse their motives. It would be simplistic to try to argue that the working class voted for the communists and the middle class for the Nazis, since the NSDAP enjoyed a broad cross-sectional appeal. Dick Geary argued that it was not simply the unemployed or narrow sectional interests that were economically motivated in their voting behaviour, but it was a cross-section of society who felt a common sense of grievance. Each group, and even different regions, as Ian Kershaw discovered, could produce quite different motives for supporting the Nazis. The traditional view, that one could identify male, young, Protestant and lower-middle-class voters as Nazi supporters has now been revised. The Nazis were a genuine *Volkspartei* (people's party) drawn from a range of classes and backgrounds. The majority of Nazi voters were also female.

> ### COMMENT:
> To the question: 'Who voted Nazi?' we might pertinently retort: 'Who didn't vote for them?'. Too often there is glib assumption that the German people flocked to Hitler's banners, but millions did not. The issue is important if we are ever to solve the enigma to just how the Nazis took power, and what responsibility the German public share for the horrors of Nazism.

Propaganda and opportunism assisted the Nazis
David Welch emphasised the impact of propaganda on support for the Nazis, which is evident in many eye-witnesses' accounts. For example, Hitler's message that democracy was 'a morass' was recorded at the time by Frau Luise Solmitz. She, like many others, believed that Hitler was a 'saviour' of Germany, suggesting the effectiveness of Hitler's delivery. The scale of popular support, and the speed of Hitler's acquisition of power has left historians speculating about how much calculation went into the process, and how much skill Hitler possessed in being able to exploit grievances and weaknesses so effectively. It might appear that Hitler's rise to power was inevitable, but there is much evidence to suggest that it was really a case of opportunism. Hitler tried and failed to become leader of Germany in the presidential elections of 1932, and was not selected as Chancellor until the very end. Perhaps there is danger in trying to credit Hitler with a skill he did not possess, when it really comes down to circumstances.

Conclusion

The records and eye-witnesses that historians use provide an indication that Hitler's appeal was cross sectional, and that the Nazis paid attention to, and exploited existing grievances in German society. Arguably their most popular appeal was anti-Weimar, and young people especially liked the radicalism of the movement. By contrast, the elites seemed to have been reluctant to appoint Hitler, not because they wished to preserve democracy, but because they feared the radicals within the Nazi party. These elites appeared to have wittingly, or unwittingly, worked towards the destruction of Weimar, regardless of the popular appeal of the Nazis, or the feelings of the masses towards the regime.

Tutorial

Progress questions

1. What piece of legislation gave Hitler 'emergency powers' in 1933?

2. What did the Nazis do in the 'co-ordination' phase of their take-over?

3. Why were the SA purged in 1934?

4. What errors did the Weimar politicians make, according to historians?

Discussion points

1. The charge of 'political corruption' could be made about the fall of the Weimar system. Yet Weimar's constitution was one of the strongest democratic constitutions in Europe. Gustav Stresemann was one of its most popular politicians, and had been conciliatory to Western leaders. What was less certain were his views on Eastern Europe and Russia. Is it in any sense valid to regard Weimar as weak? Were circumstances to blame, or individuals? Which individual was most to blame for the fall of the Weimar Republic? Were there continuities in Weimar's foreign policy, or was it that it was not nationalistic enough that helped discredit the Republic?

2. Marxist historians claimed that the economic crisis in Germany determined the formation and rise of the Nazis. Does this mean that in every economic crisis we can expect an attempted coup d'état or a revolution? If not, does that indicate that the economic factors were a cause of the Nazi seizure of power, or just a catalyst? Does the Nazi takeover follow a Marxist explanation of revolution?

3. Many have focused on the violence of the SA, and the direct action which the Nazis employed. However, in our own time, direct action is still popular. Terrorists regard 'direct action' as a justifiable method of pursuing a political aim. Demonstrations and strikes are a form of direct action, and animal rights activists fall into this category. Are these activities ever justifiable? Was the decision to lift the ban on the SA understandable? What were the consequences expected to be if the Nazis were denied power?

4. The German media made much of one by-election result at Lippe-Detmold in 1932 which the Nazis won. In many ways this coloured public opinion, even though this result was not necessarily reflective of the support for Nazism. It is interesting to test the significance of this historical event by examining what would have happened if this had been a non-Nazi area, or a Nazi 'safe seat' that was lost. What part did propaganda play in the Nazi takeover, and how important were the election results in assisting the Nazis into power?

Practical assignment

Read the extracts and answer the questions which follow.

A. Hitler and Otto Strasser, 1930

'All that is very simple for you, Herr Hitler', Strasser continued, 'but it only serves to emphasise the profound difference in our revolutionary and Socialist ideas. The reason you give for destroying the Kampfverlag [Strasser's publishing House] I take to be only pretexts. The real reason is that you want to strangle the social revolution for the sake of legality and your new collaboration with the parties of the Right.'

At this Hitler grew violent.

'I am a socialist, and a very different kind of socialist than your rich friend Reventlow. I was once an ordinary working-man. I would not allow my chauffeur to eat worse than myself. But your kind of socialism is nothing but Marxism. The mass of the working classes want nothing but bread and games. They will never understand the meaning of an ideal, and we cannot hope to win them over to one. What we have to do is select from a new master-class men who will not allow themselves to be guided, like you, by the morality of pity. Those who rule must know they have the right to rule because they belong to a superior race. They must maintain that right and ruthlessly consolidate it. . .'

B. Account from the diary of Frau Luise Solmitz of an election meeting, 1932
He censured the system (I want to know what is left to be ruined in this state!)
'On the way here Socialists confronted me with a poster, "Turn Back, Adolph
Hitler". Thirteen years ago I was a simple unknown soldier. I went my way. I
never turned back. Nor shall I turn back now.' Otherwise he made no
personal attacks, nor any promises vague or definite. His voice was hoarse
after all his speaking during the previous days. When the speech was over,
there was roaring enthusiasm and applause. Hitler saluted, gave his thanks,
the Horst Wessel song sounded out across the course. Hitler was helped into
his coat. Then he went. – How many look up to him with touching faith! as
their helper, their saviour, their deliverer from unbearable distress – to him
who rescues the Prussian prince, the scholar, the clergyman, the farmer, the
worker, the unemployed, who rescues them from the parties back into the
nation.

**C. Extract from Goebbels' diary on the meeting between Hitler and
Hindenburg, 13 August 1932.**
…The Führer is back in under half an hour. So it has ended in failure. He
has gained nothing. Papen is to remain Chancellor and the Führer has to
content himself with the position of Vice-Chancellor!

A solution leading to no result! It is out of the question to accept such a
proposal. There is no alternative but to refuse. The Führer did so immediately.
Like the rest of us, he is fully aware of the consequences. It will mean a hard
struggle but we shall triumph in the end…

A grim task, but we have to go through with it. There is no other way. The
idea of the Führer as Vice-Chancellor of a bourgeois party is too ludicrous to
be treated seriously…

**D. Otto Meissner's account at the Nuremberg Tribunal on the developments
that led to Hitler's appointment as Chancellor**.
He [Hindenburg] wanted to have Papen again as Chancellor. Papen finally
won him over to Hitler with the argument that the representatives of the
other parties which would belong to the government would restrict Hitler's
freedom of action. In addition Papen expressed misgivings that, if the present
opportunity were again missed, a revolt of National Socialists and civil war
were likely.

1. Explain Hitler's understanding of the term Socialism (source A).

2. Compare sources A and B. How successfully did Hitler convey his ideas on Socialism and national regeneration in these extracts?

3. Using all the sources and your wider knowledge, examine the view that 'Hitler gained the Chancellorship more as a result of political intrigue than popular ideology'.

Study tips

1. Make two lists of causes of the Nazi take-over under the headings 'Short term' and 'Long term'. Aim to find about four or five for each list.

2. Don't be tempted to *describe* the rise to power of the Nazis, but take an analytical view by trying to explain each of the factors in your lists.

3. Look up and include in your studies the *concepts* from this chapter (such as *Gleichschaltung*, or the various forms of dictatorship). Using concepts in your work will impress lecturers and examiners more than descriptions.

4. Add the views of other historians, even if you don't agree with them. This will show that are able to acknowledge different opinions, and refuting them makes your own work more analytical.

5

The National Socialist ...

One-minute overview – The Nazis quickly established their auth...
Hitler was the sole leader in a one-party state. He relied on a combinati... of coercion
and persuasion to stay in power. The apparatus of terror and dictatorship is well
documented. However, the degree to which this constitutes a fully totalitarian
system is open to debate. Michael Burleigh has revealed how much collaboration
there was with the regime. However, there has been a great deal of disagreement
amongst historians over the relative importance of Hitler in the decision-making of
the Third Reich. Many have argued that Hitler was a very weak dictator who relied
on the state and his subordinates in the party. Others have pointed to Hitler's
abilities as a propagandist, and his forceful character, which drove the regime
forward. The debate is not easily resolved because it depends on whether Hitler can
be regarded as a man of ability, or of mediocrity, which has implications about the
gullibility of the German people and the role of Hitler's subordinates.

In this chapter you will learn:
- ▶ *How Hitler's dictatorship worked.*
- ▶ *The historical controversy which surrounds the leadership of the Third Reich.*

This section contains two sub-divisions:

a. how Hitler's dictatorship functioned
b. the Nazis' means of controlling society.

How Hitler's dictatorship worked

There are three ways of examining Hitler's dictatorship:

(i)   Hitler's form of leadership
(ii) the hierarchy of government
(iii) the historical controversy over Hitler's leadership.

itler's form of leadership in theory and practice

The theory: unlimited power

Theoretically, Hitler had all the powers which had been formerly ascribed to the President and the Chancellor in the Weimar Republic. However, Hans Frank, the Head of the Association of German Lawyers, stated that Hitler's powers went beyond any constitutional limits which had previously been imposed on German rulers. Hitler's power was defined as being derived from the will of the people. Hitler's actions were therefore taken on their behalf and could not be challenged. Moreover, Frank argued, Hitler's power was unfettered and therefore able to be totally creative.

The practice: chaos

Figure 45. Indolent Führer: Hitler at the Berghof.

The reality was quite different. Although Hitler had all the powers of the state, he was uncomfortable with its procedures and chose to superimpose the party structure over the state. The civil service therefore found itself by-passed by party members. Worse still, Hitler chose when to work and when to be at leisure, and was frequently unavailable when decisions had to be taken. By the late 1930s, Hitler's routine of work had almost broken down as he rose at lunchtime and ceased the business of state by late afternoon. He preferred to watch feature films or take walks and rarely read official documents. Casual remarks were made by Hitler which became directives of the state, since no other avenue for decision-making existed. His indolence did not suit a state that relied on one individual to make decisions on its behalf. Hitler could not be in a position to know all the details of state business anyway, and subordinates often withheld unpalatable information since they feared his rage or his disapproval. Hugh Trevor-Roper likened Hitler's government to a twelfth-century court, since it eventually consisted of Hitler's closest associates who knew how to handle him.

The hierarchy of government

The theoretical structure
In theory, the government was organised in a strict hierarchy like an army. At the apex was the Führer with unlimited powers and total responsibility for the direction of Germany. Below him was the Reich Cabinet, whose job it was to ratify the Führer's decisions and frame them into laws. The Cabinet's Ministers each took responsibility for a certain area of administration, such as the economy, labour, or defence. Serving them were the civil service. However, working directly to the Führer were the provincial governors of the party, or *Gauleiters*. Added to this senior team was the party leadership, co-ordinated by the party secretary. Under the *Gauleiters* were the district leaders, or *Kreisleiters*. Below them were the *Ortleiters*, down to the *Zelleiters* (cell leaders) and *Blockwarte* (block wardens for flats, or a street). In theory, party and state worked together to solve Germany's problems. If there were clashes or overlaps, one would assume responsibility depending on whether the issue was political or administrative.

The practice: competition
In practice, Hitler would generate competition where it didn't already exist between departments, by simply creating new appointments or responsibilities. He took the view that if someone in authority was challenged, they should deal with it firmly, or be replaced by the challenger. Hitler would appeal directly to subordinates if it suited him, and miss out, contradict and overrule *Gauleiters*, particularly if he couldn't get his way. If there were disputes, he would often remain aloof and intervene if and when he felt like it, sometimes without success. Even at the highest levels there was no unity. Around the Führer gathered the Chancellory (*Kanzlerei*), a group of Nazis who could best be described as his friends and favourites. They were adept at dealing with Hitler, but this meant that his chauffeurs (often given the rank of general) and adjutants often had more influence and power than the *Gauleiters*. Some ministers were simply not seen by Hitler because he didn't get on with them. Those who knew they did not have Hitler's favour would appoint adjutants to be in Hitler's presence at the Berghof, his holiday residence. The result was a chaotic regime, full of competing groups. Historians have described the Third Reich as a polycratic (many rulers) system.

The Nazis' means of controlling society

The Nazis' means of controlling German society can be summarised as:

(i)   the secret police (Gestapo)

(ii) informers

(iii) the law and the Third Reich

(iv) the SS

(v)   the concentration camps.

The secret police (Gestapo)

The Third Reich was a form of police state. The police were granted new powers and given new roles in monitoring the activities of the people. Subversive behaviour and criticism of the state was criminalised from 1933, and the secret police could imprison any suspect without trial. The secret police were a branch of the SS, and feared for their brutality and routine torture. Quite innocent expressions of discontent could lead to interrogation and a prison term of hard labour. When the Nazis took over the civil police of the Weimar Republic, they inherited all the files on the population. It was therefore a relatively easy matter to track down and intimidate potential opponents. The structure of the Nazi regime's secret police and civil-police network was as follows.

Himmler (Chief of Police and *Reichsführer* SS) was in command of police services overall. Each department was then divided as follows:

Sipo	The security police concerned with internal security
Orpo	The regular police force
SD	(*Sicherheitsdienst*) The SS security service (overseas and Germany)
RSHA	(*Reichssicherheitshauptamt*) The Reich security department
VOMI	(*Volksdeutsche Mittelstelle*) The Reference Officer for Racial Germans, an office that decided on the suitability of one ethnic origin for service in the state
RKF	(*Reichskommissar fur die Festigung Deutschen Volktums*) The Commissioner for strengthening Germanism, a similar task to VOMI
WVHA	(*Wirtschafts- und Verwaltungshauptamt*) The Economic and Administration department
The SS	Subdivided into the *Verfügungstruppen* and *Totenkopf* units. The armed version of the SS was known as the *Waffen SS*
Gestapo	The secret police with responsibility for political crimes
Kripo	The secret police tasked with dealing with other criminal activity

Informers

It would be impossible for a police force to be able to control the entire population of a country by its own efforts. The chilling fact of totalitarian regimes (where control of society is total) is the degree of willing and unwitting participation of the mass of the population for reasons of self preservation, promotion, or fear. The method used in Nazi Germany was that individuals were approached to 'inform' the authorities about any unusual or unpatriotic comments or activities by neighbours. By approaching several individuals, a whole network of informers could be set up. However, the effect of one or two successful outcomes where 'subversives' were arrested, was out of all proportion to the input. Within months, people feared that almost everyone was an informer. People dared not say anything out of the official line lest even their children inform on them. In fact, it was safer to become an informer than to wait until one was informed upon. The net effect was to create a climate of fear and isolation. In George Orwell's novel, *1984*, a fictional society regulated itself because of a fear of informers and it was based on a combination of Hitler's Germany and Stalin's Soviet Union.

The law and the Third Reich

▶ *The Nazis made use of the law.*
It would be fair to say that objectivity and independence in the law were lost under the Nazi regime. The Nazis altered the law to suit their priorities, best summed up in the phrase 'protection of the state'. As early as 17 February 1933, the Nazis had legalised the 'shooting' of 'enemies of the state' with impunity. Thus the law would ensure the discipline of its own people, and for Hitler, who had seen Germany collapse from internal rebellion during the First World War, this would be a vital factor in winning the next war.

▶ *There was collaboration by the judges.*
Many of the judges favoured the right wing before Hitler came to power because they feared communism. At Hitler's trial in 1924, the judges had looked upon his patriotic Putsch with sympathy. Many could therefore be relied upon to implement Hitler's 'police state' without opposition. Under the Nazis, 'race' became a legal concept. The civil service took an oath of loyalty in 1934, and the Supreme Court was abolished. Judges were obliged to wear the Swastika badge. There was an increase in the use of the death penalty and sentences for 'social undesirables' and political opponents included sexual sterilisation. These measures tell us that the Nazis aimed to use the law as a weapon against the left and against Germany's 'biological enemies'.

Hitler appointed as Chancellor: January 1933
Reichstag Fire: 27 February 1933 (prior to election)
Election: 5 March 1933
Enabling Law for emergency powers

▶ Police and new auxiliary police seize and imprison potential revolutionaries.
▶ Destruction of other parties and trade unions.
▶ First action against Jews: boycott.
▶ Police action against all potential opponents and the free press.

However, growing threat of SA destroying elites or German society and provoking reaction before Hitler had full power.

▶ Pressure from army and SS to take action against SA.

Night of the Long Knives: 30 June 1934
President Hindenburg died: August 1934 Hitler became Führer

Figure 46. The role of the SS and SA in the *Gleichschaltung* (co-ordination).

The SS

Originally a branch of the SA, the SS were a paramilitary unit with the special task of protecting Hitler. Their members were recruited on the basis of their physical appearance and their fierce loyalty to Hitler, but they grew rapidly in number, and gradually assumed a more important role in the regime. This was largely because they acted with Hitler's authority, and, as Hitler's authority assumed a new importance after the death of Hindenburg on 2 August 1934, so too did the authority of the SS. Hitler felt that he was fulfilling an historic mission, the creation of a *Volksgemeinschaft* for the Aryan race, and therefore his authority

was above the state. Hitler could legitimatise all actions. The SS were the executive arm of Hitler's power, and the SS therefore asserted itself within the state, especially in the realms of internal security, then later in resettlement and population policies, and, after 1939, in the occupied territories.

Figure 47. SS rally.

Two areas need particular explanation:

(i)   the rise of the SS
(ii) new roles for the SS.

The rise of the SS
In February 1933, the SS became auxiliary policemen. With Hitler's authority as Reich Chancellor, and with Frick and Goering in command of the police, the actions of the SS were legalised. They took part in the arrest of communist leaders after the *Reichstag* Fire (27 February 1933), and set up their own concentration camps after the election of March 1933. Whilst SA camp personnel tended to bully their opponents, the SS carried out routine torture and maintained a stricter security. In the early days of the regime, some SS units actually mutinied and Hitler threatened to use the army's artillery against them. This indiscipline was soon crushed and the SS remained steadfastly loyal to Hitler to the bitter end.

▶ *The rivalry of the SA turned to bloodshed.*
   It was the SA that was the most outspoken in their criticism of the new regime. Many were impatient for jobs, local powers, revenge against their enemies and possessed a vague, revolutionary spirit of wanting to 'settle a few scores' against the middle classes. But the SA was something of a rival organisation to the SS. The administration of the state could not be divided between the two groups, and tension built up throughout the hierarchy of the regime. The SS played on the army leaders' fears that the SA was planning to carry out a revolution with considerable bloodshed. Roehm had proposed that the SA replace the army, and the SS used Roehm's inflammatory remarks as evidence that he was planning a coup. A conflict was forestalled by Hitler's purge of the SA in the Night of the Long Knives (30 June 1934). The SS were provided with arms and transport by the army, and they helped to round up the SA leadership and execute them.

▶ *The result of the purge of the SA was undisputed supremacy by the SS.*
   The purge placed Himmler in a more powerful position, but he was still only one of the 'inner circle' of Hitler's entourage. With him was Heydrich who established a security service element to the SS. Their task was to acquire intelligence on potential enemies in their bodyguard duties. This was the first development of their role since they were first established as a group only 100 strong, and, with the purge, it showed how they had departed from the revolutionary bands of the SA, and how they had integrated themselves into the state apparatus.

Bodyguards to Hitler, 100 strong.

Auxiliary police in 1933
    Made arrests
    Ran **concentration camps** – discipline
                                   – torture
                                   – execution

Night of the Long Knives
    Killed the leaders of the rival SA

Established a **secret police force**
    Gradually took over all internal security

Waffen SS formed as a military wing in 1939

All other police units absorbed and integrated
    Secret police acted above the law using Hitler's authority

Took over **industries** during the war and terrorised the people

The instrument of **anti-Semitic policies** and the **Holocaust**

Figure 48. The rise of the SS.

New roles for the SS

▶ *The early role of the SS was as a police service.*
   After 1933 the SS gradually incorporated police activities, and after 1934 they assumed responsibility for all concentration camps. On 17 June 1936, Himmler was created Chief of Police as well as head of the SS. This had been in response to Frick's demands to Hitler that there should be a clarification of policing in Germany since the SS tended to overlap the responsibilities of Frick's policemen. However, Frick was surprised that Himmler, not himself, was granted full control. The secret police immediately assumed control of all policemen in the Reich and the files on virtually every German citizen, which made the targeting of their enemies even more efficient. In October 1939, the police and SS were amalgamated. The SS also raised a new armed unit, the *Waffen SS*, to rival the army, and to spearhead it with a racial elite.

▶ *The new role of the SS was as a vessel for breeding a super race.*
   Himmler defined the role and position of the SS in 1937 in a statement called 'The Nature and Task of the SS and Police'. Essentially they were to maintain law and order to avoid a repeat of the 'stab in the back', a euphemism for civilian agitation against war in 1918–19. But the SS was also designed to secure the organic life of the Aryan race and its institutions against the Jewish-Bolshevik threat of destruction and decomposition. Hitler prophetically warned that the next war would be an 'ideological war' against Bolshevism which had aimed at 'the destruction of the whole world'.

Concentration camps

In the initial seizure of power a large number of camps sprang up to house the massive influx of internees, since the existing prisons could not cope. In Bavaria, 27,512 people were imprisoned in this way between March 1933 and November 1937, but the majority served relatively short sentences and the peak period was between 1933 and 1935. When Himmler took over, the system was rationalised and there were fewer, but larger camps under SS control.

▶ *The profile of prisoners illustrates Nazi prejudices.*

The profile of prisoners' cases illustrates Nazi thinking. The overwhelming number of prisoners were Jews. They were more likely to be taken into custody because they could not belong to the nation as citizens, and therefore constituted a potential threat. Other 'asocial' groups, or *Gemeinschaftsfremde*, could include gypsies, criminals, homosexuals, tramps, the mentally ill and a broad category simply called the 'work-shy'. Anyone who refused the offer of a job from the regime could find themselves in this group and consequently in a concentration camp. The KZ (concentration camp initials) were certainly known to the general public and there was widespread fear of being sent to one. However, it cannot be assumed that German people had knowledge of the later death camps in the same way.

▶ *Camp discipline was tough.*

Discipline and regulations were strict and rigidly enforced. From 1 August 1933 SS regulations applied to every camp, and in the first instance gave almost unlimited powers to the camp commandant. Flogging or solitary confinement were the responses to minor misdemeanours, such a grumbling, or sending letters which contained criticism of the regime. Hanging was applied to potential or actual resistance, but could equally apply to anyone who was caught discussing politics, formed a clique, loitered around with other prisoners, or transmitted information about conditions in the camp by any means. Any physical attack on a guard or discussion during a march to a labour task would result in the offender being shot on the spot. Other punishments ranged from withholding food and beatings, to drilling or reprimands. Even camp guards were liable to severe punishment if they failed to carry out an execution instantaneously.

COMMENT:
What distinguishes the most successful writing is the ability to conceptualise and to analyse. The ability to apply concepts (such as power, totalitarianism, or causation) to solve historical problems, and the skill to argue for or against more than one interpretation of the past, are the hallmarks of outstanding work.

Designed to encourage participation:

- The RAD
- *Volksgemeinschaft* (Winter Aid and *Eintopfsuppe*)
- SA, NSBO
- Holidays and events
- Women's movements
- Youth movements
- Party membership and promotion

Designed to control by fear:

- Secret police and SS
- The law
- Informers
- Concentration camps

Figure 49. Nazi policies of control.

The historical controversy over Hitler's leadership: 'weak dictator' or 'master of the Third Reich'

The dispute between historians called Intentionalists and Functionalists/ Structuralists resurfaces here and centres around the question 'was Hitler a strong or weak dictator?' The current debate on Hitler's role and importance in Nazism has certainly been around since the late 1960s and shows no sign of abating. After the Second World War, anguished German scholars found it difficult to discuss Hitler, and a generation after the war found it too emotional an issue for the dispassionate rigour of history.

Hitler as a relatively important factor

Fest believed Hitler was the product of the times and of his supporters

Joachim Fest was one of the first to try to put Hitler in his economic and social context. In fact he was really resurrecting some of the ideas of contemporaries on the left wing, suggesting that Hitler's rise to power was the outcome of specific, local, socio-economic factors prevailing in Germany after the First World War. However, Fest adapted the crude 'agent' approach (the idea that Hitler was really little more than the tool of the capitalists, such as Krupps, which was the classic Marxist interpretation). He analysed the grass roots Nazi supporters, and not the industrialists, examining their occupations and economic background and played down the other approaches of the 1960s which stressed Hitler's quasi-hypnotic powers. Fest approached the problem of Hitler's rise to power from the point of view of the people's reactions to him, rather than Hitler's personality.

Fest resolved the problem of leadership in the Third Reich
Nevertheless, Nazi foreign policy, and economic and social policies were still beyond the realm of popular pressure, Fest believed. Hitler's personality was important insofar as it reflected the anxieties, hopes, and fears of an economically depressed society, but Hitler also imparted racialist ideas and an aggressive foreign policy to Germany, and *Mein Kampf* provides us with the evidence for this (see explanations of anti-Semitism and *Lebensraum* in Chapter 2). However, the traditional elites in Germany, the civil service, army, and industrialists, managed to retain considerable power, or their positions, by co-operation with Hitler's schemes. But if you want a contrasting view to Fest's thesis, then look at Lucy Dawidowicz's work in which Dawidowicz returns to Hitler's central role and his demonism.

Hitler as the most important factor

Historians who regard Hitler as exceptional, and somehow gifted with certain skills which make him central to the fate of Nazism and the Third Reich, include Alan Bullock, R. G. Waite, K. Hildebrand and W. Langer. There is little doubt that Hitler definitely had an important role, and his drive in the rise to power, and his position in the Third Reich confirm this. His powers were unlimited and eyewitnesses reported that individuals did not stand up to Hitler as he was too overbearing. Furthermore, they worked towards Hitler's goals voluntarily, since they feared Hitler's disapproval, or were inspired by him. A better understanding of crowd psychology and mass hysteria have dispelled the ludicrous notions that Hitler was possessed of an evil genius, and show that people's reactions to him were illustrations of a sense of collective desperation. More recently, the bizarre theorists have concentrated on Hitler's childhood as an explanation for the Holocaust, but there is little or no evidence for their claims.

Figure 50. Germania: Hitler's plan for a new Berlin – a fantasy realm to which he frequently escaped.

Hitler as an unimportant factor

Hitler was a weak dictator
Martin Broszat saw Hitler as a rather weak figure, unable to control his
subordinates, and the Third Reich was a somewhat ramshackle and disorganised
affair. Departments were duplicated and became rivals; subordinates became
bitter enemies and struggled with each other for Hitler's approval to the detriment
of the country. Hitler was rather lazy, and failed to intervene at critical moments
to settle disputes and establish policy, but interfered (with disastrous results as in
the case of the order that denied General Paulus' Sixth Army the chance to make
a tactical withdrawal from Stalingrad, leading to their defeat in 1943). The
strongest advocate of Hitler as a weak figure, controlled by the rivalries of his
subordinates who fed him information as they chose, was Hans Mommsen. He
identified a 'cumulative radicalisation' process, whereby subordinates, in their
desire to fulfil a programme of Hitler's imagination became bitter rivals and
competed, not for Hitler's approval, but with each other. As a result, programmes
developed a momentum of their own which Hitler, the weak dictator, was unable
to control. The regime lurched out of control and produced war and genocide.

The most recent debate has focused on Hitler's leadership qualities. It is now
acknowledged that Hitler was exceptional and 'driven' by certain ideas, but he
lacked the qualities associated with good leadership. Ian Kershaw has shown that
he led by force of personality and he provided a 'vision'. However, some structures
and people he introduced exacerbated the confusion of government and led to a
dynamic. This reminds us that responses to Hitler (including the reactions of
voters) is also important. Michael Burleigh has identified a quasi-religious
following for Hitler that reflects a German cultural crisis. Robert Gellately argues
that many 'ordinary Germans' embraced Nazi politics and Hitler's
authoritarianism. Nevertheless, it is impossible to generalise about the reactions
of the German people, especially when the evidence is so thin. It is simply
unreliable to view cheering crowds at rallies and assume that *all* Germans felt the
same way as these party faithful. Moreover, within the regime, there were those
who actively 'worked towards the Führer', as Kershaw put it, to achieve favours
from Hitler or simply because there were no orders. In the final analysis,
historians are clear that, whatever the system, Hitler was ultimately responsible
for the crimes committed in the 1930s and 1940s. He presided over a system that
was as brutal as it was inefficient. Orbiting around him were men eager either to
fulfil the Nationalist Socialist agenda, like Himmler and Goebbels, or those who

wanted a share of power and privilege, like Bormann and Goering, but it was Hitler who governed.

The weak leader	The strong leader
Couldn't control everything	Total power
Subject to limits on information	Powers above the law
Hitler was ineffective	Powers above the state
Persuaded to act by subordinates	He took the crucial decisions
Structure of regime dictated	He intended certain outcomes
Structuralists	**Intentionalists**

Figure 51. The polarities of the Intentionalist-Structuralist interpretations.

Tutorial

Progress questions

1. How was the Third Reich led in theory?

2. What differences were there in practice?

3. List the historians who believe that Hitler was (a) strong and (b) weak. How convincing are their approaches?

4. To what extent was Nazi Germany an efficient 'police state'?

Discussion points

1. How satisfactorily were conflicts resolved in the policies of the Nazi movement in the early days (1920–33)?

2. How effectively did Hitler deal with those who opposed him?

3. In the seizure of power, what was Hitler's contribution? To what extent did 'circumstance' intervene for him? Does this make him a 'strong' leader?

4. How well was Hitler supported by his subordinates? After further research consider Goebbels, Goering, Roehm, and Himmler.

5. Did the Nazi 'revolution' occur when, or after, they had taken power?

Practical assignment

Study the following account by Fritz Wiedermann, one of Hitler's adjutants.

> 'In 1935, Hitler kept a fairly ordered routine. Gradually... this broke down.
> Later Hitler normally appeared shortly before lunch, read quickly
> through Reich Press Chief Dietrich's press cuttings, and then went into
> lunch. ...When Hitler stayed at the Obersaltzburg it was even worse. There
> he never left his room before 2.00pm. Then he went to lunch. He spent most
> of his afternoons taking a walk, in the evenings, straight after dinner, there
> were films. ...He disliked the study of documents. I have sometimes
> secured decisions from him, even on important matters, without his ever
> asking to see the relevant files.'

1. Which historiographical approach to Hitler's leadership is most closely
    represented in this account?

2. What were the advantages and disadvantages of these methods to decision-
    making in the Third Reich?

Study tips

1. Understanding this chapter is central to all the others because it involves how
    decisions were made in the Nazi regime. Try to remember the Intentionalist
    and Functionalist approaches, and offer a resolution to the debate.

2. Look back over Hitler's rise to power and the consolidation phase. List the
    episodes that fit the Intentionalist or Functionalist approach.

3. If you write out one example in more detail, and find both approaches within
    it, you can use this example in your essays and studies.

4. Try to remember the different parts of the apparatus of dictatorship. When
    you examine resistance to the regime, you will need to acknowledge the
    power of the system the dissidents faced.

6

Nazi Propaganda and Social Policy

One-minute overview – *Hitler's priorities, once his power had been firmly established, was to regenerate the economy, and set up the institutions necessary to prepare the German people for the coming 'racial struggle'. However, despite the efficient propaganda, popular social movements and a massive increase in production, there were a number of fissures in German society. The regime was never able to release its grip of terror, and therefore it would be true to say that the regime was reliant on coercion. However, not all Germans cowered beneath the secret police, and there was some degree of consensus and compliance. Nazi social policies and propaganda can explain some of the reasons for collaboration, but it should be borne in mind that individual experiences were widely different.*

In this chapter you will learn:
▶ *How the Nazis attempted to control and regenerate German society.*
▶ *About the themes and techniques of Nazi propaganda.*

The Nazis' attempted regeneration of German society

The Nazis' vision of a new Germany was founded on the ideas Hitler had expressed in *Mein Kampf*. Broadly, these can be divided into:

a. the *Volksgemeinschaft* (people-centred community)
b. public institutions
c. womanhood in the Third Reich
d. youth movements.

The *Volksgemeinschaft* (people-centred community)

The Nazis believed in 'community'
The concept of a people-centred community was the closest the Nazis got to implementing a socialist programme. It was an attempt to create a sense of belonging and mutual good-neighbourliness in German society. Radicals had

Figure 52. The propaganda myth: Hitler as saviour of Germany.

grown tired of the materialism of capitalism, which had divided society with inequalities of wealth and property. The *Volksgemeinschaft* approach would re-establish a folk-community, something approximating to the atmosphere one might have found in a village. The Nazis established a Winter Aid project, where volunteers collected warm clothing for the elderly from the rest of the local community. Periodically, citizens would be encouraged to eat *Eintopfsuppe* (one-pot soup) together, rather than eating separately, as a demonstration of solidarity with the poorer members of society and a signal that Nazism believed in some form of equality.

'Folk-community' was a propaganda ploy
But the concept was little more than wishful thinking, or, as David Welch believes, a propaganda ploy. The Nazi elite continued to enjoy their privileges throughout the period. Herman Goering, for example, acquired a particularly comfortable existence. Meanwhile, the Nazis' economic programme depressed people's standard of living artificially. Furthermore, those that fell foul of the regime were regarded as falling outside the *Volksgemeinschaft*, and therefore were no longer entitled to legal protection or other liberties. Most important of all was the fact that only ethnic Germans could participate in the *Volksgemeinschaft* anyway. Jews and other minorities were excluded. The best that can be said about the programme was that it emphasised an existing community spirit and gave it publicity.

Public institutions

Most public institutions in Nazi Germany centred around the building of a sense of national identity over and above traditional regional loyalties, and the promotion of public health. This coincided with Hitler's aim to make the German people the vessels for the racial struggle. This would require Germans to be radically nationalistic thereby helping them to identify racial enemies as different and inferior. It would also assist them to be as healthy as possible to assist in the procreation of more Aryan children.

These can be summarised as follows:

(i) German Labour Service
(ii) national holidays and national symbolism.

German Labour Service

The RAD (*Reichsarbeitdienst*) or German Labour Service was an organisation not simply designed to absorb the army of unemployed which the regime inherited in 1933. Hitler envisaged a new dignity for the manual labourer, and a prestige which would replace the condescending attitude which had existed under the Weimar Republic. In order to gain full citizenship, Hitler had written in *Mein Kampf*, the individual would have to perform some service in the ranks of the SA and the army. Citizenship was a privilege to be earned, and the

Figure 53. Parade of the *Reichsarbeitdienst* (RAD) – the Labour Service.

Labour Service was planned to be a compulsory first step to that prize.

Ritual days: national holidays and national symbolism

The Nazis sought to reinforce conformity and a sense of collective identity by enforcing the Hitler salute, the hanging out of flags for official Nazi dates in the calendar, and by the celebration of key events such as Hitler's birthday. Such conformity tended to produce apathy and a sense of resignation, rather than total enthusiasm, except perhaps in the younger generation. This, according to J. Noakes and G. Pridham, worked to the regime's advantage in that its survival relied not just on terror, but a certain degree of consensus.

Figure 54. Party headquarters in Munich: the Brown House.

Womanhood in the Third Reich

Women: the childbearers

Hitler was not exactly disparaging about women, but they hardly featured at all in his theories. In *Mein Kampf* they barely appear at all, but it is not a simple case of male chauvinist arrogance which some historians often expect to find. Hitler saw women as bearers of children, and given the central position of race to his ideas, he saw women as fulfilling a crucial role across the generations. Whilst he saw the men doing the fighting against Marxism, he saw women producing as many healthy Aryan babies as possible. In the biological war against world Jewry, Hitler felt that the Aryans would have to 'out-breed' their opponents. Women were not second-rate citizens in this sense, but linked inextricably to his master plan.

Hitler opposed women's liberation

He regarded women's liberation as a nonsense because he could not understand why women should want to be liberated from their natural role of having children. This can raise passions in debate, but there seems to be a more balanced view prevailing now that women should be able to choose, and be able to have both a career and a family. However, this is a recent view and we are in danger of being historicist if we try to impose our own views upon the past. For many women the traditions of *Kinder, Kuche und Kirche* (children, kitchen and church) were the norm, which is why Scholtz-Klink, the leader of the women's movement, had so much trouble recruiting women into party activities. Hitler believed that the compass of female interest should be to cherish her husband, her family and her home. Yet Hitler also spoke of the female role in *Volksgemeinschaft*, a community where he felt women had an important part to play. Given that women were a crucial component of the economic fabric of the Third Reich, the contradictions of the Nazi view of women were clear: women were supposed to be equal but subordinate to men, and they were supposed to be in the home but were needed in the workplace.

Figure 55. The Führer myth: Hitler portrayed as a friend of animals and children.

Female employment profiles reflected the nation's needs
Women's employment profiles reveal a traditional pattern before and after 1933, reflecting the demands of the country's economy rather than social engineering. The majority of women remained in agriculture, with a steady rise in clerical and administrative appointments during the war years. In 1933, women made up half of the 8.9 million strong agricultural workforce, and 1.2 million were engaged in domestic service. They were strongly represented in nursing, welfare services, churches and religious institutions, catering, clothing manufacture and the tobacco or confectionary industries. Nevertheless, Hitler banned married women from the higher ranks of medicine, legal posts and the civil service. All women were forbidden to enter politics. Loans were offered to married couples if the woman would withdraw from the labour market, and there were tax breaks too. In the first years of the war, female employment fell across all sectors (except administrative work), illustrating Nazi efforts to get them out of employment, but the figures rose again by 1944, partly because female employees were cheaper. Thus by the end of the war there were 5.7 million in agriculture and forestry, 3.6 million in industry, 2.1 million in finance and transport, 1.2 million in domestic service and 1.7 million in administration.

Women's groups were class-based
Hitler, like many Nazis, resented the promiscuity of the years before 1933, especially in Berlin. He also objected to the rights accorded to women by the Weimar Republic's constitution. Nazi views of women were often based on traditional middle-class moral standards. The activities of the female youth groups reflected this concern to create idealised versions of women. They were to be beautiful, physically honed, and yet courageous and determined, thereby complementing their Nazi menfolk. The Nazis stated that they intended to increase the Aryan German population and actively encouraged women to have large families. Medals were awarded to the most fecund. The number of marriages and births did increase after 1932 (marriages rose from 516,793 to 618,971 in 1937, whilst births rose from 993,126 to 1.27 million in the same period). However, according to Tim Mason, some of this may have been due to the improved economic situation after the Depression and the financial bribes. Yet the fact is that many German women, like the men, participated in the Third Reich in the hope that they were contributing to the improvement of their country. Many joined the Nazi women's groups. The NS-F (*Nationale Sozialistische Frauenschaft*) was the elite (leadership) group numbering 2.8 million in 1938, whilst the wider DFW (*Deutsches Frauenwerk*) numbered 4 million by the same

Figure 56. Poster: The Hitler Youth.

date. The BDM (*Bund Deutscher Mädel*) was more popular and enlisted girls of 14–18, while the JM (*Jungmädelbund*) targeted the 10–14 year olds.

Youth movements

The structure and values of the Hitler Youth were militaristic
For boys and young men there was a comprehensive structure which Hitler had outlined in *Mein Kampf*. He stated that young men should do service in youth organisations where basic skills could be taught and Nazi values learnt. Then they would graduate to the SA until some physical fitness and skills in agility could be honed prior to joining the army. After military service citizenship rights would be earned (not granted) and party service (for the ablest) would follow. In reality boys of 10–14 joined the DJ or *Pimpfen* (*Deutsches Jungvolk* or 'cubs'), then the HJ or *Hitler Jugend* (Hitler Youth, 14–18). The select few would attend one of the Adolf Hitler Schools to become a future party leader. The leader of the youth organisations was Baldur Schirach, and his organisation numbered 50,000 in 1931 rising to some 7.2 million (out of 8.8 million young people aged between 10 and 18) in 1939.

Figure 57. The Hitler Youth: marching was regarded as an essential part of youth training.

The Hitler Youth was popular compared with other groups
Existing organisations, such as Roman Catholic groups and Scouting, suffered a fall in membership. The aim was to create and sustain a mass organisation, with an emphasis on camps, drill, uniforms, the values of patriotism, courage and discipline which would create social conformity and replace the emphasis on

academic achievement (where people would learn to be critical, or challenge oppression) with an emphasis on sport. Ian Kershaw argues that many of the Nazi initiatives were positive, and popular, and young people enjoyed the anti-Weimar flavour of the early days, but membership declined as the years passed because conformity and discipline were emphasised at the expense of its early radicalism.

The themes and techniques of Nazi propaganda

Propaganda in the Third Reich can be examined as a set of techniques, but also as an illustration of the Nazi 'message' of what they stood for. There are two further questions generally asked of propaganda: how effective was it? And how important was it? To answer the first question it is important to know by what criteria it can be measured. It is not easy to assess 'effectiveness' or 'success' because people's decision-making was complex and not based solely on what they were told. The importance of propaganda ought to be assessed by its position in relative terms to other factors, especially in deciding what it was that made Hitler so popular in the early 1930s, for example. It should also be borne in mind that propaganda is only really effective when it tunes in to, or exaggerates people's existing fears, desires and prejudices.

This section will therefore be divided as follows:

a.   The aim of Nazi propaganda.
b.   Nazi propaganda techniques.
c.   The themes.
d.   The effect of Nazi propaganda.
e.   Historical controversy on Nazi propaganda.

The aim of Nazi propaganda

We should not forget that Chief of Propaganda was Hitler's first appointment in the early Nazi party. He believed that the German propaganda machine of the First World War had been weak compared to the Allies' effort. He also believed that the battle for the hearts and minds of the German people had been lost to pacifists and left wingers, and to the Jews, who had set out to undermine the German war effort, and therefore the nation. Hitler believed that propaganda was essential to rebuild national confidence, to unite the German people and to galvanise and propel them towards the Nazi goals. If obedience could be engendered, then all aspects of Nazi policy would be achievable, and obedience would begin with propaganda. In the event of war, there would be no repeat of the collapse of 1918. Goebbels, who became Minister for Popular Enlightenment and Propaganda, was unhappy with the title of his ministry because of the negative connotations it contained. However, Hitler had his way, and fulfilled much of what he had expressed in *Mein Kampf* as the essentials of propaganda.

Figure 58. Hitler at the Nuremberg Party Rally, 1934.

Propaganda was well organised

The systematic organisation of propaganda was striking. There was total control of the media, whose staff was drawn from racial Germans, in radio, literature, theatre, films, and in the newspapers. Censorship was imposed, and foreign information tightly regulated. The emphasis given to this kind of control is more understandable when one considers the adage 'information is power'. Resistance was certainly more difficult when information was difficult to obtain.

> COMMENT:
> *The message, not the medium, is of the greatest importance. Many dictatorships in the 1930s used similar techniques – but not all produced the same ideas: it is this which makes Nazism hideously unique.*

Nazi propaganda techniques

The techniques of Nazi propaganda are well known. Slogans were common and could be an accepted salute such as *Sieg Heil*, or the greeting *Heil Hitler*. Slogans might also adorn public spaces. An unpleasant anti-Semitic slogan found across Germany was *Juden sind hier unerwünscht* (Jews are not wanted here). There were other repetitive messages especially on the radio and weekly *Wochenschau* (Weekly Newsreel). The Hitler salutes, uniforms, stirring military music, and dynamic public speaking characterised the rallies and other public events. There was a great deal of emphasis on marching in groups, a technique which fostered bonds of solidarity, but also prepared the marchers for military drill. The singing of familiar songs was encouraged, often designed as an accompaniment to marching.

Figure 59. Stage management: a party rally of the 1930s.

Radio and film techniques preferred subtlety to obvious propaganda
There was an effort to harness modern technology in the form of mass-produced
and cheap wireless radio sets called 'People's Receivers'. As a fashionable and
modern item, they were eagerly acquired. Goebbels was particularly keen to use
radio to its maximum effect, and prevented the broadcast of overtly military
music in favour of more interesting and subtle programmes. Public address
systems were also relatively new pieces of technology, and radios were linked up to
broadcast into the streets. Feature films occasionally appeared amongst the staple
diet of dramas and romances, and whilst some were quite obviously propagandist
such *Triumph of the Will* (1934), others were more extreme as in the case of *Der
Ewige Jude* (*The Eternal Jew*, 1940). The latter was named after an exhibition on
the Jews in 1937, which purported to show the Jews as parasites and in the film,
images of Jews are shown alongside those of rats.

Advertising techniques were used
It should not be forgotten that propaganda came into other aspects of everyday
life. Messages appeared in shops, lessons and textbooks in education, and at the
ritualised, annual party rallies. It was even superimposed on the traditional May

Figure 60. The 'People's Receiver': cheap radio sets for the masses.

Day and Christmas celebrations, which continued with Nazi motifs, whilst new holidays such as Labour Day, the anniversary of the Putsch, and the *Machtergreifung* (the seizure of power) were created. The most important of all these was Hitler's birthday. Robin Lenman believes the Nazis understood modern advertising techniques and exploited them very effectively.

The themes of Nazi propaganda

These can be summed up as:

(i)   the Führer myth
(ii) national solidarity.

The Führer myth
▶ *The purpose of the personality cult was to generate loyalty.*
Perhaps the most important theme of all was the creation of the Führer myth. Eyewitnesses referred to Hitler as an important reason for supporting the Nazis. The techniques Goebbels used to popularise Hitler still feature in 'personality-politics': people identify strongly with a politician or a leader, rather than an agenda, especially when all parties crowd into the centre and offer much the same policies. However, Hitler was portrayed as 'above' politics, and as a man of the people with a special father-like pathos. In 1939, the *Wochenschau* explained its technique in covering Hitler's fiftieth birthday parade: 'The camera lingers lovingly on the Goebbels children, all clothed in white, who stand, curious but well behaved, next to Hitler, thus strengthening his reputation as a true lover of children.'

Figure 61. Hitler addressing the party at Nuremberg.

▶ *Hitler was portrayed as the people's leader.* Hitler was shown in all walks of life, so that all could identify with him. Hitler was carefully marketed as a friend of the workers by showing him digging soil for the new motorways (class solidarity), he was shown surrounded by women (implying that he was an attractive sex symbol), by children (trustworthy, father-like), with babies (caring), with soldiers or in uniform (the patriot and the head of a strong army), with Bavarian friends (traditional, cultured, middle class), with adoring fans (popular), at parades with the scowl of concentration, and at ease with multitudinous crowds. It was not uncommon for people who felt a grievance with local Nazi leaders or the system, to continue to reserve respect and admiration for Hitler personally. David Welch believes this was Goebbels' main achievement.

National solidarity

Ritual events were both invented and hijacked. Rituals created a sense of belonging and could also be a collective comfort. In this case the aim was to create a national unity over traditional regional differences. Parades for the fallen of the Great War were useful reminders of national grief and a sense of injustice with the terms of the Treaty of Versailles. Yet there was also a sinister context to the rituals. The burning of 'Jewish' books by students on 10 May 1933 in Berlin was cleverly orchestrated to appear spontaneous. It was portrayed as a purging of German culture to remove its impure contents, which one German philosopher, Heine, had aptly prophesied in the epithet: 'Where one burns books, there one ultimately burns people'.

Figure 62. The burning of books, 10 May 1933.

The effect of Nazi propaganda

The effects can be summarised as follows:

(i)   grievances and fears exploited by the Nazis
(ii) the neutralising of opposition.

Grievances and fears exploited by the Nazis

▶ *The themes of Nazi propaganda reinforced Hitler's ideas.*
   The themes of Nazi propaganda equated to their ideological agenda, but it
   should be noted that some concepts were more popular than others. Despite
   Daniel Goldhagen's assertion that the majority of Germans had a pathological
   hatred of the Jews, there still does not seem to be compelling evidence to
   suggest that this was the case. Instead, many Germans seemed to have
   believed that the more intolerant messages of Nazism were the views of a few
   hotheads, and that in contrast, Adolf Hitler seemed to a fair and moderate man
   who had a strong sense of injustice about the way that Germans had been
   treated. Certainly the Versailles settlement was unpopular. Unemployment
   was universally feared, and this affected all classes with even the middle
   classes perched on the edge of the abyss of poverty.

▶ *German people's fears have been underestimated.*
   Some historians used to like to argue that the Germans were inherently Nazi

because their standard of living
was intact when they became
Nazis, but this view fails to
empathise with all those
Germans who were fearful of the
future and bitter about the past.
Many remembered the
hyperinflation of 1923, and so
when the Depression began to
affect so many millions, it was
fear that drove them away from
the Weimar government.

Figure 63. Hitler at a party rally.

▶ *The fear of communism was widespread and Nazism was an antidote.*
   We should also acknowledge the fear of communism throughout Germany.
   Marxist-Leninist revolutionaries had seized parts of north Germany and

Bavaria in 1919, and it was no secret that the KPD took its instructions from Moscow. The communists also made little attempt to hide their contempt for the middle class and longed for the collapse of capitalism and, therefore, of Germany. The shocking tactics of massacre, terror and atrocities meted out in Russia between 1917 and 1924 were not easily forgotten. The turmoil on the streets and the Depression convinced many that communism was a greater threat than the NSDAP which offered regeneration, a fresh start, and an end to political chaos in Germany. Weimar seemed to have little to offer by comparison.

The neutralising of opposition
During the later 1930s, a sense of indifference to politics developed since active opposition was likely to end in severe punishment. Whilst all official information was suspected of being altered, the absence of any alternative sources made this impossible to verify. Only in the case of opposition to euthanasia do historians have any concrete information that propaganda failed. Considering all these factors, it is difficult to be certain which was the more important to the individual: propaganda or personal considerations.

▶ *The contribution of Goebbels was significant.*
Finally we should not discount Goebbels himself. The effectiveness of his propaganda, or his direction is difficult to measure, but Goebbels was undoubtedly skilful, earning the grudging respect of his opponents. When Berlin and other German cities were bombed, it was Goebbels who visited the ruins and called for a *Totaler Krieg* (total war) or the full mobilisation of all of Germany's resources. He was also successful in organising the *Reichskristallnacht* in 1938, and maintained Germany's propaganda offensive right into 1944. His success was to create the illusion of national solidarity that the German public dared not oppose, even after the war was lost.

Historical controversies on Nazi propaganda

Historians take differing lines on propaganda. Ian Kershaw feels that the uniformity of the message did not conceal the antagonisms and divisions which remained inside the party, and certainly within the nation. Whilst Hitler was a 'man for all seasons', he could not please 'all of the people all of the time'. Geoff Layton regards propaganda as 'crucial', revealing as it does Hitler's ideals and techniques. D. Orlow regards propaganda as trying to find 'an answer for all grievances', hence the wide content in arts, literature and other media. J. Noakes and G. Pridham focus on the structure of propaganda, and how this ensured control, which they regard as the priority. Richard Grunberger tends to emphasise the role of the Hitler myth as the most crucial element. He wrote, 'in the spring of 1945, in the minds of many Germans, Hitler still ranked as lord over life and death'. This perhaps implies that Hitler was the most important element of Nazism, for without him the movement would not have been what it was. There is a strong argument to suggest that, in the same way, Hitler's ideas also shaped Germany's fortunes.

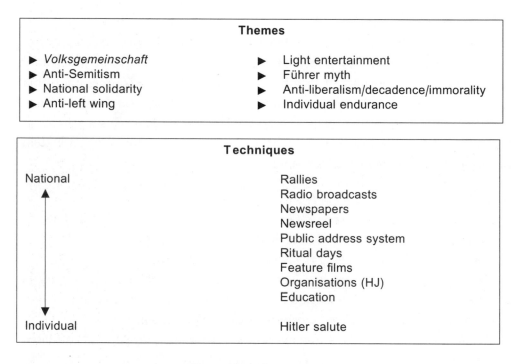

Figure 64. Nazi propaganda.

A verdict on Nazi propaganda

It is important not to be blinded by the techniques and 'special effects' of propaganda (as Goebbels once complained had happened to some of those who supported the party), but one should instead try to understand the 'message' as these were the indicators of what the Nazis, or rather Hitler, intended to do. Finally, in trying to measure the effect of Nazi propaganda, it is important to assess the levels of coercion in the Third Reich and the degree of resistance and opposition.

Figure 65. Plebiscite poster, 1935.

Tutorial

Progress questions

1. What happened to the profile of female employment?

2. What effect would Nazi ideas have had on the birth rate? Could couples profit from having more children, and what might the penalties be?

3. What were the functions of youth movements? What positive benefits did they bring?

4. How did the Nazis use the youth movements to control education?

5. What were the Nazi propaganda techniques?

Discussion points

1. Were the Nazis successful in fulfilling their aims in the youth movements?

2. What sort of society did the Nazis manage to create? Did this society meet their expectations?

3. How successful were the methods the Nazis used to control society?

4. How effective was Nazi propaganda? (Consider how an historian can measure this and some of the considerations that must be made: what other factors may have made people behave the way they did? Were people motivated by economic factors, or by the propaganda itself?)

Practical assignment

Compose an essay on the following: To what extent did the Third Reich achieve its objectives with regard to women and young people in Nazi Germany?

Study tips

1. It is tempting to simply describe Nazi propaganda techniques, and to be distracted by the rallies, and newsreel clips of ecstatic crowds. To avoid this approach, structure essays around the themes or 'messages' of Nazi propaganda and try to say if the techniques used were effective or not.

2. Make a list of the brand new technologies the Nazis incorporated into their propaganda. Note how this gave the impression that Nazism was 'new', and it appealed to young people.

3.   Consider the long-term objectives of the regime. Describe the features of this Nazi Society in two paragraphs.

4.   Try to sum up each chapter of this book so far in two paragraphs for each chapter. Highlight the names and dates. Use the opening paragraphs (one-minute overviews) to help you.

The Nazi Economic Programme

One-minute overview – *The Nazis seem to have begun rearmament in Germany almost as soon as they took power, suggesting aggressive ambitions. However, there were several stages in their economic policies, the result of changing demands, and a critical imbalance of trade. The Nazis' first priority was to deliver a 'recovery' from the Depression. In fact, Germany benefited from the recovery of world trade in 1935–6, although the Nazis were quick to claim the credit for themselves. Nevertheless, Dr Schacht, the economics expert, tried in vain to fulfil Hitler's calls for simultaneous rearmament and recovery, even though Germany's economic weaknesses threatened to pitch the country back into depression. Hitler's views remained constant even though rearmament dislocated the economy and depressed living standards across the country. Moreover, there were major contradictions in Nazi economic policies, and Hitler's leadership in resolving these problems was often ineffectual. Either as a result of this, or as part of a longer term programme, Hitler began to orient the German economy for a war of plunder after 1936.*

In this chapter you will learn:
▶ *Why the Nazis' economic programme failed.*
▶ *The historical controversy surrounding the Nazi economic programme.*

This chapter is divided into the following sections:

a. Hitler's economic aims.
b. The New Plan.
c. The Four Year Plan.
d. Results of the plans.
e. Historical controversy on Nazi economics.

Hitler's economic aims

Hitler had immediate priorities when taking power

When Hitler was appointed Chancellor in January 1933, Germany was in economic turmoil. Six million were unemployed, dole payments were inadequate, and industries and banks had gone bankrupt. A nationalistic organisation like Hitler's would not countenance going back to the Americans for loans, so Germany would have to find the means for its own recovery. Industrialists and workers alike had high expectations. It is clear that Hitler passionately believed in the ability of the German people to effect their own recovery. He was convinced that it was financial institutions and dependence on foreign imports or loans that rendered Germany weak. If the Germans were freed from the constraints imposed on them, and taught to work hard, then Germany would prosper. However, Hitler also intended to put people to work by force, to remove 'racial enemies' from the workplace, and, ultimately, find new markets and agricultural lands in Eastern Europe so that the German people were no longer confined within the narrow borders of the Reich.

Hitler's immediate priorities were therefore to:

▶ provide food for the workforce
▶ create jobs and reduce unemployment.

Hitler's ideological aims

The 'racial struggle' was Hitler's guiding concept in planning his economic programme. The problems of the Depression which the Third Reich had inherited were to be overcome in the same way that he aimed to overcome all other problems in Germany, namely the force of the political 'will'. Once accomplished, Hitler believed that Germany must prepare itself for the final confrontation with the forces of Bolshevism which he regarded as the strongest manifestation of the Jewish threat. There was a time imperative to this. Hitler argued that: 'Since the French Revolution [1789], the world has been moving with ever-increasing speed towards a new conflict, the most extreme solution of which is Bolshevism; and the essence and goal of Bolshevism is the elimination of those strata of mankind which have hitherto provided the leadership and their replacement by world-wide Jewry.' He warned that: 'the military resources of this aggressive will [in Russia] are in the meantime rapidly increasing from year to year'. He stated confidently that this: 'crisis can not and will not fail to occur'.

Hitler's policy created problems

Hitler responded to this threat by demanding rearmament, but this tended to dislocate the economy. Although rearmament provided employment, the production of military goods could not be sold (this tends to produce inflation). Its demands on imports tended to come at the expense of other goods, especially consumer products. Hitler's solution was autarky (economic self sufficiency) which attempted to make Germany independent of foreign exchange. Finally, when rearmament threatened to precipitate a financial crisis and force Germans to accept rationing, Hitler embarked on his programme of conquest for resources prematurely.

Schacht's initial economic programme

Schacht had to raise capital
In March 1933, Hitler appointed Dr Hjalmar Schacht as President of the *Reichsbank*. At this early stage, Hitler seemed content to focus only on winning popular support and was at pains not to make explicit any details of his economic programme. Schacht was simply to avoid the restrictions on government spending which had characterised the Weimar Republic. However, Schacht quickly found the capital Hitler required for his rearmament programme by 'deficit financing' (a practice where the government spent money, even if it didn't have any, to kick-start the economy and thus find its way out of depression by generating economic growth). One method was to encourage the purchase of bonds. Any citizen or firm could invest in the government and literally loan it some money, and expect some return when the government had made a profit several years later. The concept had been used by the German government during the First World War. In order to avoid foreign suspicion that this money would be used for rearmament (in defiance of the terms of the Treaty of Versailles), the bonds were called *Mefo-wechsel*.

The financial crisis of 1934

Schacht delayed making repayments on loans
However, although the war reparations had been cancelled by the Weimar Republic in June 1932 with the Allies' agreement, there were still considerable interest payments and other loans to repay. Schacht managed to delay repayments and only paid partial amounts when forced to do so, and then finally abolished repayments except in the form of bonds which would be honoured at some future date.

Imports were increasing

The continuing Depression tended to mask Germany's rearmament funding which continued apace in secret. But this only created a second problem. The demand for raw materials for its rearmament caused an increase in imports and the strength of the *Reichsmark* meant that these imports were expensive, especially when other countries had thrown up protective tariffs. Exports were also less competitive and consequently the volume of exported goods continued to fall. Hitler's drive for work creation schemes had also caused an increase in consumer demand, and this caused an overall increase in imports. In effect, Germany was sinking deeper into debt.

Schacht set up bilateral agreements and barter deals

Schacht also set up bilateral trade agreements with neighbouring Eastern European countries, hoping to get the advantage of any deal. However, the Germans' bullying approach merely alienated the Czechs and Hungarians, although there was some limited success with barter agreements (where Germany did not buy goods with scarce foreign currency but offered to exchange goods for other commodities, such as timber).

The New Plan

Schacht's solution to the economic problems was the New Plan

The net effect of the increase of imports was a trade deficit and a serious balance of payments problem which developed during the summer of 1934. To solve the problem, Schacht launched the New Plan in September 1934. In this Schacht gave the government the powers to regulate imports by forcing importers to apply for permission to import goods before a transaction. The government gave priority to two things: raw materials and foodstuffs. Consumer goods were to be relegated in importance, but, if sustained, the risk was of a fall in standard of living (and consumer spending) and a housing shortage.

The problem of financing rearmament

The financial problems of 1935 continued as imports rose and exports fell

A second balance of payments deficit crisis began in 1935 and by early 1936 looked set to cripple the German economy. Imports rose by 9%, exports fell by the same percentage. Added to this problem, a conflict arose between the consumer

demand for the import of fats and meat, and the
rearmament requirement for raw materials,
especially lead and copper.

Schacht was replaced
Schacht was replaced (officially, in 1937) because he
tried to solve economic problems using
conventional economic measures. Hitler removed
him for failing to find a solution to the financial
crisis. Hitler appointed Goering as Plenipotentiary
of the Four Year Plan because he was more
compliant. At first Goering continued with the New
Plan policy of prioritisation of raw materials and

Figure 66. Hermann Goering in
the uniform of the *Luftwaffe*
circa 1939.

food. However, to avoid rationing, Goering decided not to reduce foodstuffs. Yet
there was pressure on him not to slow down the pace of rearmament either, so
more alternatives were sought. Attempts were made to increase agricultural
production, but this had a negligible effect. More effort was placed on cutting
imports and pushing exports, but this policy was toned down as it was unlikely to
succeed with European neighbours for long.

Hitler's solution was in autarky
The alternative was to produce synthetic goods and research was carried out into
the feasibility of producing cheap synthetic oil and rubber. Schacht had opposed
the moves towards synthetics, arguing that they cost more to produce than to
import. Hitler was attracted by the idea of autarky (economic self-sufficiency
through synthetic products) as it appealed to his patriotism. During the First
World War, Germany had been blockaded by the Royal Navy, its resources had
dwindled, and as a result it had lost its capacity to wage a total war. He refused to
see the rearmament programme jeopardised and so he overruled Schacht and
announced the launch of the Four Year Plan.

The Four Year Plan (1936)

The aim of the Plan was to prepare for a war of plunder

The Four Year Plan stated that a war with the forces of Bolshevism was inevitable
and Germany must be prepared to fight in four years' time (in other words, in
1940). Hitler believed that there were limits to how far the standard of living of the
German people could be depressed before people died of starvation, but the

lowest acceptable limit was necessary to avoid a drain on rearmament. A transition phase would then occur, before a final solution could be found in the exploitation of resources in the 'living space' to the east. The transition phase gave absolute priority to readiness for war, even above the stockpiling of goods and raw materials. Hitler seemed to envisage the conquest of others as the solution to scarce resources.

The implications of the Plan

Every effort was to be made in the field of autarky, regardless of cost, and production was to be increased in a number of key areas. Goering was put in charge of the Plan, but a number of influential private capitalists collaborated. Despite the remarks of Soviet historians that this proved a link between capitalism and fascism, the fact that the Nazis tolerated the capitalists only until they had outlived their usefulness, or they had failed to reach agreed targets, would tend to refute this assertion.

Results of the Plan

In the early years there was an expectation that the Nazi regime would ensure economic recovery. However, the rearmament programme seriously affected the economy. By 1939, the spending power of the German citizen was less than that of 1929, before the Depression. The effects of the Nazis' economic programme can be summarised in three areas.

(i)   production
(ii) German capitalism
(iii) life for the working class.

Production
The following table reveals the Nazis' achievements and failures:

Commodity	*1936*	*1938*	*1942*	*Plan Target (1940)*
	(Output in thousands of tons)			
Mineral oil	1,790	2,340	6,260	13,830
Aluminium	98	166	260	273
Buna rubber	0.7	5	96	120
Nitrogen	770	914	930	1,040
Explosives	18	45	300	223

Powder	20	26	150	217
Steel	19,216	22,656	20,480	24,000
Iron ore	2,255	3,360	4,137	5,549
Brown coal	161,382	194,985	245,918	240,500
Hard coal	158,400	186,186	166,059	213,000

There is no data available on the year 1940 when the Plan was supposed to be fulfilled. However, even by 1942, it is clear that targets were rarely met. Yet, whilst this appears to be a failure, it should be noted that the targets were set artificially high. This was to create a propaganda effect (rivalling the targets being set by the USSR in its Five Year Plans), and to encourage the people of Germany to strive for improved results. The fact is that production increased in every case, and, in this sense, the Plan succeeded in its aim. The figures also conceal the complete neglect of the consumer sector, including housing, or levels of consumer income.

Index of average earnings
Real wages per week (1936 = 100)

1914	94.6
1928	102.2
1933	92.5
1936	100
1938	107.5
1940	111

These figures indicate that whilst the spending power of the workforce increased, its rise was sluggish and took until c.1937 to reach the pre-Depression levels. The impact of the Depression is also clear, given that real wages were well below what they had been before the First World War.

German capitalism

There was optimism amongst capitalists at first
Here there was a radical change. Rejecting an economy of purely entrepreneurial initiative (which had created mass unemployment), the Nazis chose instead what Richard Overy calls the 'managed economy'. It was one which demanded subservience – not to market forces or ideology, but to the political will. The state decided on prices and distribution. This begs the question, what difference was there between this and communism? This was not a Soviet-style 'command

economy', because, although the state directed aspects of the economy (such as those linked to rearmament), it allowed capitalists to compete and to run industry, and left the rest to the free market.

Businessmen hoped that they could use Nazi beliefs to their advantage. For example, Jewish competitors would be removed. Rearmament profits were welcomed too. Personal contacts were established with leading Nazis, such as Goering. Many joined the party, but collaboration was usually for profit rather than belief.

The capitalists were dismayed by state takeovers
But things could, and did, go wrong. Fritz Thyssen (an 'iron baron' or iron manufacturer) anticipated success under the regime but fled to Switzerland in 1939 because all his assets had been seized and nationalised. Goering warned that industrialists that failed to co-operate would have their firms taken over by the state. In fact, Goering amassed a personal fortune through bribes and takeovers. Workers and plant were simply expropriated by the *Reichswerks Hermann Goering* if it suited him. This was all part of Goering's desire to live the life of an aristocrat, but more sinister state takeovers also took place.

The SS began to create their own economic empire
By 1944, the SS had begun to supersede party interests as they responded to the war, Germany's territorial and economic expansion, and a trend of increasing racism. Overy identifies this radicalisation as the manifestation of greater SS influence in economic life. By the end of the war, the SS were running their own factories and businesses as if they were a state within a state. The SS was the biggest 'employer' of slave labour. Speer was sidelined in 1944 as Hitler's personal economic advisor (as well as architect), whilst the SS leader, Himmler, received all the latest war weapons, and organised the defence of German industry. Hitler was increasingly absorbed by the dilemma that the war was a struggle for economic resources and the economy had to support the war effort. However, that did not stop him from giving free rein to the SS as they constructed their own economic empire in Germany and the occupied eastern territories.

> ### COMMENT:
> *The Nazis benefited from the world economic recovery, and the German domestic economy profited in spite of (not because of) Nazi economic policies. However, the structural flaws remained and Hitler sought more radical solutions to them – namely war and conquest.*

Figure 67. The giant armaments firm, Krupps.

Case study: Daimler-Benz

Using archive material from Daimler-Benz in Stuttgart, Neil Gregor has shown how one company adapted to the Third Reich. The company's aim was stability and profit. It was resentful of the regime's restrictions on the import of raw materials and their forcible reduction in the number of car makes the company could produce. However, the company also kept its investments in the occupied eastern territories to a minimum, believing that they would not last. Nevertheless, they freely made use of the new labour disciplines imposed on the workforce to maximise profit. Forced labourers were used for the same reason. Jews were used, specifically to reduce production costs, and, in common with other industries, when they had outlived their usefulness and were no longer productive, they were handed over for execution. The archives show that the living and working conditions of the labourers were appalling and there was concern that this was affecting product quality. As the war came to an end, the company dispersed its machinery so as to restart production as soon as the war had ended. The company was well placed to recommence production and prospered once it was freed on the inefficiency that had characterised Nazi government interference. What is shocking about this case study is how little moral scruple entered into the company's thinking. The priority was simply profit, or survival.

Life for the working class

The effect on the working class
The Nazis' economic programme had two key effects on the working classes in Germany, a reduction in the standard of living and a lowering of their morale.

Consumer demand was deliberately suppressed
Hitler had made clear in the Four Year plan that the standard of living should be depressed within certain limits to suppress consumer demand and thus relieve pressure on imports, releasing more money for the rearmament programme. Statistics help to illustrate this. Although Germany's GNP increased from 1932 to 1939 from 58 billions of *Reichsmarks* to 130 billion, this was almost exclusively

produced by military production and expenditure. Investment in the civilian economy (such as agriculture, light industry, communications and civilian construction) grew very slowly during the Nazi regime and in 1938 had not even reached its pre-Depression level (1928, 9.3 billion *Reichsmarks*; 1938, 8 billion *Reichsmarks*). Goering stated that the Germans had to get used to 'Guns, not butter!'

The wider problems for the working class

An SPD analyst commented in 1938 that construction of housing had been neglected that a long-term, chronic shortage was building up. This seemed particularly hard to understand given the Nazis' policy of trying to encourage an increase in the birth rate and consequently a larger population that would, in time, need more housing. All consumer industries were suppressed, and the regime imposed a ban on the issuing of mortgages making it impossible for working-class people to buy homes.

The workforce was exploited

The Nazis demanded higher production in all sectors of the economy connected with rearmament. The regulation of a maximum eight-hour day was abolished, allowing employers to exploit their workforces. Women were forced to take up employment, despite the Nazis' aim to keep them at home to raise children, since families needed to maintain their income by having both parents working.

Although it was Hitler's boast that the German worker had an average of 100–120 Marks a month in pay in 1936, compared with only 50 Marks a month in 1933, Hitler did not acknowledge that the 100 Marks was actually worth less than before. In other words, the spending power of the consumer had been reduced as food prices increased, and this was a direct result of the Nazis' squeeze of the import of foodstuffs.

Figure 68. Advert encouraging Germans to save for a KdF car: the money was siphoned off for rearmament.

Morale was lowered

The morale of the workforce was seriously affected. The Nazis attempted to raise interest and support by promises that every German family would be able to own their own cheap motor car. The *KdF-wagen* could be purchased at the end of a savings scheme period. Each month, Germans paid money for the promise of a car in the near future. Propaganda films showed the cars in production, and prototypes were produced, but the cars were never manufactured on a mass scale. Instead the government redirected the money being raised into the production of armoured fighting vehicles, and the war was blamed for the interruption to production.

Farmers were angry
Farmers grew angry about the Nazis' attempts to cream off a profit from their produce. In Oldenburg and East Friesland, for example, farmers received 4 to 6 *Pfennigs* less per litre for milk in 1934 than they had before the Nazis came to power. However, at the same time, the consumer was paying 4 *Pfennigs* more, so the government, which had set up its own 'Central Co-operative' was taking the difference for itself. In addition, the Nazis passed an Entailed Farm Law which placed restrictions on the sale or division of the property. Although it was designed to protect the peasant farmer, it seemed to be a step towards collectivisation of agriculture and caused some discontent.

The Nazi unions were a sham
It soon became clear that the replacement of the Trade Unions with the NSBO (The Factory Cells Organisation) and the government's arbitration service in the form of the Trustees of Labour offered little protection to the individual worker. The Trustees favoured the employers, and even SA men enjoyed little respite from their duties in the factories and workplaces. They were expected to work by day and carry out auxiliary police duties after hours. Workers felt unable to grumble about their conditions for fear of arrest. The result was a feeling of apathy for most, and a competitive striving against fellow workers for the rest.

Jobs were more important after the Depression
One key area of propaganda was very effective in keeping the workers quiet: jobs. Hitler wanted to create jobs and reduce unemployment and this was largely achieved. The extent this was appreciated by workers was noted by secret SPD reports. Fear of official punishments for refusing a job, or the relief at being employed and having a wage, however small, after the Depression years, was a powerful factor in ensuring workers' loyalty. However, the Nazis were able to reduce unemployment by drafting men into the armed forces or the Labour Service, removing Jews and other groups from the lists of unemployed, or simply not counting the inmates of concentration camps. However, the expansion of

heavy industry and the recovery of world trade undoubtedly helped in the reduction of unemployment too. From 6 million in 1932–33 (30 per cent of the workforce), the figures fell steadily to 52,000 in 1939 (0.2 per cent).

The historical controversy on Nazi economics

The views of Richard Overy

The paramountcy of economics
Richard Overy believes that economics are central to our understanding of Nazism. He states that there was a direct relationship between economics and the ideology of *Lebensraum*, which was to provide prosperity for the German people. All the military objectives were to seize new economic resources, and therefore the invasion of Russia in 1941 was economically motivated. The economy of the new order was a system based on exploitation, but also aimed for Germany to be at the centre of a new European economy. Even the regime's racism, Overy states, was economically motivated. The discrimination against Jewish businesses in 1933 was followed by the removal of Jewish managers, closures and seizures of property. In Vienna this process was completed in just eight months, and all the spoils went to party men and the state. During the war there was an economic-racial hierarchy, where goods were distributed to Germans as a priority. The German working class was the most prosperous, whilst the rest were condemned to an agrarian life in the east, or slavery.

Overy's verdict is that economics are central to Nazism
Overy concludes that the economy was important for practical considerations (jobs, recovery) in the short term, and in this phase, the business world was important. But during the 1930s the interests changed as war, racism and an expansionist agenda became ascendant. Whichever way you approach the history of Nazism, Overy believes that it was economically motivated.

An alternative argument

Ideology and preparation for war
There are some areas of Overy's thesis which other historians would contest. Economic determinism is rarely popular, since it relegates the part played in history by individuals. It is dispiriting to believe that we are all mere cells in some grander economic organism; victims of circumstance perhaps. It is possible to

question whether it valid to say that all of the decisions taken in Nazi Germany were economically 'determined'. Note that a counter-argument would be seriously devalued if it tried to rule out that some decisions were taken with economic considerations in mind. However, some examination of Hitler himself might provide us with alternatives. Overy takes the connection Hitler made between race and economics and gives the emphasis to economics. But in fact, it could be seen the other way around.

Hitler's Plan was ideologically motivated

In Hitler's opening pages of the Four Year Plan, he dwells less on the economic imperative, and more on the biological one. Population growth, the continuing process of miscegenation and therefore degeneration, and the Jewish-Marxist threat are the themes he deals with. Hitler also spent a disproportionate amount of time discussing race in *Mein Kampf*, not economics. If one takes the view that Hitler saw all issues through 'racist spectacles' then a different interpretation emerges than a purely economic one.

Hitler saw the war as a racial struggle

For Hitler the war was not just an economic struggle seen in crude materialistic terms, but a titanic final confrontation with the racial enemies of Germany. The policy of exterminating Soviet Commissars, eastern Europeans and Jews was a waste of manpower and a captive labour force in economic terms, but was a necessity to the Nazis' racial struggle if they were to arrest the breeding of a new generation of racial enemies. Although Overy's work on the economy is excellent, he seems to give an inadequate explanation of the strategy, and yet, this decision-making is significant.

Is Overy an economic determinist?

Overy claims that he is not an economic determinist, but economics were just the most important factor. He explains the lack of economic preparation for war before 1936 as 'obvious', since Germany feared three factors; the intervention of other powers, the undermining of its economic development, and the fact that the army was still reorganising (and hoping to avoid interference from the regime).

1936 was a turning point

Overy states that the economic changes (trade control, banking, investment in roads and housing) prior to 1936 were in no way geared to war. However, the idea that motorways were constructed only to find employment for the unemployed seems a little unconvincing. Surely the *Autobahnen*, which cost so much, were for the efficient movement of military vehicles and supplies from one front to the other without undue pressure on the rail network (as Hitler had observed in the First World War)? Nevertheless, Overy claims the shift to preparation for war in the summer of 1936 was sudden and dramatic, and primarily focused on *Lebensraum* for economic reasons. It is here he provides persuasive statistical evidence for the shift.

Summary of the Nazi economy

The initial problems had been:

▶ unemployment
▶ social unrest
▶ balance of trade favoured too many imports
▶ government had no capital.

The New Plan consisted of:

▶ prioritisation of food and raw materials through regulated imports
▶ bilateral agreements with neighbouring states.

The Four Year Plan was as follows:

▶ food production was to be maximised
▶ increase production (see page 115–116)
▶ rearmament
▶ suppression of consumer demand
▶ high targets were set to match the threat of the Soviet Union's economy
▶ conquest was a solution and the armed forces were to be readied for war
▶ autarky was to be attempted.

Tutorial

Progress questions

1. What were Hitler's strategic aims?

2. How did Schacht deal with the crisis of 1934?

3. What were the advantages, in Hitler's mind, of autarky?

4. What were the effects of Nazi economic policies on the working classes?

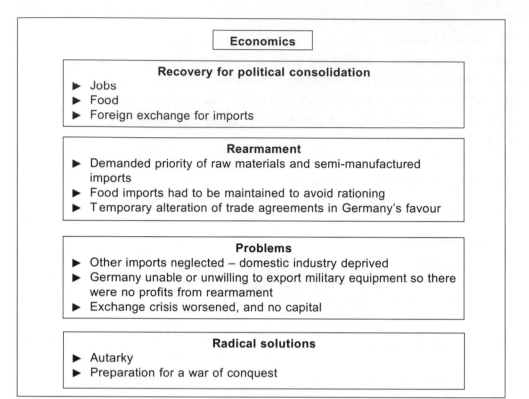

Figure 69. The Four Year Plan.

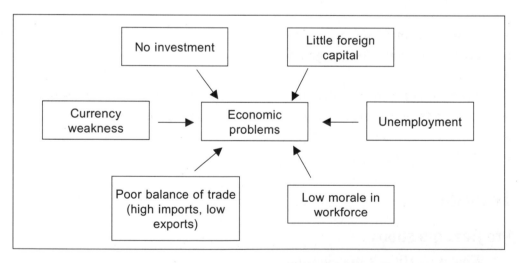

Figure 70. The Nazis' economic problems.

Discussion points

1. Did the Nazis create their own economic problems, for which war was the only solution?

2. Did rearmament solve their problems in the short term? Alternatively, was the world economy recovering anyway?

3. Did Hitler's way of viewing the economy affect his policy, and in what ways?

Practical assignment

Take a sheet of A4 paper and map out a plan of what you could include in an essay on the following questions from this chapter. Try to think of how you could present alternative points of view, by dividing the paper in half and sketching out the evidence to support each side. Using coloured pens to highlight or underline key points will help to decide on the final format of the essay.

1. How far can it be argued that the 'essential decisions in the Third Reich were taken by Hitler, and consequently responsibility for the failure of Nazi economic policy lay with Hitler alone'?

2. How much credit for Germany's economic recovery should go to the Nazis?

Study tips

1. Maintain a glossary of terms such as *Lebensraum* and autarky, and their definitions. A list is provided at the end of this book to help you.

2. Draw up a list of successes and failures in Nazi economic policy.

3. Apply an Intentionalist argument to economic policy. List the points that support or refute this line of argument in a wire diagram.

4. The Four Year Plan aspects were as follows:
   - *food* production was to be maximised;
   - there was to be an *increase* of production;
   - rearmament was the central focus;
   - *suppression* of the consumer was required;
   - the *threat* of the Soviet Union's economy was to be matched;
   - *conquest* was a solution;
   - *autarky* was to be attempted where feasible;
   - *no* increase in exports was expected.

   These form the Mnemonic: FIRSTCAN.

8

Anti-Semitism and Persecution

One-minute overview – *The persecution of minorities, in particular the Jews, are amongst the darkest annals of the Third Reich. The Nazis justified their oppression with ideas which predated the 1930s, but Hitler's speeches gave the actions of radical racists official sanction. However, some Germans were resistant to anti-Semitism, which forced the regime to be more cautious in its approach to 'the Jewish Question'. The persecution emerged as a process, often piecemeal, rather than a carefully worked out policy or programme. New controversies have arisen in recent years about the role of 'ordinary Germans' in the persecution.*

In this chapter you will learn:
▶ *How the Nazis persecuted Jews.*
▶ *The Nazis' actions against other minorities.*
▶ *The historical controversy surrounding the Nazi persecution of the Jews.*

The Nazi persecution of the Jews

This section will be organised in three parts:

a. the stages in the persecution of the Jews from 1933 to 1941
b. the action taken against other minorities
c. the historical controversy surrounding anti-Semitism.

The stages in the persecution of the Jews from 1933 to 1941 were:

(i)   Boycott of Jewish shops in 1933.
(ii) The Nuremberg Laws of 1935.
(iii) The 'lull' of 1936.
(iv) The radicalisation of 1937: Aryanisation of Jewish business.
(v)   'The Night of Broken Glass', 1938.

Boycott of Jewish shops, 1933

The initial action against the Jews was badly planned
The process of Nazi persecution between 1933 and 1941 was never systematic and

emerged in a piecemeal fashion. When Hitler came to power in 1933, radical racists in the party were eager to humiliate Jews and remove them from German society. The party leadership appear to have had no plans for the Jews at all, beyond a vague understanding that the Jewish people were the root of all Germany's problems. In other words, it was recognised that Jews were to be dealt with, but few had worked out in detail what should be done. There were approximately 500,000 Jews in Germany, many of whom were engaged in commerce, self employed occupations or in public services. This meant that Jews enjoyed a disproportionate percentage of 'white collar' jobs. For example, 15% of working Germans were engaged in commerce, but 48% of Jews were in this line of work, a total of 2.48% of the whole population.

There was a radical view of the Jews

The SA, with a large number of working class members tended to see the Jews as 'bourgeois' and unfairly over-represented in better paid jobs. There were a number of spontaneous attacks on Jews in March 1933, but Hitler was keen not to lose control of his movement at this early stage. He therefore agreed to let Julius Streicher, 'the Jew-baiter' and the *Gauleiter* of Upper Franconia, organise a boycott of Jewish shops and businesses.

Figure 71. Boycott of Jewish shops and businesses, 1 April, 1933.

Radicalism was unpopular and failed

The boycott was designed to last indefinitely, and was justified as a reaction to 'Jewish, foreign propaganda'. Nevertheless, the President managed to persuade Hitler to limit the action to one day in order to avoid adverse foreign attention. The boycott, on 1 April 1933, aroused only hostility or indifference in the German public and this made Hitler's decision to end it much easier. However, professionals, such as doctors, civil servants, lawyers and academics, were suspended or dismissed, or physically attacked throughout the Reich. Hitler tried to regulate and prevent these actions 'from below', but failed. In schools, attempts to genuinely reduce overcrowding were used as excuses to exclude Jewish children. However, the Editors Law (4 October 1933) specifically discriminated against Jews in publishing and the media.

Hitler did not exercise much control over the policy

These events in 1933 suggest the spontaneous and radical nature of anti-Semitism was almost beyond the control of the party leadership, or that at best they tacitly approved of the sentiment. Hitler grew concerned though that anti-Semitism might disrupt the economic recovery which was the first priority of the regime in the early years.

There was a lull in actions against the Jews in 1934

There was a lull in 1934 in both state-sanctioned anti-Semitic activities and in legislation, although individual acts of discrimination and violence occurred. Historians have not fully or adequately explained this lull, but the regime may have decided to avoid angering the German public with overt and unpopular measures. In March 1935, some Jews responded to the local violence with a boycott, only to be met with counter-boycotts and violence which gathered in intensity throughout 1935. This may have stemmed in part from a growing resentment from the lower ranks of the party with the apparent endless concern of the party leaders to appease the elites. Nor had the Night of the Long Knives (1934) caused this feeling to abate. Attacks on the Jews by SA men may have been the result of this frustration with a lack of progress towards a 'social revolution'.

The Nuremberg Laws of 1935

Schacht continued to protest that these attacks might affect the economy, particularly foreign trade, and so the Nazi government passed the Nuremberg Laws to fulfil a part of the old party programme and placate the radicals. The first law (26 April 1935) defined Jews as different from Germans on grounds of race

Figure 72. Anti-Semitic poster.

rather than religion, and decreed that they should be excluded from German citizenship rights. A subsequent law (15 September 1935) banned sexual relations between Jews and non-Jews, and crucially Hitler left some clauses deliberately vague. With these laws Hitler seemed keen to pass more radical anti-Jewish legislation, and he appeared to be impatient with the bureaucracy. The anti-Semitic aspects of the definition of citizenship in the Reich, were the only sections of the original party principles on citizenship that were actually implemented.

Jews were not regarded as citizens of the state
In *Mein Kampf,* Hitler had argued that people would have to earn their

Figure 73. *The Eternal Jew.* Poster advertising an anti-Semitic film.

citizenship, and that Jews would be excluded. However, there was still a great deal of doubt about the status of Jews. This allowed Hitler and the radicals to erode Jewish rights gradually. It was a more effective method of achieving their aims and satisfying demands than a confrontational approach which had failed so spectacularly on 1 April 1933.

There were problems in defining the Jews
Difficulties arose over the issue of parentage and grandparentage. Did one Jewish grandmother affect her descendants' rights in the same way as a 'full Jew'? A Supplementary Decree on 14 November 1935 tried to resolve the problem of *Mischlinge* (mixed race) and suspended judgement on whether or not the regime should force couples in mixed marriages to divorce. Hundreds were tried under this law for the crime of *Rassenschande* (racial shame) and prison sentences varied from one to six years.

The lull of 1936

The Berlin Olympics caused a suspension of anti-Semitism at a national level
The Olympics are usually cited as a reason for the down-playing of persecution in 1936, but this can be misleading. Two factors served to limit the policy of anti-Semitism – fear of a foreign boycott of the Berlin Olympics and an adverse effect on economic

Figure 74. The Nazi Olympic Games, 1936.

recovery. It should be noted that Julius Streicher and Josef Goebbels (Propaganda) were active in making sure that the propaganda offensive against the Jews was relentless. *Die Stürmer* was an especially virulent anti-Semitic newspaper. J. Noakes and G. Pridham believe that the effect was limited, but stereotypes were reinforced.

Persecution continued
Nevertheless, other legislation continued to discriminate. On 9 October 1936, civil servants were no longer permitted to use Jewish doctors or hospitals. By 1938, the SS had begun to assert itself in framing anti-Semitic policy. In 1935, they had proposed mass emigration of Jews. One option that was suggested later was to transport all Jews to Madagascar (the idea was dropped because of a fear of foreign intervention). The SD branch of the SS aimed to implement mass emigration by 1937, and, at the same time desired to limit the participation of Jews in German society.

The radicalisation of 1937–38

The Aryanisation of Jewish businesses
With an apparently more secure economy by late 1937, Hitler felt confident about the future of the Reich and carried out a wave of dismissals of the elites. At the same time, the removal of Schacht and others who had claimed that anti-Semitism would damage the economy, opened the way for a new radical agenda. Goering was appointed to execute the new economic programme, and began by pressuring Jewish businessmen to sell their firms to Germans. This 'Aryanisation' of business was welcomed by German entrepreneurs who stood to make considerable profits.

After the annexation of Austria (1938), the radicalisation of anti-Semitism was accelerated. Deportations increased, and initiated a flood of voluntary emigrations to other European countries or America. But behind the scenes the pressure was still mounting for radical and physical action against Jews.

Reichskristallnacht: **The Night of Broken Glass**

Figure 75. The aftermath of *Reichskristallnacht*: a gutted synagogue.

On 7 November 1938, Ernst von Rath, a minor diplomatic official in Paris, was shot dead by a Polish Jew, Herschel Grünspan. In response, Goebbels orchestrated a violent anti-Jewish demonstration which, in line with Hitler's wishes, was to appear 'spontaneous', but which Goebbels organised to coincide with the anniversary of the Munich Putsch on 9 November. Initially at least, there seems to have been a desire to limit the action to the breaking of shop windows and the burning of synagogues, but rank and file Nazis got out of control and 91 Jews were killed. Twenty thousand Jewish men were arrested and taken to concentration camps. The German public were generally shocked, and it is likely few were convinced by the official explanation that this was a spontaneous uprising of the 'national will'. Jews were later forced to pay for the damage. This was later extended by Goering to include a tax that could be used for rearmament.

The historical significance was the crossing of a threshold of violence
The *Reichskristallnacht* was a defining moment in that a threshold of almost unprecedented violence had been crossed. It is true to say that pogroms (riots) against Jews were not new in Europe, but the scale of this incident and the inability of the German people to prevent it recurring, could be seen to be a clear indication of the power of the regime to impose itself upon minorities, and the absence of any accountability. When the state had sanctioned murder of Jewish German citizens, the way was open for a further radicalisation of anti-Semitic activity.

1933

▶ Boycott of shops: 1 April
▶ Burning of Jewish books (Berlin)
▶ Dismissal of professionals
▶ Editors Law against Jews in the media
▶ Exclusion of Jewish children from schools

1934–35

▶ Control of anti-Semitism through fear of damage to the economy but local persecution continued
▶ Attacks increased after the Night of the Long Knives
▶ The Nuremberg Laws defined Jews and half-Jews

1936

▶ Olympic Games offers a lull, but persecution continued at local level

---

1937–38

▶ Aryanisation of businesses
▶ Deportations
▶ *Reichskristallnacht*: mass arrests and 91 killed

Verdict

Intentionalists:
Logical outcome of racial hatred in 1920s which led to the Holocaust

Functionalists:
Holocaust was not inevitable but resulted from ever-increasing radicalism and Hitler's poor leadership

---

Figure 76. The stages in the persecution of the Jews.

The persecution of other minorities

The Nazis had a particular dislike of most foreigners and their ideology purposely built up the myth that the Aryan German was superior in every respect to other races.

1. Within the German borders, the former migrants of Eastern Europe such as the gypsies were particularly loathed as 'ethnically inferior'.

2. Homosexuals found themselves imprisoned in concentration camps for their 'moral offensiveness'.

3.   Quakers and conscientious objectors were branded as traitors and
     imprisoned.

4.   The 'feeble-minded' became a category to be despised.

5.   Any south-east European nationalities collectively known as Slavs were also
     thought to be 'inferior'.

In January 1940, the German press was told to present the Poles as objects of
'lasting revulsion', and that 'Gypsies, Jews and Poles ought to be treated on the
same level'. The same directive envisaged a time when Poles would serve as
agricultural labourers in Germany and there was concern that fraternisation
might develop unless Germans were taught to regard them as inferior. It should be
noted that the nationality that suffered the largest single casualty figure in the
death camps were the Poles, of which 2.9 million were Jewish.

The historical controversy surrounding Nazi persecution

There are controversies concerning:

(i)   The 'straight road' to the Holocaust.
(ii)   Solutions to the historical problem.
(iii) Alternative approaches.
(iv)   Jews and sexuality.

The 'straight road' to the Holocaust

Racism was central to Nazism
Racism was an essential component of Nazism. The racialist ideology reached its
ultimate and terrible conclusion in the mass extermination of the Reich's
enemies, the largest single group being the Jews. The term Holocaust (first coined
in 1943), with all its religious and apocalyptic overtones, has been almost
universally accepted as its description rather than the usual 'genocide'.

The Holocaust was the world's worst crime against humanity
The Holocaust sets Nazism aside as a different phenomenon than other preceding
attacks on social groups because of its scale, and because of the 'scientific'
justifications Nazis offered, and, most of all, because, as Volker Berghahn put it, 'it
was the application of the processes of the production-line' to mass destruction.

In 1945 it was termed a 'crime against humanity', and dealt a severe blow to the confidence of the West, and called into question its claim to civilisation.

There are fierce debates between historians
The historical debate over this aspect of Nazism is one of the most fierce. Memoirs continue to surface from survivors, or victims, and they mingle with those historians who have tried to explain the inexplicable – why did a modern, advanced and formerly democratic society turn to the barbarity of genocide? Who were the executioners?

Was there a 'straight road' to Auschwitz?
Lucy Dawidowicz argued that there was a 'straight road' to Auschwitz, implying that Nazi policies were consistent and aimed at annihilating the Jews from the outset. She wrote that the extermination of the Jews was both *systematic* and *inevitable*. These two simple words carry a whole range of questions which the historian is compelled to consider.

1. At what point did the genocide become inevitable?
2. What preconditions existed to enable this to happen?
3. How was dissent silenced?
4. How was it systematically organised?
5. Does systemisation imply pre-planning and the involvement of millions of people?
6. Or was it down to only a handful of dedicated Nazi extremists?

Solutions to the historical problem

There was a dynamic effect in anti-Semitic behaviour
Kershaw addressed the problem of anti-Semitism from the point of view of the debate into how the Nazi regime functioned. To reiterate, there are historians who believe that the regime's leaders intended all that happened, and pre-planned its agenda and simply put this into practice over the 12 years that it was in power. This is the Intentionalist view (shared by Dawidowicz, and G. Fleming). The Structuralists (Hans Mommsen and M. Broszat) in contrast believe that it was the system that the Nazis constructed that created a dynamic of its own that no one person or group could halt, but was a by-product of half-baked ideas and vague instructions, or even no instructions at all.

Ian Kershaw's research balances Intentionalism and Functionalism
Kershaw explained how he has explored the Soviet archives and discovered the reason why no order existed from Hitler ordering the mass extermination of Jews. This is tied in to the failure of the euthanasia programme, and centres on a document dated 18 December 1941 from Himmler to Hitler, agreeing that the Jews are to be 'executed as [if they are] partisans'. Hitler had already given a chilling prophesy as early as January 1939 in the *Reichstag* when he announced that another war would be the fault of the Jews and as a result they would be annihilated. Whilst this may have been pure rhetoric, the war made extreme solutions more acceptable. Moreover, as Hitler's utterances had to be read as policy statements (in the absence of any organised system for getting decisions out of Hitler), then many leading Nazis would have regarded violent persecution of the Jews as a natural extension of what had gone before. The war then radicalised that interpretation still further. Kershaw therefore modifies the Intentionalist-Structuralist debate. One should see him as part of the group that now feels that the Nazi regime was polycratic, and lurched between programmes, as rival groups fought for Hitler's approval, but Hitler was still capable of leading the country, however vaguely, in certain directions. The 'polycrats' also include Christopher Browning, Mary Fulbrook and Phillippe Currin.

> **COMMENT:**
> One of the shocking characteristics of Nazism was its racism. There is no doubt that it was intrinsic of Nazism, from Hitler downwards. Whether there was ever a 'blueprint' for violence against German Jews and Eastern Europeans is unlikely, as the policies emerged piecemeal over several years. It was not a 'straight road' to the Holocaust, but a 'twisted path'.

The Goldhagen controversy

Daniel Goldhagen dived into this debate and claimed that all the Germans willingly joined in the orgy of violence against the Jews. He provided some useful new material on the ancillary staff of the Holocaust, particularly on the 'death marches' at the end of the war (where camp guards refused to give up their inmates despite official orders to do so).

Goldhagen exaggerated
However, Goldhagen's thesis was weak in one crucial respect. He refused to acknowledge the contrary evidence of German opposition to the regime, or the

central role of Hitler, his ideology and the terrorising effect of the regime on ordinary citizens. The work was much sensationalised. By contrast, Saul Friedländer stresses the 'central role' that Hitler played, whilst acknowledging the frailties of individuals. This seems to suggest that the debate has returned to Hitler, which is really where it began.

The weaknesses of the Goldhagen thesis is its generalised assumptions
The chief problem with Goldhagen's view that the Germans were 'inherently' anti-Semitic and therefore, to follow his logic, inherently murderous on the grand scale, is that we would have to question whether this is only applicable to Germans. If we did think this, as he does, then we are little better than the Nazis themselves, as we would be singling out one ethnic group as particularly vicious and deserving of our contempt. If we do not, then we would have to seek other historical examples. Was racism 'inherent' (and murderous) in eighteenth-century England as black slaves were transported to the Americas? If so, why was slavery abolished in the 1790s and across the empire in 1833? Can we really construct an historical model for later genocides in Rwanda and Cambodia?

The debate after Goldhagen

The debate after Goldhagen's work has focused on 'ordinary Germans'
The question that Goldhagen raised was: how far were ordinary German citizens involved in anti-Semitic activity? Not surprisingly, many Germans would have liked to have distanced themselves from Nazism, but in Germany there is a full and frank debate about the generation of the 1940s. Saul Friedländer records with sadness the vicious anti-Semitism of the period that occurred at grass roots level. In one example, he explains how the mayor of Düsseldorf banned Jews from the local swimming baths. At first this seems like a Nazi official imposing anti-Semitic policy, but Friedlander reveals that the mayor acted this way after a barrage of letters from 'ordinary citizens' who feared being contaminated by 'dirty Jews' whilst swimming.

Prejudice at local level was not the road to the Holocaust
However, anti-Semitic prejudice in the 1930s does not automatically mean that the German people would endorse the mass murder of the Jews. Even if the radicalising effect of the war is taken into account, the death camps would have been unthinkable to the German people. It is for this reason that the death camps were often concealed within SS barracks (as at Dachau) or in remote areas.

Eyewitnesses testified to the danger of trying to enquire too much about the government's secret business, even when rumours circulated that the Jews were being systematically killed.

'Jewishness' was a tool for terror
We might have to seek other ways of examining the problem, for if we begin with the Holocaust and look back for its origins, we are in danger of assuming that it was inevitable, and we will ignore contrary evidence. The origins of anti-Semitism were largely religious, but Germany in the 1930s was relatively secular, so the Nazis redefined the Jews in racial terms. Jews were in fact defined rather vaguely, but generally they were regarded by the rest of the German population as different on grounds of *both* race (ethnicity) and religion (although not all Jews were practising/orthodox). This Nazi vagueness was in itself a tool to coerce society. Unpatriotic persons might be deemed as being somewhat 'Jewish', a stigma that most wished to avoid. Nationalism was very important to most Germans and to all Nazis, but anti-Semitism was less accepted (as the boycott of shops in 1933 demonstrated). Jews were the scapegoats, and this may have arisen naturally as economic conditions worsened or was a deliberate policy, encouraged and officially sanctioned by the regime.

Employment imbalance
Taking the idea that anti-Semitism was embedded in German thinking for a moment, one would need to seek causes of the extreme version which presumably arose in the short term. One is immediately drawn to the defeat of Germany in the First World War. To hold the Jews responsible for this is irrational, but Nazis were willing to accept that Jews, whom they saw in Government

„Hier, Kleiner, halt du etwas ganz Süßes! Aber dafür müßt ihr beide mit mir gehen…"

Figure 77. Caricature of a Jew with paedophile connotations.

appointments, in the communist party, amongst the revolutionaries, and in big business, were responsible for the catastrophe. Employment was a more rational grievance. A glance at the profile of Jews and occupations shows a high proportion in white collar work. It was easy to accuse Jews of stealing jobs and, in a climate of high unemployment, this was especially irksome. For the poorest Germans, Jewish employers or landlords were an unpopular group.

'Scientific' explanations were common
The Nazis also believed there were scientific grounds for the differences between Jews and Germans. During the Third Reich they carried out extensive research. But they found Jews so hard to define that the laws against Jews were in danger of inconsistency. They therefore chose the arbitrary date of 1750 after which Jews could be located in family trees.

Figure 78. 'Jews are criminals': anti-Jewish poster.

Some historians have sought to ridicule this Nazi embarrassment, but be cautious of this approach. We should not forget that the Nazis thought in terms of the distant generations, and not just the present. An active breeding programme, and perhaps a planned solution to the Jewish question (through exile or extermination), would mean that eventually the old Germans who might be 'tainted' with Jewish blood, would be bred out and replaced by the new generations of pure Aryans. Perhaps this is why the Nazis spoke of 'a thousand year Reich'.

There was a curious lack of systemisation and consistency in Nazi policy
The biggest problem with the Intentionalist view is that the anti-Semitic programme was hardly systematic in the early years of the Reich. In fact it was piecemeal and even chaotic. If anti-Semitism was integral, why did it take so long to be implemented? Mass executions did not begin in Russia until 1941 and the Holocaust itself did not get underway until 1943. The policy could have been implemented for the sake of the Nazi elites, or it could have been to maintain the interests and energies of the radicals as in the case of the boycott of Jewish businesses at the beginning of the regime.

Jews and sexuality

One area of Nazi Germany not yet fully explored is the issue of sexuality. Nazi doctrines denied sexual activity amongst its youth movements, and homosexuals were singled out as criminals and sent to concentration camps. The anti-Semitic policies also have sexual overtones (see Figure 77).

The great fears were of miscegenation – racial mixing, and the corruption of women. There is something Wagnarian about damsels in distress, pursued by unscrupulous barbarians intent on rape. The portrayal of the Jew as sexual predators was lurid and as offensive as possible in Nazi newspapers. A glimpse at this can be seen in the Nuremberg Laws where only female (never male) Jewish housekeepers over a certain age would be tolerated.

Summary

▶ Anti-Semitic prejudice in Germany predated the Nazis.

▶ In 1933, radical elements wanted to 'punish' the Jews.

▶ After the failure of the boycott (it was unpopular with the German people), the Nazis switched to more cautious policies, and used legislation.

▶ The Nazis defined Jews in religious and racial terms.

▶ 1938 was a turning point because of the degree of violence that was unleashed.

▶ Historians do not agree on whether there was a consistent policy that ended in the Holocaust.

Tutorial

Progress questions

1. Briefly outline the stages in Nazi persecution of the Jews on an annotated timeline.

2. Why was Goebbels so keen to orchestrate the violence of the *Reichskristallnacht* in 1938 rather than before?

3. What action did the Nazis take against other minorities they disliked?

4. Why do historians disagree so fiercely when it comes to the origins of the Holocaust?

Discussion points

1. Why were the actions against Jews implemented in a piecemeal fashion? What lessons had been learned from the boycott of 1933?

2. Why is the *Reichskristallnacht* regarded as an event of so much importance?

3. Do Hitler's actions against the Jews between 1934 and 1937 strengthen or weaken the Structuralists' arguments?

Practical assignment

1. Consider the argument that all aspects of Nazism were motivated by a racist interpretation of history and society. Can all aspects of policy-making in the Third Reich be explained in this way in practice? Draw up a list of policies in which racism can be detected as the overriding consideration, or as a secondary factor.

2. Divide a page in half and list on one side the Intentionalists, and Functionalists on the other. Taking each aspect of Nazi persecution between 1933 and 1938, assess whether they can be explained by means of the two approaches. Add subsequent findings from the genocide covered in Chapter 11.

Document questions

A. **The Law for the Protection of German Blood and German Honour, 15 September 1935**
   Entirely convinced that the purity of German blood is essential to the further existence of the German people, and inspired by uncompromising determination to safeguard the future of the German nation, the *Reichstag* has unanimously adopted the following law:

   1. Marriages between Jews and citizens of German blood are forbidden.
   2. Sexual relations outside marriage between Jews and nationals of German blood are forbidden.

B. **Hitler to the *Reichstag*, 30 January 1939**
   If the international Jewish financiers outside Europe should succeed in plunging the nations once more into war, then the result will be not the Bolshevising of the earth and the victory of world-wide Jewry, but the annihilation of the Jewish race in Europe.

C. **Martin Housden, Resistance and Conformity in the Third Reich (1996)**
    In the context of a society in which racism formed the background feature of
    everyday life, many ordinary Germans indeed played small parts in making a
    flawed system function. During peacetime, some people passively accepted
    and others actively supported racial policies and actions which stopped short
    of the wholesale violence of *Reichskristallnacht*. With the nation at war,
    increasingly extreme racial policy grew into something people learned to live
    with. It was for most people a matter of indifference. If their job dictated some
    sort of collaboration in the implementation of racial policy, by and large they
    conformed to the demand.

Progress questions

1. Explain the reference to *Reichskristallnacht* in C.

2. Compare sources B and C. What similarities and differences are there
    surrounding Germany's attitude towards the Jews in these sources?

3. Using your wider knowledge, analyse how far these sources show that
    Germans were fully involved in supporting Hitler's racial aspirations.

Study tips

1. Anti-Semitism and persecution are topics worth knowing in some detail as it
    is regarded as the most significant phenomenon of the Nazi period.

2. Don't assume that the Holocaust was simply the inevitable outcome of the
    legislation of the 1930s. Many students fail to recognise the hesitant and
    rather disorganised nature of the persecution before the war.

3. Adopt an analytical approach by acknowledging the historians who are
    important in this field, and assess their views critically. Phrases like
    'Dawidowicz neglects to mention . . .' or 'Goldhagen is convincing
    because . . .' can add to the authority of your own views.

9

Opposition and Resistance

One-minute overview – *State terror, despite Goebbels' protestations that Germans would be won over by propaganda, was an intrinsic part of the Third Reich from the beginning. As the regime gradually tightened its grip during the 1930s, the ability of the opposition to organise and make itself felt grew more distant. All agencies capable of resisting the state were subject to coercion, even sections of the Nazis' own movement, such as the SA. The Nazis justified their brutality with the ideology Hitler had developed in the 1920s. However, Nazi policies did not go unchallenged. Although the state possessed considerable powers of physical coercion, including the formidable SS and Gestapo, some Germans took enormous risks to oppose the regime.*

In this chapter you will learn:
▶ *The problems of opposing the Third Reich.*

The problems of opposing the Third Reich

Any opposition to the regime was an enormous risk, and for the majority there was a desire to avoid the coercion of the Nazis by keeping a low profile. Inevitably some Germans chose to collaborate, but just as many chose to oppose the regime, even in the most subtle ways. The failure of the boycott against Jewish shops was an early example of passive non-co-operation. The Church and the left wing provide some examples of more active opposition. Many individual acts of courage, such as concealing Jews or other 'enemies of the state' will never be known since, by their nature, no records were kept. There are four sections:

a.   Action against potential opposition
b.   Disincentives to opposition.
c.   Actual opposition: the church.
d.   Actual opposition: the Left.

Action against potential opposition

The first question for the Nazi party was how to eliminate the opposition. Hitler planned to operate without opposition, a factor which made Nazism distinctive from Wilhelmine Germany which had been a limited democracy. The methods that the Nazis employed included mass arrests and punitive legislation. Laws ended the trade union movement on 2 May 1933. All political parties and all opposition was illegal from 14 July 1933. In addition, there was a threat of draconian action against those who might defy the regime and the early concentration camps were designed to intimidate more than their inmates. It should also be noted that all forums of debate and opposition were removed from February 1933. All media was in state hands. Demonstrators at public protest meetings would have been rounded up and imprisoned. Even grumbling in the workplace was likely to be reported. Kershaw believed that all opposition ended in March 1933, and that the KPD was the last effective agency of resistance.

The weakness of the opposition

Why was opposition so weak? In many ways this question assumes that all the citizens of a state, or the majority at least, would be willing to act against the legitimate government. In fact this is quite rare. When the regime is undemocratic and has no scruples about the crushing of its opponents, then opposition is almost impossible. Ironically the form of government that it is easiest to oppose is a democracy. The communist and fascist systems sought to remove all opposition by whatever means necessary, whilst democracy encourages the alternative view *within* its system. Apathy is perhaps the greatest threat to democracy, but terror is the greatest threat in a dictatorship.

Disincentives to opposition

Information was controlled

When a regime controls all sources of information, it is difficult to get any reliable opposing views. This was certainly true of the Third Reich which went to great lengths to organise and control the media. By contrast the opposition to Nazism was itself divided. Communists, conservatives, democrats and socialists were unlikely to co-operate. Opposition was made even more difficult when Hitler claimed to represent Germany in himself. Any action against Hitler or the party thus became automatically a crime against Germany.

Fear was a deterrent

At first many Germans embraced the idea of national regeneration, and jobs were eagerly taken up. Patriotism and an almost universal fear of Bolshevism ensured

Figure 79. National Socialism: 'The organised will of the Nation'.

the compliance of many others. Whilst all eventually had their own grumbles and complaints, it was safer to become apolitical and avoid getting into trouble. Terror, or the fear of its application, was often enough to ensure people kept their mouths shut. Few wished to attract attention to themselves, even when neighbours were arrested. This, more than anything else, proves that all have a responsibility to take care of the interests of others, or they will pay the price for their isolation.

The cost to the individual

Any assessment of the failure of opposition needs to take account of the strength of the Nazis even at the early stage of the regime's history. It was difficult to resist the massed ranks of the SA. When the Nazis had the advantage of being able to invoke the law on their side it was even more difficult to oppose the regime without recourse to violence. The social implications of such actions were beyond the realm of the majority of citizens, since they did not want to lose their jobs or their families. The regime was well informed, having inherited all of Germany's police records, and well organised. In the early days at least, few Germans expected the brutality which followed.

Actual opposition to Nazism: the church

The opposition by Christian churches provides a useful example of how the Nazis were defied or accepted. The churches remained one of the few organised bodies that remained intact, but they were handicapped by two factors. First, they were divided in their response to Nazism, and second, they tended to take the view that events in the present, however terrible, would be rectified by God in the hereafter. Faith provided a comfort and consolation, but it offered little hope of successful resistance. There are six aspects to consider:

(i)   The ideology of Christianity that opposed Nazism.
(ii)   The Protestant church.
(iii) The Roman Catholic church.
(iv)   The state church.
(v)   Other groups.
(vi)   Nazi morality.

Christianity opposed Nazi ideology

Ironically, Hitler admired Christianity. But he was not interested in its values, merely the effect it had on society. He was impressed by its endurance, such as its heritage of over 1,000 years without changes in its fundamental principles, and by the way that it could unite millions of devotees, and mobilise them in 'blind faith' to an idea. These parallels between Nazism and Christianity thankfully end there.

The churches were suited to resistance
The churches (there were several branches of Christianity) were the only agencies in Germany that successfully resisted the Nazis. The Christian church gave a good account of itself in mustering support against the euthanasia programme until the authorities stepped in, and it was a churchman, Dietrich Bonhoffer, who assisted in the army's attempt to assassinate Hitler in July 1944, and who was executed. It was the special character of the church which enabled it to oppose the Nazis where others failed.

A strong ideology in the church sustained many Germans against Nazism
Bonhoffer believed that it was the duty of Germans to protect everyone in society, and in particular it was the responsibility of society to care for the weak. This fundamental Christian view proved a compelling ideology and one might suggest that the reason for the weakness of the other agencies of opposition was that they lacked a robust, or coherent, ideology. But this must be challenged by the fact that trades unions and the KPD had firm ideological beliefs that opposed Nazism. Moreover, Christian groups were divided over their interpretation of the Bible, although they were, with one or two exceptions, united on its fundamentals. Likewise, the SPD and other democrats had a strong and carefully constructed set of anti-Nazi beliefs. If anything, it was the Nazis, not the Left, that suffered from a lack of a coherent ideology. Even if it was not ideology, then the individual or collective courage of the members of the church must be acknowledged as an important factor in sustaining opposition to Nazism.

The Protestant church
▶ *There was collaboration by some churchmen, but not all.*
   Bonhoffer's colleagues belonged to the confessional church, a group who broke away from the more conservative Protestant churches which had acquiesced in the Nazi takeover. The confessional congregations believed that the Bible was fundamentally immutable and homoeostatic. Christ's message was clear, only through faith in Him could one be saved from the inevitable consequence of sin, and belief carried obligations to love God and one's 'neighbour'. The Protestant and Lutheran church had some background of anti-Semitism, partly because of some outspoken remarks by Martin Luther

himself in the sixteenth century to the effect that Jews had been so obsessed by the Law of Moses that they had failed to accept Christ, and murdered him by turning him over the Roman authorities for execution by crucifixion. Nevertheless the motives of the Protestant church leaders was less ideological than pragmatic. Their aim was to survive.

▶ *The instinct of survival fostered stalemate.*
The church was not a set of buildings, or even an institution, but a congregation of people. They dared not show disloyalty to their country, and moreover they feared the communists who had carried out a reign of terror in Russia against all churches after 1917. At least, they reasoned, the Nazis would not abolish the church if they knew that Protestants would not resist them. If the Nazis could be made to see that Protestantism meant loyalty to one's county and a desire to preserve conservative values, such as a strong sense of morality and culture, then the church would survive.

The Roman Catholic church
▶ *The Catholic church tolerated the Nazis.*
The Catholic church reasoned in much the same way as the Protestants, although Hitler was suspicious of Germans who seemed to owe their first loyalty to Rome, and not to Germany. The Catholic church had survived many regimes; Wilhelmine Germany's authoritarian monarchy, Bismarck's assault on Catholicism in the 1870s through the law (the *Kulturkampf*), the revolutionary upheaval after the First World War, the socialist, and therefore secular, government of the Weimar Republic, and the Third Reich. Accusations of collaboration with the Nazis have been made against Catholics because of the Concordat of Pope Pius XII (a deal that Daniel Goldhagen has criticised), which effectively was an agreement of mutual non-interference. This has been reinforced by evidence that the Catholic Centre Party agreed to co-operate with the Nazi takeover, although it should be noted that this was in return for the survival of various Catholic institutions including youth groups.

▶ *Galen's resistance was significant.*
Bishop Galen's speech of 3 August 1941 in protest at the secret killing of 'unproductive people' sheds some light on the dilemma for Catholics. 'It is true that there are definite commandments in Catholic moral doctrine which are no longer applicable if their fulfilment involves too many difficulties. However, there are sacred obligations of conscience from which no one has the power to

release us and which we must fulfil even if it costs us our lives...' Galen's outburst against the euthanasia programme gained widespread support in Westphalia, but the regime was only restrained from hanging Galen because of the effect it may have had on the war effort and support for the regime.

▶ *The limitations of Catholic doctrine meant resistance was passive.*
Ideologically, Catholics were expected to focus on the life to come, that is after death, with God; but at the same time Catholics were to live in the world which was seen as inherently sinful and 'broken'. Constant reaffirmations of faith were required, and compromise with the world is not usually tolerated. Catholics continued to resist contraception, abortion, divorce and other aspects of immorality. In this sense, whilst their ideology was resilient and saved them from Nazism, it was also self-limiting. To participate in active resistance was to defy a Papal Bull, an order from God's representative on earth, which had promised not to interfere with the Nazis' plans. The fact that the Nazis had broken their side of the agreement did not give Catholics license to do the same.

The state church
The *Reichskirche* was an attempt to undermine the existing churches and to explore the ways that Christianity could be altered. One considerable problem for the Nazis was the fact the first section of the Christian Bible is also the Jewish Torah. The *Reichskirche* therefore became a secular 'church', using the motifs of religion or spirituality, but using only Nazi themes. It was not a great success. However, newly-weds were given a copy of *Mein Kampf* and engaged couples offered secular marriage services. The failure of the *Reichskirche* tells us that resistance to Nazism was perhaps more passive and subtle, since other forms of physical opposition were deemed impossible.

▶ *Other religious groups were regarded as disloyal.*
Minority religious groups were persecuted, which served to remind the bigger churches of the threat. Jehovah's Witnesses, many Nonconformists, and Quakers were imprisoned and attempts made at re-education. Their refusal to bear arms was a significant factor in their categorisation. 'Disloyalty' to Germany, and failure to conform, seemed to be the most important criteria for the decision to intern them in concentration camps.

▶ *Nazi morality – the Nazi 'will'.*

The Nazis put great store on sexual morality although some never lived up to it. Goebbels had an affair with a Czech actress, Lida Baarova, until Hitler intervened. But the Nazis lacked any compunction when it came to the execution of thousands of people. They tried to suppress, marginalise or usurp the existing churches. This indicates that they were afraid of the churches. Why? Hitler talked of the need to overcome feelings of pity, and to have an iron will. These seem to refer to the ambition to alter the biological structure of the German people over several generations, but equally might refer to mental preparation for the 'struggle' of war, and the ability of the German population to endure another round of heavy casualties as they had done in the First World War.

▶ *The Nazis promoted 'Aryan qualities'.*

The most compelling argument returns to Hitler's long-term plans for Germany and the Aryan race, and of the special qualities which he admired in his view of the typical Aryan. Courage, endurance, and determination would complement Hitler's concept of 'spiritual re-education'. In effect this was little more than training his soldiers to kill civilians and other non-combatants exactly as if they were enemy troops which constituted a military threat. To Hitler, of course, they were a threat in the biological sense.

> *COMMENT:*
> *Resistance to a dictatorship was a dangerous business. Since no state agency was accountable, there was arbitrary imprisonment, torture and murder in Nazi Germany. Only a few were affected, but it was enough to convince the majority not to challenge the regime.*

Figure 80. The Left v. Hitler: communist demonstration against Hitler.

Actual opposition: the Left

Although the SPD had been banned in 1933, and despite their lack of preparation for resistance, they managed to offer a form of opposition. They actively encouraged not physical resistance, but the dissemination of information to combat Nazi propaganda. This was done by means of a whispering campaign, which the Gestapo acknowledged as 'the most effective illegal work against the State'. The information largely concerned price increases, low wages, exploitation, corruption and brutality. The secret police found it almost impossible to catch the perpetrators as no information was ever written down. Nevertheless, while such a campaign raised the morale of those who came into contact with it, it cannot really be classed as 'resistance', and its effect was probably quite small.

Resistance to Hitler
The boundary between opposition and resistance in the Third Reich is difficult to draw. During the war, a growth of activities that could be identified as 'resistance' is identifiable.

The White Rose was a small and brave group of pamphleteers
The White Rose was a small group of university students in Munich who organised a pamphlet campaign condemning Nazism and the war. A total of six pamphlets were produced between 1942 and February 1943, and the group distributed these and daubed anti-Nazi graffiti on public buildings in eight cities at night. Amongst their criticisms was the condemnation of the 'bestial manner' in which 300,000 Jews had been murdered in Poland. After the disaster at Stalingrad, Paul Giesler, the *Gauleiter* of Munich criticised the university students for failing to support the war effort. Although hecklers were arrested, a demonstration took place in the city. The Gestapo surveillance that followed meant that the White Rose group were caught distributing pamphlets in the university. In February 1943, all the remaining members were arrested and executed. The White Rose letter and pamphlet campaign is regarded by J. P. Stern as a courageous and significant effort, but Ian Kershaw points out that the failure of the group, and the short-lived nature of the campaign, shows just how hopeless this kind of resistance was.

The Edelweiss Pirates' opposition developed during the Third Reich
Some young people, dissatisfied with the Hitler Youth, formed gangs called 'Packs', 'Pirates' and 'Edelweiss' which prompted concern in the regime that a few young men were becoming delinquents. At first, the 'Pirates' were concerned only with jazz and swing music and wanted to escape the regimentation of the Hitler Youth, especially when it became compulsory to join in late 1939. They were easy to identify as they wore their hair long, sported checked jackets and shorts (men) or white jumpers and socks (women). Gang warfare against the Hitler Youth was common. However, once the war broke out, the Pirates' opposition became more

serious. They wrote anti-Nazi graffiti, and ignored movement restrictions to take part in camping expeditions where they could criticise the regime and its leaders freely. In 1942, as some Pirates joined communist cells and participated in more serious acts of sabotage, the Gestapo cracked down on them. In four industrial cities, 739 Pirates were arrested on one day in December 1942. In 1944, after SS directives against youth gangs, some Pirates were publicly executed by hanging.

There were a number of resistance groups

Thousands of individuals resisted the Nazi policies against the Jews, and in Berlin, a group calling itself 'Uncle Emil' smuggled and hid 5,000 Jews and others wanted by the Gestapo. A cell called the Red Chapel was also uncovered in the Air Ministry. However, an important unit was the *Abwehr*, the Military Intelligence wing of the German Foreign Office. The *Abwehr* collected information about war crimes and transmitted information about the regime which might be useful to the Allies to London. However, Admiral Canaris, chief of the *Abwehr*, was eventually arrested by the Gestapo and Major General Oster, another leading figure, was also discovered. Both were executed in April 1945.

The most serious threat to Hitler came from the German Army

The army abandoned its attempt to remove Hitler in 1940 following the fall of France, but a group of army officers who were dissatisfied with Hitler's leadership in the war formed a group called the Kreisau Circle. It attracted the support of churchmen, members of the Foreign Office and some aristocrats. Although dismissed as an ineffectual think-tank, the Kreisau Circle provided the focus for a group of conspirators to meet and formulate a post-Hitlerite Germany. The Gestapo succeeded in penetrating the group in 1944, arresting some of its leaders, but this merely provided the impetus to further action.

The July Plot was an attempt to blow up Hitler

A plot was hatched to kill Hitler and establish a democratic and federal Germany. Amidst great secrecy, Claus von Stauffenberg was given a post within Hitler's headquarters. He decided to try to kill Hitler by exploding a bomb at his headquarters at the 'Wolf's Lair' near Rastenberg. Hitler was injured in the explosion on 20 July 1944, but the announcement of a takeover by the plotters was bungled. In the confusion, Goebbels took command of the Berlin garrison and made announcements that the Führer was still in command. The Nazis then quickly hunted down the conspirators. They were tried in a public trial, tortured and executed. One of them was Dietrich Bonhoffer, a Protestant minister.

The failure of the Plot led to an increase of Nazi terror
In the aftermath of the July Plot, 5,000 people were arrested and killed, amongst them many aristocratic officers of the army high command who had nothing to do with the conspiracy but whom the Nazis hated. The army was also given a number of National Socialist Leadership Officers who would ensure the political loyalty of the armed forces. The Plot was a tragic failure, and led to a tightening of Nazi persecution and terror against anyone who showed even the remotest sign of dissent. There are estimates that 12,000 people were executed by the secret police during the period of the Third Reich.

Historians disagree on the significance of the resistance groups
Martin Broszat carried out an excellent and detailed examination of resistance to Hitler in Bavaria between 1933 and 1945. He concluded that there were many forms of opposition and resistance that ranged in type and seriousness. Following this study Allan Merson carried out research into communist resistance in the belief that this area had been neglected by West German historians because of the Cold War prejudice against the Left. Although Merson praised the communists' 'moral triumph', Kershaw regarded their efforts as another 'tragic failure'.

The youth groups also failed
The same conclusion could be drawn about the youth groups. Detlev Peukert believes the Edelweiss Pirates and swing/jazz gangs represented a complete rejection of Nazism. However, their effectiveness must be questioned when one considers that they were easily contained by the Gestapo. Moreover, it has to be said that less than 1% of the population were engaged in active resistance, even though it is acknowledged that many more were involved in some passive forms of dissent. The reason for this need not be that the German people were pro-Nazi, but that they were afraid of the regime. Given what happened to the dissidents who were caught, this fear was well founded.

Tutorial

Progress questions

1. What was the White Rose organisation?

2. What deterred German citizens from opposing the regime?

3. How did members of the Catholic church resist the Nazis?

4. How effective were the resistance movements against Hitler?

Discussion points

1. Why was there no general strike by the trade unions as there had been in 1920 in the defeat of Dr Kapp's Putsch?

2. Why was there no rising of the communists in 1933–34 as there had been in 1919?

3. Why didn't the army resist the takeover of the state?

4. Why didn't the SA rebel when their demands were ignored?

5. Why did the democrats, both conservative and socialist, fail to act together against the Nazis?

6. How successful was the opposition of the church?

Practical assignments

1. Add to the list of coercion by the regime in this chapter by re-examining propaganda, and the use of anti-Semitism. Write two or three paragraphs to explain how the Nazis used these methods to reinforce their coercion.

2. Evaluate the position of the Catholic Centre Party in 1933, and the calculations it made in supporting the Enabling Law. Compare the position of the churches in 1939. What pressures continued to bear on the church leaders to ensure their loyalty to the state? List all the factors from this chapter as well as your own ideas.

3. Use a graph to examine the degree of threat posed by the different opposition groups. On the x axis, plot the danger of the threat, and the on the y axis, plot the level of popular support. Within the graph use icons to represent different groups or individuals. For example, von Stauffenberg would be a dangerous threat but was not someone who enjoyed popular support.

Study tips

1. Make sure that you are familiar with the role and effect of the SS and other security forces. They were the most important terror agencies of the Third Reich.

2. Use diagrams to help you remember the reasons why Germans found it difficult to resist the regime.

3. Create, and then check, your own notes on this chapter on the success of the opposition and resistance groups with the actions of the SS, Gestapo and other security services in the period 1933–45.

10

Foreign Policy and War, 1934–42

One-minute overview – Hitler's foreign policy has been the subject of much debate by historians as they try to piece together how the world's most devastating conflict broke out. There is much evidence which points to Hitler's planning for a war from the beginning. He was pragmatic in the sense that he knew Germany had no chance of victory in 1934, but by 1939, Hitler was eager to make use of the advantages he had secured through a rapid rearmament policy. His contingency plans reveal something of his opportunism, but also his long-term aims. The war he unleashed on the West in 1940 involved the new tactics of Blitzkrieg where armoured divisions, supported by aircraft, punched through enemy lines and drove deep into the rear causing panic and confusion. The war in the East was also a new departure. Civilians were either regarded as a resource, or an inconvenience, and Hitler's ideal of Lebensraum (living space) was implemented at the expense of thousands of lives and properties.

In this chapter you will learn:
▶ *How Nazi ideology and foreign policy led to war.*
▶ *About the war in Western Europe in 1940.*
▶ *About the war in Eastern Europe between 1941 and 1942.*
▶ *About the other theatres of operations, such as North Africa.*
▶ *What the effects were on the German home front.*

Nazi ideology and foreign policy, 1933–39

Hitler's foreign policy began cautiously as Germany's weaknesses were considerable. However, there was an early attempt to annex Austria which failed because of the opposition of Italy. Taking advantage of the Abyssinia Crisis, Hitler reoccupied the demilitarised Rhineland in 1936 and took steps to forge a closer relationship with Italy's dictator, Mussolini. However, it was not until 1938 that Hitler felt that Germany could make a start towards the fulfilment of his grandiose plans for Eastern Europe. He annexed Austria in March 1938, the Sudetenland in November 1938 at the Munich conference, and Czechoslovakia in March 1939. Having secured the assurance that Stalin would not intervene, and

Figure 81. Hitler's ally, Benito Mussolini in Rome.

ignoring the warnings of France and Britain, he invaded Poland in September 1939, thereby precipitating a general war in Europe. This section will be divided into the following parts:

a. The League of Nations and the attempted *Anschluss*.
b. The Saar Plebiscite and the Anglo-German Naval Agreement, 1935.
c. Abyssinia, the Rhineland, and Italy, 1936.
d. The Spanish Civil War and the Hossbach Memorandum, 1937.
e. The annexation of Austria, 1938.
f. The Czech Crisis and the Munich Conference, 1938.
g. The invasion of Czechoslovakia, 1939.
h. The invasion of Poland, 1939.
i. Historical controversy on the causes of the war.

The League of Nations and the attempted *Anschluss*

The aim of the League of Nations was to resolve conflict
The League of Nations was formed in 1919, as an agency designed to preserve peace and prevent a recurrence of the First World War. Although there were 42 nations that were signatories, it relied on the participation of Britain and France, the two leading Great Powers to emerge from the First World War, to be effective. Russia was diplomatically isolated as a Bolshevik country, the Austrian empire had ceased to exist, and America had turned its back on European affairs in an isolationist policy. Although many of the countries were democracies, the League had no mandate to interfere in the domestic issues of any country. It was concerned only with acts of aggression between countries and the resolution of conflict by negotiation. These were limited aims.

The League's methods were designed to avert war
The means by which war would be made less likely was through world disarmament. Economic sanctions would be levied at countries which did not comply, and gradually it was expected that the denial of vital raw materials and

foodstuffs would bring any modern state to reason. Only as a last resort would the League force another state to comply, and in practice it was clear that this task would fall to Britain and France. In 1923, France had demonstrated its power by invading the Ruhr industrial region in order to force Germany to pay for reparations, or damages payments, from the First World War. It was clear to Hitler that France intended to uphold the provisions of the Treaty of Versailles, the peace terms which Germany had been obliged to sign in 1919.

Hitler's aim was to destroy the peace settlement of 1919

Hitler loathed the treaty and in 1933 he told the district army commanders that foreign policy was 'the battle against Versailles'. Yet this was never the limit of his ambitions. He stated that he aimed to build up the armed forces and asked 'How is political power to be used when it has been gained? ... Perhaps fighting for new export possibilities, perhaps – and probably better – the conquest of new living space in the east and its ruthless Germanisation'.

Hitler aimed to annex Austria

Hitler's first move seemed to be consistent with his desire to revise the terms of the Treaty of Versailles. He decided to break the encirclement policy France had adopted by allying with Poland, by negotiating a non-aggression pact with the Poles himself. But his first attempt to establish self-determination for Germans (the right to choose which state a people could belong to), by unifying Austria and Germany failed. It was clear that the majority of conservative and socialist Austrians did not want an *Anschluss* (union) with Germany, but a brief civil war in 1934 seemed to herald an opportunity for a handful of Austrian Nazis who attempted to seize power in July that year. The Austrian Chancellor, Engelbert Dollfuss, was killed, but the Austrian army defeated the revolt.

There was opposition from Italy

More significantly, Mussolini, the fascist dictator of Italy, threatened Germany with war if it attempted to annex Austria. Mussolini felt that such a move would threaten his northern borders, and he boasted that the 'Brenner [Pass] will bristle with bayonets'. Britain and France felt that they could rely on Mussolini as an ally against the new Germany and in April 1935, the three powers signed a pact at Stresa to uphold Austrian independence.

The Saar Plebiscite and the Anglo-German Naval Agreement, 1935

Hitler had only limited success in 1935
In January 1935, the people of the Saar, a small industrial area administered by the League of Nations, voted overwhelmingly to rejoin Germany. This small victory for the Nazis served to emphasise the success of their policy of returning Germans to their homeland. In March 1935, Hitler announced compulsory military service had been reintroduced in Germany and Goering stated that the *Luftwaffe* (air force) was again in existence, both of which contravened the Treaty of Versailles. The existence of the 'Stresa Front' and the alliances quickly concluded between France and Russia, and joined by Czechoslovakia, seemed to indicate that Germany could still be limited in her actions.

Hitler hoped for Britain's assistance
However, Britain reached an agreement with Germany over the size of the German *Kriegsmarine* (navy). It was decided that the German navy could rearm to 35% of the size of the Royal Navy. This may seem modest, but Britain had unilaterally abandoned a term of Versailles which had stated that Germany should be limited to a coastal defence flotilla. Hitler was delighted and hoped that this was the first step in securing a racial and military alliance with Britain whom he saw as fellow Aryans.

Abyssinia, the Rhineland, and Italy, 1936

The Italian invasion of Abyssinia was Hitler's opportunity to obtain concessions
In October 1935, Mussolini's forces invaded Abyssinia in an attempt to carve out an African empire. Whilst claiming public disapproval, the British and French governments sought to appease Mussolini and prevent the collapse of the Stresa Front. However, Hitler used the opportunity to reoccupy the demilitarised Rhineland adjacent to France with his troops in March 1936. He was prepared to abandon the operation if France showed any signs of resistance, because he knew that the German army was weak, but the moment passed. British politicians justified Hitler's actions as the reoccupation of his own country and argued that the League could hardly act against Germany in this 'domestic' issue. Hitler knew that the League seemed unwilling to act against him.

Italy became an ally
This became more apparent when Mussolini, successful against Abyssinia in May 1936, and convinced that he had established influence over Albania and

Spain in a new Mediterranean empire, saw Germany as a potential ally in northern Europe. In November 1936, talks between Italy and Germany led to an understanding called the Rome-Berlin Axis. Hitler had now broken the Stresa Front and weakened any chance of collective action against him. Moreover, in November 1936, Hitler concluded the Anti-Comintern Pact with Japan. This was a treaty which was aimed at opposing Russia's influence, and Hitler regarded such an arrangement essential in a future conflict with Russia since it would split Russian forces on two fronts several hundred miles apart.

The Spanish Civil War and the Hossbach Memorandum, 1937

The Spanish Civil War was a testing ground for German forces
The Spanish Civil War broke out when a right-wing coup in July 1936 by General Franco against a left-wing government escalated into a major conflict between two groups of allies. The Nationalists, right-wing parties, the army, the church and landowners rallied behind Franco, whilst the Popular Front represented trade unionists, socialists, communists and anarchists. Mussolini sent troops and munitions to help Franco, but Hitler was more selective. His main contribution was the Condor Legion, an air force that used the Spanish Civil War as a testing ground for its planes and pilots. In the media, the bombing of the Basque town of Guernica seemed to indicate the new power of air warfare and its devastating effects on civilians' lives and property.

The Hossbach Memorandum: a plan for war?
The Hossbach Memorandum was a set of notes drawn up by one of Hitler's adjutants on contingencies which Hitler outlined to his chiefs of staff in November 1937. Although Hitler did not explicitly mention the policy towards Russia, he alluded to *Lebensraum* as follows, 'the aim of German policy was to make secure and to preserve the racial community and to enlarge it. It was therefore a question of space. The question for Germany was: where could it achieve the greatest gain at the lowest cost?' The document went on to specify that 1943–45 would be the 'waning point of the regime' unless this question was solved. It continued 'it was his unalterable determination to solve Germany's problem of space by 1943–45 at the latest'.

The Hossbach Memorandum remains controversial
Hitler specified that the immediate aim was to overthrow Austria and Czechoslovakia, before engaging in a war against the West. What makes the

document more ambiguous is the reference to anticipated conflict between France and Italy, which would draw in Britain, and which would make Hitler's attack on Austria and Czechoslovakia possible. Explanations have been offered that the document is merely one of many searches Hitler made for a solution to a fluid diplomatic scene, but others have seen this as the blueprint for a European war.

An anti-communist pact was established
In November 1937 Italy joined the Anti-Comintern Pact, whilst Japan was engaged in a war against China, threatening the stability of the Far East. It was clear that Britain and France lacked the military strength to deal with the threats which now existed from Japan, Italy and Germany combined. Their non-intervention in the Spanish Civil War only served to underline this weakness.

The annexation of Austria, 1938

Hitler used blatant aggression against Austria
Austrian Nazis continued to agitate for a share of power, but the Chancellor, Kurt Schussnigg, refused. Schussnigg was aware that Hitler intended to annex Austria, having been summoned to Berchtesgaden (Hitler's frontier residence) and threatened by Hitler personally. To forestall military intervention, Schussnigg called for a plebiscite (9 March 1938) in which Austrians would decide their future and he gave just three days' notice. Goering was as anxious as Hitler to take over and neither dare risk a vote against them. Goering gave the order to invade, but the troops were not to fire unless fired upon. Hitler contacted Mussolini and sent a reassuring note that the Brenner Pass represented a permanent boarder between them. This indicated that Hitler had no intention of making the South Tyrol (with a German-speaking population) a source of conflict with his Italian ally. Schussnigg called off the plebiscite in the hope of a German reprieve, but the invasion began on the 12 March 1938.

The speed of annexation was a surprise
The speed of the annexation took Europeans by surprise. Many Austrians welcomed the *Anschluss* (union) announced on the 13 March, but half the population had been socialist voters and opposed the move. The treatment of Schussnigg showed that Hitler applied new rules to diplomacy. The personal summons and the intimidation of leaders was designed to terrify others into submission. However Schussnigg's actions seemed to be based more on the

relative strengths of Germany and Austria, and his attempts to avoid a war that his country could not win.

The Czech Crisis and the Munich Conference, 1938

Hitler hated Czechoslovakia
Hitler again used Nazi agitators in his move against the Czech Sudetenland. There were a number of reasons why Hitler coveted this region. First, it contained a majority of ethnic Germans who had been alienated from the Czech state by the effects of the Depression, and who had been convinced by the arguments of Konrad Henlein (Sudeten German Party) of the benefits of association with Germany. Second, the Sudetenland was a mountainous region, heavily fortified and, as such, represented a serious obstacle to his plans of eastward expansion. Third, Hitler resented the Czechs. He was familiar with them from his days in Vienna, and he felt that they had no place in a racially German state. Moreover, he was no doubt piqued by the fact that Czechoslovakia was a successful democracy in an eastern European sea of dictatorships.

Hitler wanted a short war to terrorise Europe
Recent evidence suggests that Hitler planned a short war against the Czechs to test his army, and to send a signal to other European states that he was not to be resisted. Hitler demanded a solution to the Sudeten problem. Opinions on Prime Minister Neville Chamberlain's motives are divided. He made a declaration that Britain would not support France if France went to the military aid of Czechoslovakia. This meant that the French were reluctant to act alone, and the French-Czech alliance was a sham. Chamberlain may have done this to avoid war. He may also have realised Britain was unable to fight as it was ill-prepared, and that Czechoslovakia, land-locked in eastern Europe, was impossible to reach. He resolved to end the problem by negotiation.

Chamberlain tried to preserve peace
German troops concentrated on the border and the Czechs responded by mobilising in May. On 12 September, Hitler demanded self-determination for the Sudeten Germans. Was he hoping for another 'Saar plebiscite' response, or a short conflict which might involve France? On 15 September Chamberlain visited Hitler only to find him determined to solve the crisis by war. On 21 September, with French support, Chamberlain persuaded President Benes to capitulate, and cede those areas where 50% or more of the population were Sudeten Germans.

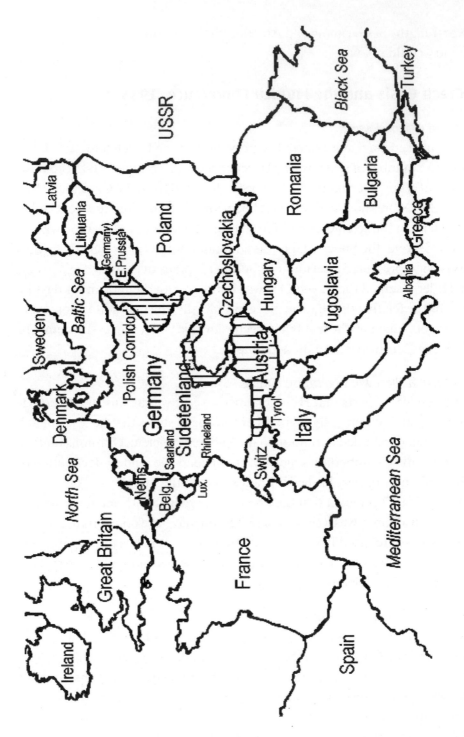

Figure 82. Europe in 1938.

War was narrowly averted

On 22 September, Chamberlain visited Hitler again at Bad Godesburg but Hitler stated that an agreement between Czechoslovakia and Germany was out of the question, since he intended to occupy the Sudeten land with troops on 1 October! He demanded the Czechs give in to German, Polish and Hungarian territorial claims. War appeared imminent. The Czechs would invoke their alliance obligations with France and a German attack would oblige Britain, as a League of Nations signatory, to fight Germany. Chamberlain chose to believe Hitler's closing remarks that Germany had 'no other territorial ambitions', and if this one issue could be resolved, then peace would be preserved.

Peace was maintained at the expense of Czechoslovakia

A Four Power Conference was proposed by Mussolini and Chamberlain leapt at this last chance. On 29 September, Chamberlain, Hitler, Daladier (the French Prime Minister) and Mussolini signed an agreement to transfer the Sudetenland to Germany. The Czechs were not invited and Benes was faced with a choice of signing, or fighting Germany without allies. He signed and resigned. Chamberlain felt peace had been preserved, but historians no longer agree that he was naive and was fooled by Hitler, since he ordered the rearmament of Britain to begin at once. On 10 October the Germans took the Czech border lands, quickly followed by Poland which took Teschen (an industrial region) and Hungary which gained lands in the south.

The invasion of Czechoslovakia, 1939

Hitler urged the Hungarians to annexe Ruthenia, one of the three states that made up the rump of Czechoslovakia. He also urged Slovakia to declare its independence of the republic, which only left Bohemia and Moravia outside foreign influence. Emil Hacha, the new Czech president, was told to place his country in the hands of the Reich, and to reinforce the point, German troops invaded the Czech republic on the 16 March 1939. One week later Slovakia also placed itself under German control.

Appeasement ended with new assurances to Poland

Chamberlain determined that Poland, also containing ethnic Germans, would not become a source of conflict, or suffer the fate of Czechoslovakia. He gave a firm assurance to Poland on 31 March 1939 that Britain would guarantee its independence. It marked the end of appeasement.

The invasion of Poland, 1939

Diplomacy was unfavourable for Poland

Hitler was convinced that Britain and France would not fight. In April 1939, following the Italian invasion of Albania, guarantees were given to Greece and Romania. On 18 April, the government of the USSR made overtures to Britain and France that it would agree to a treaty of mutual military support. But Chamberlain calculated that Russia was militarily weak, and he knew that Poland would never agree to Russian soldiers on its soil, even if Poland was invaded by Germany. Stalin's motives were unclear. Did he, in fact, intend to annex Poland himself? Or at least extract generous concessions?

Hitler isolated Poland with a Nazi-Soviet Pact

Figure 83. 'Ethnic cleansing': Jews being forced out of Warsaw.

With the fate of Poland in mind, Hitler ordered Ribbentrop (the Nazi Foreign Minister) to conclude an alliance with Russia. Molotov, the foreign minister of the USSR, signed a mutual, non-aggression pact, but secretly both powers agreed to carve up Poland. Hitler, Goering and Ribbentrop all tried to reason with Chamberlain that Poland's cause was unjust, and Germany had a fair claim to those areas lost under the terms of Versailles. Did Hitler anticipate that Britain and France would give way for the sake of peace? Hitler ordered his troops to invade on 1 September 1939, but he was furious when, two days later, Britain and France declared war.

Figure 84. David Low's cartoon of the Nazi-Soviet Pact of August 1939.

Historical controversy on the causes of the war

Was the war intended by Hitler?

Andreas Hillgruber (1965) believed Hitler was pursuing goals that he had set out in *Mein Kampf*, but Hans Mommsen sees Hitler as an opportunist, 'a man of improvisation and experiment', who was persuaded by different groups, such as the army, the party, and foreign ministry staff, to take various decisions. However, most of these groups seemed to be trying to delay or divert Hitler, rather than urging him on to war.

The war was 'accidental'?

A. J. P. Taylor (1964) believed that the war was, like many others, the product of 'accidental' factors. Errors, misunderstandings, and unintended results, led to the outbreak of war. Recently, Jeremy Black has shown that wars between so-called 'civilised states' frequently result from an intention to fight – a calculation by the leadership that war is an extension of politics by other means (to borrow the expression of the war analyst, von Clausewitz). Evidence of what Black calls 'a propensity to bellicosity' echoes Fritz Fischer's study of Germany's ambitions before the First World War. Fischer argued (1961) that Germany sought a long-term goal in the domination of Europe which had a continuity stretching back to the unification of 1871 and found its fruition in the Third Reich.

War was the result of many factors, but Germany was the aggressor
In 1986 P. M. H. Bell explored the recent historiography and argued that the origins of the Second World War can be found in ideological, economic and strategic factors across Europe. Many of the issues that caused the Second World War lay in the consequences of the First World War, a period Bell called the 'Thirty Years War'. This analysis omits the conflict in East Asia, which began in 1937, and fails to acknowledge that the USSR and the USA were not involved in a general European conflict until 1941. However, in the final analysis, the war was the result of the aggression of Germany, and to a lesser extent, Italy, and the attempt by other Europeans to resolve that aggression and then oppose it. But one enigma remains – why did Germany embark on a policy of expansion with such determination and ferocity?

The war in the West, 1940

In the West, the war progressed through three phases:

a.   The fall of Scandinavia.
b.   The fall of France.
c.   The Battle of Britain.

The fall of Scandinavia

Hitler planned to attack the West in the winter of 1939
Hitler had wanted to launch an immediate offensive in the West, when Poland
collapsed after 36 days of desperate fighting. The generals disagreed, but Hitler
was only prevented from launching a winter campaign by the intervention of the
weather. Britain's navy established a blockade of German ports but without much
effect. Sweden was content to sell its iron ore to Germany in order to avoid the
same fate as Poland. Following successful naval operations by the Royal Navy, the
British government decided to send an expeditionary force to make an
amphibious landing at Narvik in northern Norway.

German forces were directed to Scandinavia to thwart Britain
However, German forces were landed at southern Norwegian ports and many
airfields were captured intact. The British tried to redirect their land forces
further south, but they were ill-equipped and lacked sufficient air cover. Oslo
surrendered and, once again, fear of suffering the same fate as Warsaw was the
main consideration. Vidkun Quisling was appointed puppet governor by Hitler.
Denmark, unable to offer any effective resistance, also surrendered.

The fall of France

The senior French officers were not confident of victory

Before the war, Hitler had invited senior French
officers to view the *Wehrmacht* on military
exercises. This experience left them feeling
intimidated by the German army, and their
sense of despair was made worse by the fact that
many of them had fought in the First World War,
and had witnessed appalling casualties, and the
mutinies of the French army in 1917. Their
expectation was that the next war would be a
repeat of the Great War.

Figure 85. Hitler fulfils his goal
of seizing Paris, 1940.

Blitzkrieg *tactics were used against the French and British*
On 10 May 1940 Hitler launched Case Yellow, the attack on France, Belgium and
Holland. The Low Countries had expected to be spared because they had insisted
that they were neutral, but this was no protection. The German army pierced the
Anglo-French line just where it was weakest, in the Ardennes hills and forests.
French strategists had believed that the formidable Maginot Line fortifications
would be sufficiently protected on its relatively lightly protected north flank by
strong mobile reserves. Seven German armoured divisions (each with about
15,000 men), supported by the *Luftwaffe*, drove deep inside French territory,
spreading confusion and denying the Allies the chance to deploy or regroup.

The bulk of the British forces escaped at Dunkirk
A portion of the French army and the British Expeditionary Force (BEF) found
itself fighting a rearguard action towards the Channel coast. Reynaud, the French
Prime Minister since March, formed a national government, but Churchill (now
the British Prime Minister) was appalled by the mood of defeatism which
prevailed in the French administration. On 25 May, the BEF began to withdraw to
the coast for the purpose of evacuation. The Belgians pursued an armistice and
surrendered on 28 May. The Royal Navy had expected to rescue only 45,000 from
France, but the anticipated German armoured thrust against the Dunkirk
beachhead never came. German vehicles and crews needed time to rest and refit.
In total 200,000 British and 130,000 French troops escaped.

The collapse of French resistance followed
The German *Blitzkrieg* swung south, and on 22 June, Reynaud's replacement,
Marshal Petain, signed an armistice. Hitler ensured that the surrender of France
took place in the same railway carriage in which Germany had signed its
capitulation in 1918, and a few weeks later, a victory parade was staged in Paris. A
puppet regime, Vichy, was established in southern and central France, whilst the
north was occupied by German troops.

The Battle of Britain

The air war against Britain was designed to precede a landing
Hitler was astonished that Britain did not seek an immediate accord with him.
Consequently on 16 July, he issued orders for Operation Sea Lion; the invasion of
Britain. As a first step, Goering's *Luftwaffe* were to destroy the RAF, then the
Royal Navy, before launching an amphibious operation on the south coast. The

Battle of Britain began on 10 July with attacks on convoys in the Channel, but on 13 August their attentions were turned to English airfields. Losses in pilots were more difficult to replace than planes on both sides. However, on 23 August, German bombers inadvertently hit the East End of London. When British bombers retaliated with an attack on Berlin, Hitler ordered the wholesale destruction of London, and other cities.

Hitler cancelled the operation against Britain
However, it became clear that the bombing of civilians could not guarantee that morale would collapse, or that the British would sue for peace. Hitler could not secure victory in the air alone without a presence on the ground. Following a day of heavy losses on 15 September at the hands of the RAF, Hitler postponed Sea Lion on 17 September 1940, and again on 12 October, and finally abandoned it in January 1941. Hitler had calculated that, in time, U-boats and mines would starve Britain into submission and therefore she was no longer a threat. It is interesting to note that Admiral Raeder, the Naval Commander in Chief, did not think the German Navy was yet ready to defeat the British in this way.

The war in the East, 1941–42

a.   The invasion of Eastern Europe: preparation for Barbarossa.
b.   The invasion of Russia.

Hitler calculated on the weaknesses in the East
Hitler first mentioned the possibility of fighting Russia on 22 July 1940, whilst considering why Britain still refused to surrender. He was aware that Russia was a potential ally of the British against Germany. Hitler also became aware of the deteriorating relations with the Soviets because of his insistence on pressuring Rumania to accept territorial changes in the Balkans. Despite the weaknesses of the Italians in Abyssinia and North Africa, where they had been defeated by British forces, Hitler was reluctant to interfere in Mussolini's 'sphere of influence'.

Hitler prepared to attack Russia for Lebensraum
Despite Hitler's non-interference with the Russian attack on Finland and the Baltic States, his ideological aims began to resurface. He made preparations for an attack on Russia, but kept up the diplomatic pretence. J. Noakes and G. Pridham suggest that Hitler was undecided, and he may have been prepared to reach another agreement with Russia in order to secure Britain's capitulation

(since he felt that Britain would not continue without the hope of Russian support). In this way he could avoid a war on two fronts.

The invasion of Eastern Europe: preparation for Barbarossa

The fall of the Balkans was necessary because of Italy's defeats
Before Hitler could fulfil Germany's 'historic destiny' of seizing Russian territory, he was compelled to support the Italians against the Greeks following their disastrous attack on 28 October 1940. This necessity shows how far the Axis powers were working independently of each other. Hitler wanted the Balkans quiet for his invasion of Russia, but Mussolini still wanted a Mediterranean empire to rival Hitler's in the north. Italy's failure to capture Greece, and a coup d'état against the pro-Nazi government in Yugoslavia opened up the possibility of British intervention against the forthcoming operations in the Balkans and in the Russian campaign. Consequently Hitler was forced to make an attack against Greece and Yugoslavia on 9 April 1941 which delayed him by four weeks. Once again *Blitzkrieg* tactics proved very successful.

The invasion of Russia

Progression of the Russian invasion was in three stages:

(i)   Barbarossa
(ii) Sieges of Leningrad, Moscow, and Stalingrad
(iii) The Russian counter-attack from the Caucasus.

Operation Barbarossa
▶ *The invasion of Russia was on a vast scale.*
   The scale of the German attack on Russia was enormous; 153 divisions (3,050,000 men); 3,350 tanks and 7,146 guns in the artillery. But it was clear that the German forces were stretched. It actually had fewer aircraft than in the campaigns of 1940 and only 300,000 men in reserve. Two tank divisions were fighting the British in the North African desert, and occupation forces were required across Europe. Historian Martin Van Creveld has calculated that the *Wehrmacht* was seriously deficient in motor transport and faced severe supply problems.

▶ *The Germans were initially successful.*
   Nevertheless, Stalin was taken by surprise. The Russian air force was wiped out

on the ground and in three weeks, German forces had advanced up to 600 km into Russia. In two pockets at Minsk and Smolensk, 600,000 Russians were cut off, but resistance was tougher than expected. There were 200,000 German casualties in under two months, and some divisions were reduced to 50% or even 80% of their original strength. Long lines of communication and the marshy terrain of the Pripet region also added to their difficulties. The sheer number of Russian troops was also a surprise to the Nazi leadership.

Sieges of Leningrad, Moscow, and Stalingrad

▶ *There was indecision about the second phase of the operation.*
The essence of *Blitzkrieg* was the realisation that an army could not be strong all along a front line, but would concentrate in one or two thrusts in order to penetrate deeply into the interior of an enemy's territory. At Hitler's headquarters, there was some disagreement about the next phase of Barbarossa. Hitler considered linking up with Finland to obtain its nickel more easily, vital for Germany's munitions industries. However, this would mean that Leningrad would have to be captured. In the south, Hitler was equally eager to seize the rich agricultural Ukraine, and the oil-fields of the Caucasus. Moscow was less of a priority, but General Halder believed an attack here would force the Russians to commit the bulk of their forces in one area where they could be destroyed more easily.

▶ *The Germans experienced supply and climatic problems.*
At Kiev, Hitler's decision to advance in the south seemed to pay off. The Soviet South-West Front (an army group) was defeated on 24 September 1941, and 665,000 Russians became prisoners. However, German casualties in the whole campaign were over 500,000, and some units were operating at only 30% of their original strength. Hitler was determined to secure as much as possible before the winter set in, and consequently ordered an advance in the south to resume on 2 October. However, severe weather slowed the advance. There was little winter clothing since Hitler had expected total victory by the end of the summer. Supply lines broke down, and there was a shortage of trains.

▶ *The attack on Moscow failed.*
Hitler grew impatient and returned to Halder's idea of an attack on Moscow, but although leading elements had reached the suburbs, they were exhausted, inadequately supplied and depleted. A Russian counter-attack was made by fresh troops on 5 December. They were mainly drawn from Siberia and consequently they were well equipped for winter warfare. As German units

were hurled back, Hitler issued orders that there should be no withdrawals, and, having secured the resignation of the Commander in Chief, Field Marshal Brauchitsch, Hitler took over supreme command of the army himself. However, the defeat outside Moscow had proved that *Blitzkrieg* had failed.

> ## COMMENT:
> *The Eastern Front, and the battles before Moscow, Leningrad and Stalingrad, marked the high tide of German expansionism: after these engagements in 1942–43, the Nazi war machine began to break down.*

▶ *Leningrad was besieged.*
In December 1941, the German armies had completely surrounded Leningrad, and, in the south, they had reached the Sea of Rostov, if not the Caucasus. The siege of Leningrad lasted from 31 August 1941 until 27 January 1944. Approximately 1,300,000 defenders died, and despite the virtual starvation of the besieged, the long expected assault never took place. However, by March 1942, the Soviet counter-attack was exhausted and the Nazis temporary 'stabilisation' plan had worked.

▶ *Hitler ordered the capture of the Caucasus.*
In May 1942, Hitler planned a new offensive and, avoiding the temptation of splitting up his forces, he concentrated on the southern flank. He felt that one small effort might capture Leningrad, but the resources of the Caucasus were a greater prize. In addition, the capture of the oil-fields would be an excellent point of departure for a combined attack on the British in Iran and Iraq alongside the *Afrika Korps* as it advanced through Egypt.

▶ *The fighting at Stalingrad drew in German reserves.*
The Caucasus campaign, delayed until June by Russian attacks, began with a breakthrough on the lower Volga River, but did not manage to trap and destroy the Russian forces there as planned. Stalingrad was expected to fall quite easily, but resistance in the suburbs demanded the transfer of German units originally destined for a thrust to the south-east. Between 21 August and 16 October, the Germans lost 40,000 men in bitter street fighting. Every building, every apartment and every room was contested. Stalin had ordered that the defence of the city was the most important phase of the Great Patriotic War. Hitler was equally determined that the city would fall. With only one oil-field in German hands, Hitler left the other fronts dangerously weakened, and threw units into Stalingrad's ruins.

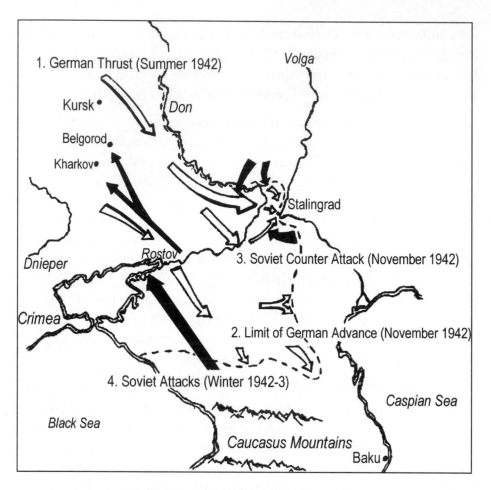

Figure 86. The turning point on the Eastern Front.

The Russian counter-attack from the Caucasus

▶ *The Russian counter-attack was successful.*

On 19 November 1942, the Russians counter-attacked to the north and south of Stalingrad and quickly surrounded the 6th Army of von Paulus. The *Luftwaffe* tried to fly in supplies for 200,000 German troops, but the Russians were able to deny any realistic attempts at relief. The German forces, 90,000 strong at the end, capitulated on 2 February 1943. Stalingrad is regarded as a turning point, and, according to Overy, was the most important engagement of the Second World War.

▶ *The Germans stabilised the line in the south.*

In early February, the Russians pressed on to Kursk, Kharkov and Belgorod, forcing the Germans to abandon the Caucasus altogether to avoid being cut off. However, on 19 February, the Germans brought up reserves, shortened their line and counter-attacked, recapturing Kharkov and Belgorod.

▶ *The Germans relied on new technology for success.*
After the spring rains, the German high command planned a new armoured pincer movement against a Russian salient (bulge in the line) around the city of Kursk. Delays were caused by Russian guerilla activities, shortages in transport and by the hope that new designs of heavy Tiger tanks would be available in larger numbers. The Germans had suffered at the hands of the Russian tanks (KVI and T34) which had thicker armour and heavier guns. The new German designs had steel skins some 80mm thick. The Russians were aware of the German build-up, and used the delays to strengthen their fortifications. Almost 3,000 German tanks were committed to a front of 320 km on 4 July 1943, but progress was limited.

▶ *The battle of Kursk.*
However, after a week, the southern German pincer was within striking distance of Kursk. On 11–12 July, the Russian armoured counter-attack met the German push head on at Pokhorova, and 900 tanks were involved on both sides. The battle lasted ten days and arguably was indecisive. However, the German offensive was halted, and from a strategic point of view, it showed that despite the Germans' best effort, they were unable to beat Russian forces. J. Noakes and G. Pridham believe that after Kursk, 'Hitler was forced to react to moves made by others'.

Other theatres of operations

a.   North Africa and the Middle East.
b.   Japan and the Far East.

North Africa and the Middle East

The war in North Africa was inconclusive
The Italian advance from their colony, Libya, into Egypt had been defeated in September 1940 and the British had pursued them as far as El Agheila by February 1941, taking 130,000 prisoners along the way. Hitler sent the DAK (*Deutsche Afrika Korps*) to prevent a complete collapse of the southern flank. By April 1941, the British had been pushed back to Tobruk and it seemed possible that Egypt might fall, and that Britain might lose control of the vital Suez Canal supply route.

The tide of the desert war was turned by the battle of El Alamein
Between November 1941 and January 1942, the British managed to push back the
Afrika Korps, who were suffering from extended lines of communication and
supply shortages because resources were diverted to Russia. But General Rommel
managed to repulse the British and drove them back inside Egypt (January to June
1942). Rommel's forces were engaged at El Alamein on 23 October 1942 by a new
British commander, General Montgomery, at precisely the moment that Hitler was
convinced that Egypt would finally fall. Montgomery's 230,000 men and 1,440
tanks defeated the 80,000 Germans and their 540 tanks. The DAK began to retreat
on 4 November. On 8 November, the Americans landed in Morocco and the British
in Algeria. The collaborative Vichy French initially resisted but then gave way. The
Germans dissolved the Vichy regime in France itself.

Japan and the Far East

Hitler's efforts were not co-ordinated with Japan. The Japanese escalation of their
war with China into an attack on the United States, merely prompted Hitler to
declare war on America himself. This was largely because he felt that America
was already so deeply involved in supporting Britain with supplies, that she was
really at war already. The Japanese offensive in south-east Asia pinned down
thousands of British troops, but it failed to divert American attention from the
European conflict as Hitler had anticipated. Hitler initially believed that Russia
would be defeated by the end of 1942, but Stalingrad was a severe set-back.

The German home front

This section examines:

a.   Public morale and Nazi government.
b.   The move towards a total war.

Public morale and Nazi government

Hitler was unchallenged as leader
Germans had serious misgivings about the outbreak of war, but the rapidity of the
fall of France surprised and delighted many. The Führer's leadership was largely
unchallenged, partly because of his inaccessibility. Hitler grew more remote and
made only three public speeches during the war, and his attention was drawn to
conducting the war, or planning grandiose architectural projects.

The power of the SS grew during the war

Goering set up a Reich Defence Council in August 1939 as a war cabinet, but it was unable to make decisions freely because of the rivalry of other factions such as the SS, or party chancellery. The SS continued to take over industries and administrative tasks, as well as responsibility for the occupied territories. The SS controlled 150 businesses by 1945 under the umbrella title *Deutsch Wirtschaftsbetriebe G.m.b.H*, and Himmler had set out to eventually replace the German capitalists altogether. The *Waffen SS*, its military wing, grew to 35 divisions. The SS extended their command of internal security to prisoners of war (who became slave labourers in many cases) and to military intelligence.

The Nazi party were the rivals of the SS

The party officials at *Gau* level became virtual dictators in their own right since they enjoyed unlimited powers to organise the defence of their provinces. The party also saw an opportunity to continue the social revolution denied to them in the 1930s. They inserted cells in the civil service, tried to get commissars into the party and they attacked the church and other 'establishment' institutions. Despite rivalry with the SS, the party members also played a part in the genocide. Under Borman's

Figure 87. Jewish children being 'evacuated' to concentration camps.

secretarial leadership, following Rudolf Hess's flight to Britain in 1941, a new radicalism was evident. Schoolteachers and judges were selected on the basis of their political reliability. In September 1944, Hitler created the *Volksturm*, a local defence militia of Hitler Youth or men too old to serve as regular soldiers. They were really a party militia, and gave party leaders the chance to brandish their own arm of coercion.

The German economy did not benefit from Lebensraum

The German public were spared the demands of total war in 1939. Attempts to cut wages met with an angry response and the government was forced to accept that it could only freeze wage levels. There were considerable reserves of food, but rationing was introduced in September 1939. Even so it was at a generous level until 1944. The conquests made little difference to the German economy, since any marginal benefits were absorbed by the army.

Towards a total war

Public morale in a total war was one of grim determination
Morale settled to what Goebbels called 'a light depression' after 1940, but the fall of Stalingrad and the American entry into the war did more damage. Goebbels called for a total war in early 1943 which proved surprisingly popular, but successive defeats and Allied bombing by day and night took their toll. The Allies' demand for unconditional surrender and the prospect of another drastic peace like Versailles served to convince the German public that they had to fight. There was an expectation that Hitler would somehow achieve a diplomatic compromise.

Albert Speer greatly assisted the German war effort
Fritz Todt, and then Albert Speer, reorganised German industry from March 1940 so successfully that production continued to increase until it suffered heavy bombing in 1944–45. Speer was successful because of his close relationship with Hitler, but he carefully distanced himself from the genocidal tendencies in the war crimes trials after the war. Speer did not have it all his own way though, and he was frequently blocked by the SS. Although Hitler reluctantly agreed to the conscription of women, which Speer had advocated, only 900,000 actually served in war industries. Where Speer redeemed himself was in his skill at preventing the execution of Hitler's order to destroy Germany and leave a desert in front of the Allies. He considered gassing Hitler in the bunker, but lacked the courage to betray his Führer.

Tutorial

Progress questions

1. What methods did Hitler use to avoid the interference of the League of Nations between 1934 and 1936?

2. Why did Hitler aim to seize the Sudetenland and crush Czechoslovakia by war?

3. Why was war perhaps 'inevitable' by 1938?

4. Why did Hitler decide to invade Russia?

Pressure to act

Economic problems

Advantage of German rearmament would be eroded when others caught up

League of Nations was weak

Pressure to delay

German army was small in 1933–37, rearmament would not be complete until 1940

Generals were pessimistic about the chances of military victory

League of Nations might intervene, Russia's reaction was unknown

Opportunities

Spanish Civil War, 1936–39: a chance to test weapons, aircraft and crews

Abyssinia Crisis, 1936: League of Nations distracted, Italy alienated from League, Rhineland remilitarised

Austrian and Sudeten Germans agitated, 1938: chance to annex territory and resources

Setbacks

Austria, 1934: Mussolini was prepared to oppose *Anschluss*

Austria, 1938: Schussnigg called a plebiscite which may have opposed the Nazi take-over

Czechoslovakia, 1938: Britain, Italy and France prevented a short war against the Czechs which was designed to force them and other Eastern Europeans to concede to Hitler's demands

Figure 88. Foreign policy: calculations.

5.   Why was Stalingrad so significant to Hitler's campaigns in the east?

Discussion points

1.   Can it be argued that Hitler launched a war to avert a domestic crisis? Richard Overy says no, which perhaps contradicts the Hossbach Memorandum of 1937. (You will remember that this is the document which hints that 1943–45 would be the 'waning point of the regime' if war had not broken out.) There certainly were tensions within Germany, especially as rearmament was artificially suppressing consumer spending power (in 1938,

consumers had less spending power than in 1929). Re-examine foreign policy
in the 1930s and try to resolve this difference of opinion.

2. Why was Germany so successful in its military operations until 1942? Is it
    possible to argue that Hitler had won the European war which had broken out
    in 1939?

3. What factors or events 'turned the tide' of the war against Germany?

Practical assignment

1. List all the causes of the war used by the historians. Prepare a series of
    questions you would need to test the theories the historians each put forward.

2. Make a sketch or copy a map. Measure a map distance of 600 km from the
    eastern border of Germany (of 1914) eastwards. Draw a line running north-
    south from this point. This area was Hitler's planned area of Germanisation
    under the concept of *Lebensraum*.

Study tips

1. Construct a timeline of the causes and events of the war, labelling each key
    event.

2. Make sure that you are able to see the weaknesses as well as the strengths of
    the Hossbach Memorandum as a document. It is not conclusive.

3. Consult a map. Familiarise yourself with each of the places mentioned in the
    text.

11

The Nazi Euthanasia Programme and the Holocaust

One-minute overview – *The euthanasia programme was an important aspect of the Third Reich, but has been overshadowed by the scale of the events in the genocide. In some respects, the T4 programme was the forerunner of the 'final solution', and the Nazis learnt a valuable lesson about the power of public opinion. The euthanasia programme attracted much hostility when news of it leaked to church leaders. Future programmes, including the Holocaust, were designed to avoid public knowledge. Death camps were generally set up in remote areas, and a stricter security was observed. The rationale behind the euthanasia programme give a further clue to Hitler's way of thinking. It may also explain why no written order has ever been found from Hitler to his subordinates. Given the comments by Himmler that the genocide was an episode that would never be recorded in history, it seems very likely that Hitler gave only verbal instructions. Even if he gave no order, leading Nazis understood Hitler's attitude towards the Jews and were eager to fulfil their 'historic mission'. The most compelling evidence has emerged from the infamous Wannsee Conference, where detailed planning to initiate the death camp 'production line' took place.*

In this chapter you will learn:
- ▶ *About the rationale behind the programme.*
- ▶ *About the implementation and reaction to the euthanasia programme.*
- ▶ *How the Holocaust was planned and executed.*

The euthanasia policy

This section will be divided into four parts:

a.   The burden of diseases.
b.   The future of Germany.
c.   The programme T4.
d.   Mental illness.

Figure 89. The image of
Hitler as war leader.

The burden of diseases

The problem of diseases
In an era before the discovery of 'genetics', genes and DNA were interpreted as 'blood'. Therefore, changes in each generation, in eyes, hair colour, and facial structure for example, were transmitted through blood. That diseases could also be passed on in this way was not difficult to understand. In our own time, AIDS, Hepatitis (A, B and C), sickle cell, and a range of other diseases are spread by contamination of the blood. The Nazis were both idealistic and fearful about the future. On the one hand they hoped to gain a better understanding of how to control changes in human beings through the application of science. They aimed to apply a Darwinist approach, the selection of the fittest and best, and grow hybrids of the human species who would be better than before. This had, after all, been done to plants and animals even before the agricultural revolution of the eighteenth century.

Why did the Nazis aim to kill 'undesirables'?
One might ask, why, if there was faith in the concept of natural selection, did they need to interfere in evolution to alter humans? The answer lay in their fear of the future because of the situation in Germany as they found it. The Nazis were concerned that the ethnic, normal German population were going to swamped by a faster growing population of 'undesirables'. These included the mentally ill, impoverished Slavs, the 'unhealthy', the physically weak, the morally corrupt, and the Jews.

The future of Germany

Fear of population growth in the future
The calculations the Nazis predicted were that the birth rate of 'normal' Germans was slowing down, but the overall population was growing. They predicted that there would be millions more handicapped and mentally ill people being born every generation, adding to an impossible social burden. Hitler was deeply troubled by the population statistics and they occur time and again throughout *Mein Kampf*. Hitler's fear was Malthusian; as the population grew, it would eventually outstrip the capacity of its food production. The solution Hitler proposed in *Mein Kampf* was the creation of more 'living space', or put another way, the seizure of more agricultural land, sufficient to feed the growing population.

The results of the programme were horrific
There are no references to the execution of the mentally ill at this stage, but we cannot assume that he did not consider the idea. Instead, it was enforced sterilisation that was proposed. This was carried out under the law of 14 July 1933 with the acceptance of doctors and nurses. Between 320,000 and 350,000 were sterilised. But the criteria, mental or hereditary illness, were widened to include chronic alcoholism and 'moral feeble-mindedness'. We should not forget that sterilisation programmes to control the population were used in India and China in the 1960s and 1970s. These were motivated by perceived economic pressures.

Figure 90. Adolf Hitler is the victory: wartime poster.

The T4 programme to kill the disabled

The programme for euthanasia was designed to be secret. There is some speculation about when Hitler decided on this policy. In a party rally in 1929, he referred to the idea that if 700,000 weak children died every year, the result would be to strengthen the German people. In 1935 he remarked that euthanasia would be taken up if war broke out, and in 1938, following a request from a parent for the mercy killing of a deformed child, Hitler ordered the programme to begin under Philip Bouhler, Head of the Chancellery. The secret programme, entitled T4 after the Tiergartenstrasse address in Berlin of its headquarters, resulted in the deaths by gassing of 70,273 mentally ill children and adults.

Hitler 'halted' the programme when its objectives were achieved
According to J. Noakes and G. Pridham, lethal injections and deliberate starvation released 93,251 beds in total. The codeword for a secret killing was 'disinfection', and although demonstrations of hostility drove Hitler to halt the programme on 24 August 1941, the 'disinfections' had already achieved their objective of freeing hospital beds for military use. In fact, it appears that the 'halt order' was little more than a change of direction, since the personnel, equipment

and techniques were transferred to the systematic execution of Jews in a programme called '14 f13'.

Mental illness

This section will examine:

(i)   The threat.
(ii) The coercive tool.
(iii) Recycling.
(iv) Rehearsal for the 'Final Solution'?

The threat
Mental illness was seen by the Nazis in several different ways. First, it was a threat. It was, as already outlined, a generation that was 'deformed' and therefore there was an emphasis on sterilising, or killing, children. Mental instability represented a loss of control, and self-control or discipline were Nazi values. Mental illness was also seen as unwholesome and self destructive (as in the case of child molesters, murderers, or pornographers). The Nazis also felt that those who actively worked against their country were 'ill', because they were in effect denying their own identity. Abstract artists were ridiculed and an exhibition opened on 'degenerate art' to show people what to avoid. Jewish scientists and academics would have been bracketed with able bodied and convicted paedophiles or psychotic killers. A painter of modern art would have been seen as no different in talent from a mentally ill patient. The aim was to contain this threat by the prevention of reproduction. The nightmare for the Nazis was the idea that in future generations, there would be millions of mentally ill patients who would all be dependent on the state, which in turn would represent an impossible financial burden for the able-bodied population.

▶ *Mental illness was a coercive tool.*
The second Nazi view of mental illness was as a device for coercion. Enemies could easily be condemned as degenerates. The accusation that a person was a homosexual, or even 'work-shy' (that is to say 'bone idle'), was enough to secure them a place in a concentration camp for a period of re-education. If one applies this device to the wider population, then it becomes a self-regulating society, not unlike George Orwell's novel *1984* (where Big Brother, the authority, didn't even have to exist, because people believed he existed, and regulated themselves through fear). It was easy enough to denounce an old

enemy, and settle a few scores. Enthusiastic and ambitious citizens, keen to impress their superiors, could become willing instruments of the regime even if they thought of themselves as simply 'getting on'.

▶ *Hospital resources and people were for 'recycling'.*
The third view was not unlike recycling. The removal of mentally ill people released money back into the economy where it might benefit the healthy. In Bishop Galen's sermon, he warned that the elderly might be killed off to avoid the burden of old people since they were no longer 'productive'. The death penalty, he argued, would be imposed equally against the sick, the old, and against loyal soldiers who had been crippled in war. The Nazis never proposed the death of the elderly per se, only if they were mentally ill. Nor did they consider the killing of injured soldiers, but they carried out their tasks against the mentally ill in a way that seemed symptomatic of a country fearful of the economic hardships of the Depression. But surely that could never merit a moral argument in its favour.

▶ *Was euthanasia a rehearsal for the 'Final Solution'?*
The euthanasia programme could be seen as something of a dry run for the extermination of the Jews. But there is no evidence that it was a dress rehearsal. If anything, the Nazis learnt some important lessons in 1941, some time before they had considered, and then decided on, the 'Final Solution'. They learnt that

Figure 91. Hartheim Euthanasia Centre.

security was paramount, and it was no surprise that the Nazis tried to conceal what was happening to the Jews. Deportation and relocation in the east were two common themes, and death camps were always well concealed from the German population in remote areas in Germany or beyond her borders in Poland. Euthanasia was carried out against Jewish prisoners who were sick or incapable of work. Three centres, Hartheim, Sonnenstein, and Bernburg, killed at least 9,500 in this way in 1941, but accurate figures are unavailable to the historian. By 1942, the figures had run into the tens of thousands.

COMMENT:
There can be no doubt that the war radicalised anti-Semitism in the Third Reich.
The attitude was that, with so many Aryans being killed on the battlefields of
Europe, the Jews should pay in equal measure in blood. Death was more acceptable
once the threshold of inter-state violence had been crossed.

How the Holocaust was planned and executed

The origins of genocide date back to 1939

The origins of the genocide against Jews and other ethnic groups can be traced to at least January 1939, if not before. Hitler had warned that another war would be the fault of the Jews and as a result they would be annihilated. Whilst this may have been pure rhetoric, the war made extreme solutions more acceptable.

The Nazis formed ghettoes
When Poland and other eastern European territories were annexed, the Nazis

Figure 92. Papers check: Kracow.

found that they had inherited more Jews. Expelling the Jews from Germany, the commanders of the occupied territories complained that they could not cope with the vast influx of Jewish civilians. In response, Heydrich ordered that Jews be concentrated into small ghettoes in urban areas. The first was established at Lodz.

Jews became slave labourers
At the same time, it was decided to make use of the Jews as a slave labour force (12 December 1939). To make recognition easier, a decree ordered that Jews wear a star of David armband. Around 500,000 Jews died as forced labourers, or from starvation and disease in the ghettoes.

Jews were executed as Bolsheviks
After the invasion of Russia had begun, Hitler had given instructions (31 March

1941) that communist secret police or political agents attached to the Red Army were dangerous and should be executed, and his orders were carried out by squads of special commandoes. These squads had a different role from the Secret Field Police or intelligence corps. Jews who were in the service of the Russian state were also to be killed. In Hitler's mind, Jews were the architects of Bolshevism so it is not surprising that he believed 'Jews' and 'Bolsheviks' were the same.

Figure 93. *Einsatzgruppe* execution squad in Russia, 1941.

Hitler gave special orders to execute Jews
The escalation of actions against Jews and commissars may have been prompted by partisan activity behind the German front lines. Ian Kershaw, who has discovered documents in the Soviet military archives, believes that Jews were 'executed as partisans' in a special verbal order from Hitler which was acknowledged in written form by Himmler. Kershaw believes Hitler had learnt how to avoid responsibility after his experience of the euthanasia protests. In response to a protest about the execution of Jews by Lohse, the Reich Commissioner for the Baltic States, the Reich Ministry of the Eastern Territories spokesman, Dr Otto Brautigam replied on 18 December 1941 that 'the Jewish question had been clarified by now through verbal discussions'.

Figure 94. Nazi executioners in Eastern Europe, 1941.

Figure 95. Officers of *Einsatzgruppe* administering the 'coup de grace'.

Jews were shot in massive numbers
Jews were in fact being herded into pits and shot in large numbers. David Ehof, an

organiser of mass shooting in the SD (*Sicherheitsdienst*), had 7,000 people killed on the first day (7 November 1941) at Borissov in occupied Russia.

The Wannsee Conference concluded planning for the 'final solution'
The *Einsatzgruppen* (execution squads) actions were only the beginning, and new methods were sought to speed up the executions. Over the winter of 1941–42, experiments were made with mobile gassing vans, and, finally with gas chambers. Since the introduction of the euthanasia programme, a small cadre of trained and experienced personnel existed. However, although systematic execution was proposed, there was still some debate about the use of Jews as forced labour. Therefore it was decided to divide Jews into productive and non-productive types. On 20 January 1942, at the Wannsee Conference, final decisions were made for the construction of camps, railway lines, barracks and extermination facilities. The conference conclusions further refined the definition of Jews and half-Jews, urged that the secrecy of the programme was to be maintained, and established the procedures for the 'Final Solution'.

Chelmo was a typical death camp
At Chelmo, between 16 January and the end May 1942, 55,000 Jews from the Lodz ghetto were gassed as well as 5,000 gypsies. The camp was closed down, but after a second phase of executions which was designed to kill all remaining Jews from the Lodz area, a total of 145,301 Jews, gypsies, Poles and Russians perished by 1943, and a further 7,176 were killed in 1944.

Belzec and Treblinka revealed cynical planning
At Belzec, 500,000 people were gassed until actions ceased in December 1942. Ninety per cent were Polish, but others came from all over Europe. Only one inmate survived the war. Sobibor camp was the scene of the executions of 150,000–200,000 Jews until a camp uprising in October 1943 convinced the Nazis to relocate the survivors. Thirty inmates survived the war. Treblinka was an example of cynical planning. It was built in the summer of 1942 and designed to resemble a railway halt in every detail. Prisoners were told this was a hygiene stop before transit to a labour camp. They left their luggage and belongings in the care of guards, undressed for the 'showers', and were gassed. Their bodies were dumped in pits. From the spring of 1943, however, the bodies were dug up and burnt to avoid any evidence. The camp was closed on 17 November 1943. Jewish workers were ordered to dismantle the camp, and then were shot. Some 900,000 people died at Treblinka.

Auschwitz-Birkenau was the largest death camp

Auschwitz was one of the largest camps ever built. The complex of barracks, camp and a farm covered 18 square miles. Part of the population of inmates was used as forced labour in the neighbouring factories run by I. G. Farben. When gassing began, the crematoria proved inadequate to burn the bodies, so a second camp was established at Birkenau. One of the two gassing

Figure 96. Entrance of Auschwitz-Birkenau.

bunkers could accommodate 1,200 people at a time. When new drafts of prisoners arrived, only 30% were extracted as fit to work. The rest were executed straight away. At the maximum level of capacity, the chambers in the crematoria killed 9,000 in 24 hours. Meanwhile in the nearby Manowitz camp 25,000 out of the 35,000 inmates were worked to death or killed and replaced.

Medical experiments were carried out by Dr Josef Mengele on prisoners too, and included sterilisation or the removal of organs from those specially executed. It is estimated that 350,000 German and Polish Jews, and 765,000 from other countries, died at Auschwitz. The Russians rescued 7,000 survivors (27 January 1945), the remaining 60,000 were

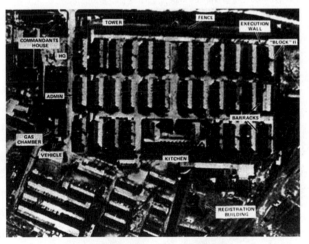

Figure 97. Aerial view of Auschwitz.

marched westwards by their guards. There were, of course, other camps, and across Europe the numbers executed have been estimated by J. Noakes and G. Pridham to be 4,194,200 or 68% of all Europe's Jewish population. The method by which these people died defies most human reasoning even today.

Figure 98. Dr Mengele, also known as 'the angel of death'

August 1939	Euthanasia programme
February 1940	Deportation of Jews from the Reich; ghettoes established
March 1941	Jews used as forced labour
July 1941	Goering ordered Heydrich to prepare for the 'Final Solution'
September 1941	First transfer to concentration camps; gassing experiments; Jews forced to wear Star of David insignia
October 1941	Himmler banned Jewish emigration
November 1941	First extermination camp operational
January 1942	Wannsee Conference – details of the 'Final Solution' worked out
March 1942	Ghettoes of southern Poland cleared; inmates are sent to extermination camps
1942–43	Death camps operated at maximum capacity, but riots by inmates caused suspension of operations at Treblinka and Auschwitz

Figure 99. The descent to the Holocaust.

Tutorial

Progress questions

1. Why did the Nazis fear a growing population of 'undesirables'?

2. How 'successful' was the T4 programme?

3. What were the Nazi views of the mentally ill?

4. Why is the Wannsee Conference so significant?

Discussion points

Figure 100. Russian Jews
hanged by the Nazis in 1942.

Today the euthanasia debate centres around mercy killing and the 'right to choose' death if old age brings unbearable pain and illness. There has been some debate about the merit of sustaining life for those in a PVS (permanently vegetative state), and the moment at which one turns off a life support machine for someone who will not recover.

1. How do the arguments contrast with the justifications offered by Nazi Germany?

2. What arguments do geneticists use to justify their actions? How do these compare?

3. How should historians approach these moral debates?

4. What do the regulations for concentration camps tell us about the regime and the practice of terror?

5. What comments can be made about Daniel Goldhagen's thesis that all Germans were 'willing executioners' of the Jews in the Nazi regime against the background of the war?

6. How can we use the examples of euthanasia and genocide to account for the rise of SS power between 1939 to 1945?

Practical assignment

Consider the following statement and compose an essay plan: 'The Nazi policy of euthanasia is an instructive example of Nazi ideology in general and laid the foundations for the Holocaust'. Do you agree?

Study tips

1. Euthanasia may have been a route the Nazis took towards the 'Final Solution', and therefore there was not simply an escalation of the legislation of the 1930s. Use this as an alternative approach in an essay.

2. Compare what you have learned about the euthanasia policy here with Bishop Galen's reaction outlined in opposition by the church in Chapter 9.

12

The Defeat of the Third Reich

One-minute overview – Why was Germany defeated? Germany lacked the resources or industrial capacity (especially in petrochemicals) to wage a long-term total war. Germany was subjected to relentless bombing and was fighting on three fronts by 1944. Russian, American and British forces outnumbered and out-gunned the Germans. The Luftwaffe lost air superiority, the Kriegsmarine lost its freedom of action at sea, and the German armies suffered a series of defeats. The German armed forces were forced to conduct a fighting retreat at every point from 1944. As the Allies reached the heartland of the Third Reich, they discovered the incomplete work of the regime's genocide policy. As the regime faced defeat, fanatical fighters made a last-ditch stand and Hitler committed suicide in his bunker in Berlin.

In this chapter you will learn:
▶ *The war in the West.*
▶ *The war in the East.*
▶ *The fall of Berlin.*

The war in the West

Italy

Figure 101. Italians surrender to the British army in North Africa, 1940.

The Allies opened a southern flank
In North Africa, Hitler tried to stem the Allied advance on Tunisia, but once men had been committed it proved impossible to evacuate them due to Allied air superiority. On 13 May 1943, Tunisia fell. It was too late in the year for the British and Americans to relocate their forces in Britain for an invasion of northern France, so it was decided to fight up through Italy instead. Sicily fell on 17 August, but already the Duce (Mussolini) had been replaced by General Badoglio amid strikes and civil unrest.

The Germans took over the defence of Italy
When the Allies landed in southern Italy on 3 September, the new government
signed an armistice (8 September 1943), but German troops disarmed Italian
units, and Hitler sent reinforcements to oppose the Allies who had landed further
up the Italian peninsula at Salerno. On 12 September, German paratroopers
rescued Mussolini, and he was installed as leader over the northern states as
Hitler's puppet, backed by German troops. The Germans' resistance was effective
and the Allies made slow progress northwards. However, their resources were
now fully stretched by the opening of this southern front.

Yugoslavia was a theatre of guerrilla resistance
Communist partisans, led by Josip Broz (Tito), overthrew the Italians in
Yugoslavia and proclaimed a revolution. Churchill decided to supply the 200,000
partisans and the Germans were forced to deploy eight divisions in fruitless anti-
guerilla warfare.

Bombing devastated German cities
Air Marshall Harris stepped up the bombing of Germany in order to destroy
German industry and lower the morale of the German people. Up to that date,
results of the bombing had been negligible, but whereas in 1942 48,000 tonnes of
bombs had been dropped, in 1943 this was increased to 207,000 tonnes by a
combination of day and night raids by the RAF and the USAAF.

The Germans lost the Battle of the Atlantic

The German U-boats threatened Allied supply routes
In 1940–41, the U-boats (submarines) and surface raiders sank 600,000 tonnes of
shipping. From bases in Norway, the German air force added to the casualty toll
of Allied ships on the arctic convoys that supplied Russia. The destruction would
certainly have been greater if the Allies had not adopted a convoy system, and the
German navy had been stronger in 1940 (Admiral Raeder did not expect the
Kriegsmarine to be at full strength until 1944.) However, German U-boats were
not easy to detect at first, and it was not until there were improvements in radar
that the tide began to turn. 'Wolf packs' of U-boats were able to overwhelm
destroyer escorts until 1941, when numbers of escort vessels were increased and
better detection equipped was developed. Thereafter, the number of U-boats that
were sunk increased dramatically.

The U-boats were less successful from 1941
Between April and December 1941, the U-boat fleet trebled in size, but the
number of Allied merchant vessels being sunk fell to its lowest number to that
date. American security was poor when it first entered the war, so U-boats
enjoyed great successes off the American coast, and subsequently against Brazil
as it too entered the war. Once again, the Allies extended the convoy system, then
established surface 'support groups' which hunted the U-boats without the
hindrance of escort duties.

The U-boats had been defeated by 1945
In early 1943, the Allies' commitment to amphibious operations in North Africa
left the Atlantic convoy escorts weakened and losses increased despite cracking
German encryptions to its U-boats. In March 1943, the Allies lost 73 ships out of
120. However, renewed efforts swung the balance and in May 1941, 41 U-boats
were sunk and only 50 merchant vessels were lost. Faced by these odds, on 22 May
the U-boats abandoned operations in the North Atlantic, except for a brief and
disastrous revival of convoy attacks in September-October 1943. In 1945 there
were still 150 U-boats operational, but the scientific advances in U-boat
technology came too late to effect a real difference. Hitler had anticipated that
U-boats would force Britain to surrender by 1941, but despite a series of crises, this
fate had been averted.

North-West Europe

Figure 102. Field Marshall Erwin
Rommel.

The Allies landed at Normandy
On 6 June 1944, the Allies launched the
largest amphibious operation in history
against the 'Atlantic Wall' defences. On the
first day, 156,000 men had fought a few miles
inland with the assistance of air superiority
and concentrated artillery support, much of
it coming from naval guns off shore. The
German Commander in Chief in the West,
von Runstedt, wanted a strong mobile reserve
to attack the landing forces once it was clear
where a landing would take place. Rommel,
who commanded northern France and the
Low Countries felt that Allied air power

would destroy von Runstedt's armoured formations, and he wanted to defeat the Allies as they tried to get ashore. Hitler tried to compromise but weakened both the 'Atlantic Wall' and the 'mobile reserve' ideas. Hitler delayed the attack of the 21 Panzer Division too long on 6 June, and its thrust was contained.

The liberation of France and Belgium soon followed
Hitler refused to consider local withdrawals and demanded that German forces hold their ground. As a result the Americans were able to turn the western flank of the German line, and as the Germans tried to escape, they were almost surrounded and suffered heavy losses in the Falaise Pocket. On 15 August, the Americans landed in southern France, and Parisians rose up against the Germans on the 16th. In August and September, the Allies continued to liberate France and Belgium, but when they were forced to re-supply and refit their units, the German units were able to slip away to positions further east.

Hitler ordered counter-attacks in the West
To seize a Rhine crossing, the British, Empire and Polish forces tried to secure the bridge at Arnhem, but they were checked. Hitler now began to put faith into special weapons he had developed: the V1 and V2 rockets. The first V1 had been fired at London on 13 June 1944, and soon numbers rose to 100 a day. Five hundred of the V2 rockets were fired, killing 2,754 people in seven months.

Figure 103. The Bridge at Arnhem.

The Germans collapsed on the Western front
Hitler's final offensive was launched on 16 December 1944 in the Ardennes during bad weather which neutralised Allied air power. Hitler's plan was to drive his armoured columns to the coast and having destroyed the Allies means of re-supply, he anticipated a negotiated peace. Having secured this, he hoped for an anti-communist crusade against the Russians, with the Allies on his side. By early 1945, the Allies defeated the Germans' armoured thrust, and they had secured the Rhine crossing. As they entered Germany, resistance began to subside.

The war in the East

The Germans failed to hold the river Dneiper

Figure 104. German troops fighting on the Eastern Front.

After Kursk in 1943, the Germans had hoped to withdraw to prepared defensive positions along the Dneiper river for the winter. However, the Russians advanced all along the southern half of the Soviet Union, and by October 1943, the Russians had crossed the Dneiper and established several bridgeheads. General Manstein tried to find reserves to stem the attack, but he was overwhelmed by the weight of numbers. Kiev was liberated on 6 November 1943 but further German counter-attacks checked another westwards advance.

The Germans were forced from the Ukraine
Hitler insisted that a narrow salient centred on Nikopol, north of the Crimea, should be held because of its mineral resources. In December 1943, Soviet forces attacked again and destroyed the salient, trapping half the defenders. In the spring, despite the weather and terrain, the Russians retook the Ukraine and the Crimea, and German units were forced to abandon their positions because of the sheer weight of the Soviet artillery. The most devastating effect was produced by artillery grouped in units of 200 guns.

The Soviets entered Poland

Figure 105. Warsaw Survivors.

In the summer of 1944, the Russians launched a new offensive in the central front of the USSR to coincide with the Allied landing in Normandy. Soviet air superiority, the weight of their firepower and an overwhelming numerical advantage in all arms assisted their advance. The

Figure 106. Recruiting poster for German Home Guard in 1945.

offensive was so successful that Russian troops reached Warsaw on 15 August. The Polish Home Army rose up against the Germans, but without Russian assistance, the Germans destroyed the Polish rising, and, on Hitler's orders, virtually razed Warsaw to the ground. Meanwhile Soviet troops captured the Baltic states. Riga was evacuated but the survivors of 20 German divisions were cut off in Courland and held out until the war ended. In the Balkans, the Russians invaded Rumania (which surrendered and changed sides) and Bulgaria. They linked up with Tito's guerillas in October. Hungary was also attacked and cleared by March 1945, and Czechoslovakia was entered in February and was secure by April 1945.

The Second World War was the most costly war in the history of mankind
The highest percentage of war dead was suffered by Poland – 17.2% of the pre-war population were killed (6.12 million). The Soviets lost a staggering 20.6 million dead or 10%, 7 million of whom were civilians. Germany lost 9.5% or 6.85 million.

The fall of Berlin

Berlin fell to the Red Army

The final advance on Berlin began on 12 January 1945 with another characteristically rapid Soviet advance which forced the Germans to abandon Warsaw (17 January) and cut off troops in East Prussia. The Russians secured bridgeheads on the river Oder and recommenced the advance on 16 April. By the 22nd of that month, Berlin was encircled. Within the defensive perimeter were 1 million troops of variable quality, a further 30,000 in the city itself along with 2 million civilians. The Russians had total command of the air, considerable artillery and 2.5 million soldiers. Seven Russian armies were used in the attack, but it took several days to fight through the streets.

Figure 107. *Reichsführer* SS Heinrich Himmler with an Aryan girl.

Hitler's suicide ended the war

Hitler took refuge in the bunker, but he had long since lost his ability to grasp the situation. As shelling began around the bunker, Hitler handed over command to Admiral Doenitz, then shot himself in the mouth on 29 April 1945. Eva Braun, his secret companion for many years, insisted on dying with him after a marriage ceremony. Goebbels and his family also died. Goering and Himmler had been tempted to takeover the leadership of the Reich, believing that Hitler was dead, but they were condemned by Hitler in the final hours of his life. In his final will and testament, Hitler blamed the German people for letting him down in the struggle against Jewry. Doenitz's attempts to set up an alternative regime were neutralised by the Allies' gunfire, and he surrendered.

Figure 108. Josef Goebbels Minister for Popular Enlightenment and Propaganda.

COMMENT:

Even in the last days, Hitler showed no remorse: he claimed he was 'lied to on all sides' and that all his subordinates 'betray me'. When news of the fall of Austria came in, his hands, his legs and his head started shaking uncontrollably – he kept repeating: 'Shoot them all! Shoot them all!'.

The eradication of Nazism

The German public were ordered to visit the death camps to see for themselves what the regime had done. There was universal shock and disgust. However, thousands of those who had supported the regime were arrested but released without trial. After the war, it was the leading Nazis who were tried for their crimes. Amongst them was Hermann Goering. He was convinced that he would be remembered with affection by the German public. He committed suicide shortly before being sentenced to hang. Rudolph Hess was imprisoned until he died in 1987. Martin Bormann was never found, nor was Heinrich Muller, the Head of the Gestapo, but Heinrich Himmler, the SS Chief, was captured disguised as a security services agent. He took cyanide to avoid a trial. Heydrich had already been killed by Czech partisans in 1942.

Figure 109. Martin Bormann, Hitler's Personal Assistant.

Many of the other Nazi personnel were tried
Albert Speer was imprisoned and then released

Figure 110. Reinhard Heydrich.

Figure 111. The ruins of Munich in 1945.

in 1966 after which he wrote two apologetic memoirs. Hjalmar Schacht was cleared of any crimes at Nuremberg. Robert Ley, the Head of the German Labour Front committed suicide in 1945 as did Philip Bouhler, the Head of the Euthanasia Programme. Hans Lammers, the Head of the Reich Chancellery was imprisoned and released in 1951. Brauchitsch, the Commander in Chief of the German Army, died of a heart attack in British custody in 1945. Otto Dietrich, the Nazi Press Chief, was imprisoned until 1949 and died the year after his release. Franz von Papen, who had served in Hitler's cabinet in 1933, was imprisoned until 1949. Hans Frank, head of the Nazi Association of Lawyers, and Wilhelm Frick, the Nazi Interior

Figure 112. Albert Speer: architect and Armaments Chief, 1944.

Minister, were both executed at Nuremberg in 1945, as was Joachim von Ribbentrop, the Nazi Foreign Minister. Admiral Doenitz was sentenced to ten years at the Nuremberg Tribunal.

The most notorious war criminals paid the penalty
Sepp Dietrich, the SS officer who had carried out the Night of the Long Knives and murders of Eastern Europeans and American prisoners of war, was imprisoned until 1959. Adolf Eichmann, the SS officer responsible for implementing the Final Solution, escaped to Argentina but he was kidnapped there by Israeli agents and executed in 1962. Josef Mengele was fortunate that the

government of Paraguay refused to allow him to be extradited despite his record of experiments on inmates of the death camps. Rudolf Hoess, the commandant of Auschwitz was captured by military police in 1946 and executed the following year in Poland. Julius Streicher, the 'Jew-Baiter' was hanged at Nuremberg in 1946.

Figure 113. 'Ordinary Germans?'
SS women camp guards captured at Belsen.

Tutorial

Progress questions

1. Why was Hitler's decision to compromise with his generals over the defence of North West Europe in 1944 so disastrous?

2. Why did the German army face defeat on every front in the Second World War?

Discussion point

Respond to the statement that: 'The Allies did too little to assist the Jews held in concentration camps between 1941 and 1945'.

Practical assignment

Answer the following question in an essay: Why did so many Germans apparently remain loyal to the Nazi regime from 1938 to 1945?

Study tips

1. Complete a timeline to the end of the war, labelling key events.

2. Finalise a list of personalities and short details on each one.

3. Create a list of reasons why the Nazis lost the war (using headings such as 'Hitler's Leadership', 'Economic capacity' or 'Military defeats').

4. Return to the notes you have made on each chapter. Use highlighting, or underlining, to help you remember each point.

5. Practise essay questions, and planning them under time pressure (five minutes). This will test your knowledge.

6. Write key details on flash cards which can be easily carried and consulted at frequent opportunities. Use colour and large headings to stimulate.

7. Construct wire diagrams to summarise each chapter.

Conclusion: The darkest chapter of human history?

Recent historiographical questions have not yet been resolved

In recent years, the historiography of Nazi Germany, and the genocide of 1941–45 in particular, has reached a stage of exponential growth. Of all the literature being poured out, it is interesting that so many studies dwell on the unique nature and extent of the Nazi period, and comparative work tends to draw examples exclusively from episodes of mass murder in the twentieth century. Often there is an acknowledgement of the patterns of cause and motive in the atrocities of Armenia in 1915, the Soviet Union in the 1930s, Cambodia in the 1970s, Rwanda in 1994 and Bosnia in 1995, and genocides have been categorised into those that are racially or ideologically motivated. Nevertheless, there has been mounting criticism of the 'Holocaust industry', and those who have profited from the memory of anti-Semitic genocide. There have also been some attempts to make relativist judgments about all genocides. How unique, then, were the mass murders perpetrated by the Nazis during the Second World War? How are historians to understand the motives of such barbaric crimes against humanity in their historical context?

What were the origins of mass murder?

Genocidal mass murders in European history can be traced back to the Crusades of the eleventh century, where Christian armies put to death numbers of Muslims and Jews as religious enemies, but there have been many examples of mass killings across world history. In war, an enemy force, essentialised as the 'other' and regarded as a threat, could be destroyed rather than merely defeated. Nevertheless, it would be wrong to blur all the boundaries between massacres and genocides. It is true that for the perpetrators of massacres a degree of 'conditioning' had taken place, often in a surprisingly short period of time, and that murder had been 'normalised' by the experience of war. However, twentieth century examples of genocide took place on a far greater scale and could occur without the xenophobic or religious antagonism that took place in the rarefied atmosphere of war. Indeed, the twentieth century examples seem to be far more abstract and ideological than earlier epochs.

Is there a difference between large-scale deaths and genocide?

In constructing some understanding of genocide, it is essential to be clear of the distinctions with other episodes of death on a large scale. Whilst famines may in some cases be the result of human mismanagement, it is harder to find examples of genocidal *intent* in them. In Irish history there are some who claim that those who died in famines in the 1840s during British rule were the victims of genocide, but, if this were the case, then a similar charge would have to be made against governments of the developing world since 1945. In fact, the famines, whilst mismanaged, owe more to the consequences of population growth, climatic extremes, and poor infrastructure. This is the situation that prevailed in Ireland and southern England in the 'hungry forties' of the nineteenth century. A more convincing case for a deliberate policy might be found in the colonisation of the western regions of the United States in the nineteenth century. The herding of nomadic populations into limited reservations, the mass culling of buffalo herds, and the waging of long and destructive military campaigns seem more characteristic of genocide. However, by far the biggest killer in the colonisation of the United States was disease, as Eurasian pathogens were transmitted into the new continent by settler populations. These diseases were not deliberately inflicted on the native peoples: they were a by-product of colonisation, not the policy of the colonisers. But no one would assert that the deaths of Eastern Europeans between 1941 and 1945 were somehow the accidental result of colonisation.

Genocides are characterised by more than random or individual acts of murder, or even of small-scale massacres

The extent of the killing, the body count to put it crudely, is an essential defining component. Yet it is also the consequence of a particular collective will to destroy *completely* another group in society. Genocides are often perpetrated by large bodies of people, rather than just by specialist units. The feelings of the mass of the population are thus a key determining factor, and would certainly be important in any analysis of why, amongst populations that have peacefully co-existed for years, there should be the appearance of sudden deadly fractures in society. Social and political conditioning is an important aspect of the process, and changes in the collective beliefs in a population may be the result of war, new threats (which

overshadow a large section of the
people), or the sanction of government
or some high authority. These factors
can be traced right down to the
individual level, where genocidal
feelings are given justification through
an abrogation of normal
responsibilities. The victims are
regarded as inferior types of humans,
or completely dehumanised, and are
associated with a threat that can only
be neutralised though a purge. Ethnic-
cleansing and deportation are not
enough, even though that may be a
stage in the process: the victims have to
be destroyed. Popular pogroms against
Jews in Russia in the 1880s degenerated
into violence and had tacit sanction
from the Tsarist state, and there were

Figure 114. Genocide.

thousands of anti-Semites across Europe who shared such a distaste of Jews that
they were prepared to advocate violent solutions. Under a definition of genocidal
tendencies listed above, these examples in Europe seem to show that a Holocaust
was likely, perhaps even inevitable. Yet such a conclusion is the result of a false
teleological reading of history. The Nazi mass murders of Jews and Eastern
Europeans (and, in some cases, of Western Europeans too) does still defy a direct
comparison with other episodes of mass murder.

Where did the Nazi process of genocide begin?

The origins of the Nazi genocide against Jews and other ethnic groups can be
traced with certainty to January 1939. Hitler had warned that another war would
be the fault of the Jews and they would be annihilated. Whilst this may have been
only for dramatic effect, the war made extreme solutions more acceptable. There
was initially some inconsistency in the way the Nazis treated the Eastern
Europeans. In the General Government Province, Polish men and women were
simply redefined as Germans, whereas other occupied territories continued to
punish, imprison and enslave all non-Germans. Crucially this indicates that

Figure 115. Concentration camp gates: 'Work liberates'.

government direction of this policy was paramount. The systematic regulation of persecution in the 1930s also lends much support to the idea that this was a calculated set of government measures and not the result of spontaneous and popular mass murder by the German people. Indeed, as the decision to make use of the Jews as a slave labour force (12 December 1939) and a decree that Jews wear a Star of David armband or badge to identify them to the authorities indicate, the leaders of the Nazi regime were setting the agenda.

The 'Final Solution' was indeed unique

The deployment of *Einsatzgruppen* into Russia and Eastern Europe in 1941 was also a policy directed by the Nazi regime. Jews and Soviet Commissars were shot in large numbers. The Wannsee Conference put the finishing touches to the concept of a 'Final Solution': decisions were made for the construction of camps,

Figure 116. Himmler and Heydrich: architects of genocide.

railway lines, barracks and extermination facilities to make mass murder more efficient. The sheer scale and systemisation of the killings lends strong support to the argument that this was a policy organised and directed from above, although it still has to be acknowledged that thousands of German personnel were involved to a greater or lesser degree. Backed by the potential of modern transport and communications infrastructure, and new weapons, the Nazi regime was able to apply the processes and systems of the industrial revolution to the business of mass murder. Although other governments have sanctioned the mass killing of their peoples on ideological grounds, namely Pol Pot in Cambodia, or Stalin in the Soviet Union, none of them reached the same level of systemisation as the Nazis. It is perhaps this, more than anything else (even when measured against the scale of it), which sets the Nazis apart from other examples of genocide. However, this fact is, in the end, of little value to scholars of mass murder: after all, our capacity for destroying vast numbers of human beings is now more efficient than at any previous epoch in world history.

Figure 117. Poison flaps at Dachau.

It is evident that the Second World War has not brought wars to an end, nor has it prevented genocides or the rise of new dictators. The United Nations, established as a consequence of the war, has proved less effective than many of its founders would have hoped. Should this be a cause for despair: are we simply unable to prevent another Hitler, another Total War, or another Holocaust? It is not the business of historians to guide the future, but in retrospect we can say that Hitler was defeated, fascism was defeated and Japanese militarism was defeated.

Figure 118. Shoes collected from victims of genocide at Auschwitz.

Despite the enormous cost, at an individual and at an international level, this outcome was just. The alternative, submission to the jackboot of tyranny, was, and surely still is, unthinkable. Consequently, in this victory, history was never better served than by the generation of the 1940s.

Figure 119. Survivors of Dachau, 1945.

Case Study of Nazism: 'Strength Through Joy'

Secondary source

The *NS Gemeinschaft Kraft durch Freude*, the National Socialist Organisation Strength through Joy, or KdF, was a section of the national German Labour Front (DAF) under the leadership of Dr Robert Ley. The KdF was designed to provide organised leisure activities for the German workforce so as to make them more loyal and productive, thus serving two purposes for the regime. Ley's organisation calculated that the working year consisted of 8,760 hours of which only 2,100 were spent actually working, 2,920 hours were spent sleeping, leaving 3,740 hours of free time. The aim of KdF was, as they themselves put it, to regiment this 'relaxation for the collection of strength for more work'. The KdF programme set about providing activities such as hiking trips, cruises, beach holidays, concerts, and cultural activities for German workers. These events were specifically directed towards the working class, and it was through the KdF that the NSDAP hoped to bring to the 'ordinary German' the pleasures once reserved only for the bourgeoisie. The calculation was that, if the working classes were happy because of novel, accessible and affordable activities, they could be lulled into being more flexible, productive and obedient at work.

Amongst the most popular aspects of the KdF programme were the international cruises on a fleet of KdF liners (one rather obviously titled the *Robert Ley*) and smaller pleasure boats. Trips were organised to the coasts of Norway, Spain, and Italy, as well as destinations on the Baltic, German and Danish coasts. KdF also organised a wide variety of other activities, including mountain and woodland retreats, day trips to famous cultural sites, extended tours, concerts, theatre and opera performances, art exhibitions (naturally of approved 'Germanic' artwork), and other ritualised cultural events, all of which were designed to create a healthier, better educated and more productive workforce, but one which also brought the masses into line with approved propaganda messages.

The KdF programme made much of the workers' 'right' to a paid holiday, a concept totally unique to the period in the world and one designed to prove to

Germans that they were better off without the confrontational trade unions which had dogged labour relations in the 1920s. Even temporary workers were granted concessions. The establishment of the NSBO (which replaced the unions) and the Trustees of Labour (a government arbitration service) was supposed to persuade the workers that the regime had their best interests at heart. The concept of a corporate state, where the government intervened to solve disputes between labour and capital, was not unique to Germany and had already been established in Fascist Italy. However, the reality was that the regime rarely, if ever, sided with the workforce. Employers were far more important to the Nazis because it was through them that pressing programmes such as rearmament and reconstruction after the Depression could be fulfilled. As long as the workers were quiescent, then the KdF had achieved its aim. Far from making the workforce happy, it was really no more than a cynical programme of social engineering.

The cynicism of KdF was exemplified in the apparent attempt to make the ownership of a car a reality for as many Germans as possible. Although the Volkswagen was designed, the elaborate saving schemes were actually a front for acquiring pre-war funds for rearmament. The Volkswagen was only used by the *Wehrmacht* during the war. Moreover, when the war began, the KdF liners were easily converted for use by the German *Kriegsmarine* as hospital ships or troopships. The largest KdF vessel, the *Wilhelm Gustloff*, was sunk in January 1945. The KdF also helped set up quarters for German troops, provided concerts and films for soldiers at the front, helped distribute food, drink and home comforts to servicemen at railway stations, ports and barracks in Germany and in occupied territory, not unlike Britain's own NAAFI (Navy, Army and Air Force Institute). All this was done in conjunction with other German social welfare organisations such as the *Deutsche Rote Kreuz*. These aspects of the KdF were genuinely popular with the troops, just as the cruises and holidays had initially been with the workers. However, certain aspects of the programme met with disapproval. In the campaign for the 'Beauty of Labour', the Nazis promised that there would be material improvements to the workplace, including plants in offices, rest areas in factories and sports facilities. These proposals were greeted with enthusiasm until the workers realised that they would have to pay for and build these facilities themselves after their working hours. As with so much of the Third Reich, all was not as it seemed.

Primary source

The extract below is from *'Das danken wir dem Führer!'* ('The thanks we owe the Führer!'). It expresses the ideas, plans and achievements of the German KdF in propagandist terms, but it gives historians a clear indication of what the Nazi KdF 'message' to German labour was supposed to be.

> The dignity of labour is evidenced by improvements in the appearance of the work place. Wherever one looks in Germany, ugly dark buildings are vanishing. The 'Beauty of Labour' movement in today's Germany is not empty talk or an impossible demand, but living reality. Large sums that formerly would have been wasted in strikes and lockouts have been used since 1933 to improve work places. 23,000 places have been transformed form soulless drudgery to pleasant places to work. 6,000 factory courtyards now offer space for real relaxation, which was not true in the past. 17,000 canteens and lounges, 13,000 shower and changing rooms have been transformed. The dirtier the work, the cleaner the workers. More than 800 community buildings and 1200 sport facilities, including over 200 swimming pools, have been established. The crew quarters in over 3500 ships have also been improved.
>
> The NS Society *Kraft durch Freude* brings cheer and pleasure to workplaces through concerts and art exhibitions. The art exhibitions alone introduced more than 2.5 million workers to the creations of true German art. Just five years ago, it was obvious that the great works of German culture belonged to a small group of the upper class. Besides the factory concerns and art exhibitions, the NS Society *Kraft durch Freude* uses theatrical performances, other concerts, singing and musical groups to introduce the creations of German art to every working German. 22 million citizens have attended theatrical performances, 5.6 million the KdF concerts, and 17 million have found relaxation in more than 40,000 cabaret and variety performances, gaining thereby new strength for their daily work.
>
> Of no less importance is the KdF's vacation programme. Earlier, German workers did not know what to do with their, at best, five days of annual holiday. They could not visit the beauties of the German landscape, much less travel abroad. The NS Society *Kraft durch Freude* gave German workers the possibility of holidaying at the beach or in the mountains, or to explore the homeland. Over 20 million have participated in KdF trips since 1934. That is

more than a quarter of Germany's population. 19 million citizens participated in 60,000 vacation trips at home. Hand to hand, they would stretch from Berlin to Tokyo. KdF trains have travelled 2,160,000 kilometres, or 54 times around the world. The nine large KdF cruise ships have covered a distance equal to twice the distance from the earth to the moon. They have carried German workers to Madeira, Italy and Norway, broadening their horizons and giving them unforgettable experiences. Three additional ships will be added the KdF's own fleet of four. A KdF resort is being built on the island of Rügen. It will not be the only one. A series of other vacation and spa resorts will be built. They will fulfil the Führer's wishes at the start of the NS Society *Kraft durch Freude*: to lead a cheerful, creative and strong people to success in the world.

Historical interpretation

After a decade of social surveys of the generation of the 1930s and 1940s in Germany, a number of German historians, including Lutz Niethammer, were prepared to draw some conclusions about life in Nazi Germany. The results seem surprising. Instead of references to persecution and terror, German workers spoke of how 'quiet' and 'normal' the 1930s had been. They had far more to say about the war years, especially shortages, bombing and the fear the war had caused. Nevertheless, oral history needs to be treated with some caution. It is surprising how often memories can be unwittingly selected and organised. There is a tendency to remember things that were 'good', and, of course, personal setbacks or loss. Moreover, the generation of the 1930s were really making comparisons between the relative 'quiet' of the years 1933 to 1939 with the chaos of the late 1920s and the trauma of the war years.

Nevertheless, there is no doubt that the respondents were impressed with the orderliness, levels of employment and absence of political matters in their lives, unless they had fallen foul of the government in some way. These views are corroborated by evidence compiled by the SPD in exile (called SOPADE) at the time. SPD analysts often despaired at the willingness of the German public to believe Nazi messages about KdF and the *Volksgemeinschaft*. This suggests that many *wanted* to believe that life under the Third Reich was better, and it seems they convinced themselves it was in reality. However, despite the claim by Richard Grunberger and David Scheonbaum that there was, in effect, a 'social revolution' in Germany that broke the old bonds of class, Tim Mason believed the Nazis had failed to destroy class divisions. What is certainly clear is that the KdF and *Volksgemeinschaft* were, at the same time, both cynical propaganda ploys to effect a change in German attitudes, but also something the Nazis dearly wanted to achieve. Hitler demanded an end to old regional and class loyalties for the sake of a 'new Germany'. That this 'new Germany' was to be a vessel for war, conquest and genocide was, of course, hardly realised by the German people in the 'quiet' years of the 1930s.

Chronology of the Third Reich

1918	9 November. Proclamation of Weimar Republic. Revoluntary unrest in Germany.
1919	September. Hitler joined the German Workers' Party (DAP).
1920	24 February. DAP published its 20-point programme and was renamed NSDAP. Foundation of *Volkischer Beobachter* newspaper.
	October. SA (*Sturmabteilung*) or Storm Troopers formed.
1923	11 January. Invasion of the Rhur.
	November. Hitler attempted to seize power in Munich Putsch.
1924	20 December. Hitler released from Lansberg having written *Mein Kampf* and Nazi Party wins seats in the *Reichstag*.
1925	June. SS formed.
	Hindenburg made President after death of Ebert.
1926	February. Hitler defeated party members who wanted a radical programme at Bamberg.
1927	July. First Nuremberg Rally.
1928	20 May. Nazi Party wins 12 seats in the *Reichstag*.
	November. Josef Goebbels appointed Propaganda Chief in the party.
	Onset of agricultural depression.
1929	November. Wall Street financial crash.
	December. Party membership reached 168,000.
1930	September. Nazi Party wins 107 seats in the *Reichstag*.
	December. Unemployment in Germany reaches 4 million.
1931	January. Ernst Roehm appointed SA Chief of Staff. Banks collapse.
1932	13 March. Presidential elections: Hindenburg defeated Hitler.
1932	April. SA temporarily banned but Nazis largest part in Prussian *Landtag*.
	31 July. Nazi Party wins 232 seats in the *Reichstag*.
	13 August. Hitler refused to take up a post under Franz von Papen.
	17 November. Papen resigned as Chancellor.
	4 December. Kurt von Schleicher appointed Chancellor.
1933	30 January. Hitler appointed Chancellor.
	27 February. *Reichstag* fire.
	March. Nazi interference in elections; Enabling Law gave Hitler emergency powers.
	March–April. Mass arrests and first concentration camps set up.
	1 April Boycott of Jewish shops and businesses proved ineffective and unpopular; establishment of the Gestapo; co-ordination period.
	7 April. Jews banned from public service employment.
1933	10 May. Burning of Jewish and left-wing books in Berlin.

	14 July. Rival parties abolished: Germany a one-party state; law passed permitting the enforced sterilisation of social 'undesirables'.
1934	29 June. Night of the Long Knives – purge of the SA leadership.
	2 August. Death of Hindenburg; Hitler proclaimed Führer.
1935	15 September. Reich Citizenship (Nuremberg) Laws define Jews and half-Jews.
1936	7 March. Reoccupation of the Rhineland.
	Goering appointed plenipotentiary of the Four Year Plan.
	1 November. Mussolini and Hitler form the Rome-Berlin Axis.
	25 November. Germany and Japan conclude Anti-Comintern Pact.
1938	13 March. *Anschluss* with Austria; Aryanisation of Jewish businesses throughout the Reich.
	August–September. Munich crisis.
	9 November. *Reichskristallnacht* pogrom against Jews.
	23 August. Hitler and Stalin concluded Nazi-Soviet Pact.
	1 September. Invasion of Poland.
	October. Euthanasia programme began.
1940	8 April. Invasion of Denmark and Norway.
	10 May. Attack on France and Belgium.
	14 June. Fall of Paris.
	13 August. Battle of Britain began.
1941	6 April. Invastion of Balkans.
	22 June. Invasion of USSR; *Einsatzgruppen* murder large numbers of Jews and Eastern Europeans.
	September. First victims killed by experimental gas chambers.
	7 December. Japan launched surprise attack on British, Dutch and American territories widening the Second World War.
1942	20 January. Wannsee Conference to settle the 'Final Solution'.
	9 April. Fall of Salonika; German control of Balkans.
	24 August. Beginning of Battle for Stalingrad.
	4 November. British victory at El Alamein.
1943	25 February. Allied air offensive against Germany by day and night.
	February. Red Army counter-offensive.
1944	6 June. Allied landings in Normandy.
	20 July. von Stauffenburg (July) plot.
	25 September. Conscription of all men.
	2 October. German army crushed Warsaw Rising.
1945	27 January. Soviet tropps liberate Auschwitz survivors.
	30 April. Hitler committed suicide.
	8 May. Surrender of Germany.
	13 August. Liberation of Belsen and Buchenwald death camps.
1946	Nuremberg trials.

Glossary

Anschluss A political union, merger or annexation, as of Austria by Germany in 1938.

Axis (line between points) euphemism for the Rome-Berlin alliance of Hitler and Mussolini.

Blitzkrieg A lightning war, a military campaign conducted with great speed.

bolshevism Revolutionary communism, as it originated in Russia.

capitalism Economic system based upon private enterprise in a free market economy.

chauvinism A prejudice.

communism The political belief in common ownership for the benefit of all citizens. In practice it means that the state owns or controls all aspects of national economic life, such as manufacturing and production, distribution, regulation and the management of labour.

coup d'état The surprise seizure of power, usually by local force of arms.

DAK *Deutsche Afrika Korps.*

Dawes Plan A financial aid package offered by the USA in 1924.

egalitarianism Belief in the fundamental right of human beings to equal treatment in all aspects of economic, social and cultural life.

Einsatzgruppe 'Reserve Squad': paramilitary murder squad.

empirical Practical, based on evidence.

'Final Solution' A more or less coded expression used in Nazi Germany to refer to the killing of the entire Jewish population after 1941.

Freikorps Paramilitaries and demobilised soliders who opposed communism.

Führer Leader.

Functionalist A school of historical thinking which argues that Hitler did not plan events, but was forced to act by the structure of the state (subordinates) or by events themselves.

Gauleiter Official responsible for controlling a region (*Gaue*).

Gemeinschaftsfremde Groups of people considered by the Nazis as 'asocial', such as Jews, gypsies, criminals, tramps, the mentally ill, and homosexuals.

Gestapo Secret police.

ghetto A zone or ward of a city used to confine Jews.

Herrenvolk Super race.

historicist Viewing past events from the modern viewpoint of hindsight, rather than from viewpoints which would have existed at the time.

historiography The study of history and historical writing.

Hitler Youth (*Hitler Jugend*) The youth organisation of the Nazi Party.

Holocaust Catastrophic destruction. The term has become indelibly associated with the Nazi genocide of Jews and other 'undesirable' social groups.

hyperinflation An extreme form of price inflation in which the national currency becomes rapidly worthless, and the economy goes out of control.

Intentionalist A school of historical thinking which argues that Hitler planned or 'intended' all the events that occurred between 1928 and 1945.

Kameradenschaft A sense of comradeship.

Kampfbund Fighting league.

KPD The German Communist Party.

Lebensraum Living space.

left wing A broad term for wishing to promote an egalitarian society through the centralised direction of economic and social affairs.

Luftwaffe The German air force.

Machtergreifung Seizure of power.

Malthusian The ideas of Thomas Malthus: population can outstrip food supply with catastrophic results.

miscegenation Racial mixing.

Mischlinge Mixed race.

Mittelstand Middle classes.

Nazi Short for *Nationalsozialistische Deutsche Arbeiterpartei*, or National Socialist German Workers Party (NSDAP).

NSBO (The Factory Cells Organisation).

NSDAP (see *Nazi*).

Ostmark Eastern region.

paramilitaries Fighters who wage military-type activities without belonging to the official state military machine.

partisans Irregular fighting forces opposed to the current regime.

plebiscite A popular vote, a referendum.

pogrom A riot.

polycratic Ruled by many different groups.

programmists Label for a group of historians who believe that Hitler was following a programme or agenda.

proletarian Relating to, or characteristic of, the mass of the people (literally urban workers).

propaganda The usually cynical use of the media to project a political message.

Putsch A sudden bid to seize political power by force, a failed *coup d'état*.

RAD (*Reichsarbeit dienst*) German Labour Service.

Rassenschande The Nazi crime of 'racial shame' for which sentences varied from one to six years.

Reich State, government, or empire.

'Reichskristallnacht' The 'night of broken glass' in November 1938, when Nazi supporters went on a murderous anti-Jewish rampage.

Reichstag Parliament or National Assembly.

Rentenmark A temporary German currency introduced at the time of hyperinflation in the 1920s.

right wing A broad term used to describe people tending to believe to a greater or lesser extent in self-reliance, private enterprise, and the market economy. But the term is also used to denote traditional and authoritarian beliefs.

Romantic Believing in the boundless possibilities of the human spirit.

SA (*Sturmabteilung*) Storm Troops, a name given to the German military formations that had achieved significant battlefield success in 1918.

SD (*Sicherheits Dienst*) Security Service, an intelligence organisation.

Slav People of broadly south-east European nationality, an ethnic definition.

Social Darwinism Application of the concept of 'survival of the fittest' to the human race.

socialism The idea in political economy that each citizen should contribute to society or the state as much as he or she can afford, and receive according to their need.

Spartakists Communist revolutionaries of 1919.

SPD Social Democratic Party.

SS (*Schutz Staffel*) A bodyguard selected from the SA on the basis on their loyalty and racial appearance.

Structuralist A school of historical thinking which argues that Hitler made decisions as a result of the structure of the state and Party.

swastika The Nazi emblem, in the form of a broken cross.

totalitarian regime A state in which the government's control of society is total.

T4 programme Code name for euthanasia in Nazi Germany.

Untermensch Sub-human.

Vichy French collaborator government of 1940–1944.

Volksgemeinschaft A sense of community.

Volksturm A local defence militia of Hitler Youth.

Waffen SS The armed version of the SS.

Wehrmacht The German army.

Further Reading

Philip Bell, *The Origins of the Second World War*. 2nd edn., London, 1997.

R. Bessel, *Life in the Third Reich*. Oxford, 1987.

Volker Berghahn, *Modern Germany*. Cambridge, 1987. Berghahn takes the long view of Nazism and its place in German history. Some of the continuities in foreign policy are striking.

Karl Bracher, *The German Dictatorship*. London, 1973. Perhaps an older work now, but still useful for an explanation of the structure of the Third Reich.

Christopher Browning, *Ordinary Men: Reserve Police Battalion 101 and the Final Solution in Poland*. London, 2001. An excellent study of paramilitaries and the genocide policy in Eastern Europe.

Alan Bullock, *Hitler: A Study in Tyranny*. London, 1962. Still a classic biography of Hitler himself. This book covers not only Hitler's career, but attempts to examine Hitler's thought processes too. Very readable.

William Carr, *Arms, Autarky and Aggression*. London, 1979. Excellent coverage of Hitler's foreign policy.

F. L. Carsten, *The Reichswehr and Politics*. Oxford, 1966. An important work examining the degree of collaboration and militarism in the German army and the political systems they served.

T. Childers, *The Nazi Voter: The Social Foundations of Fascism, 1919-33*. USA: Carolina, 1985. An attempt to answer the problem of why so many people supported the Nazism.

Richard Evans, *The Coming of the Third Reich*. London 2003, A superb new study.

Joachim Fest, *The Face of the Third Reich*. London, 1977. This book covers all the Nazi leaders and so is a useful guide to a deeper study of the Functionalist approach.

G. Fleming, *The Final Solution*. Oxford, 1986.

Robert Gellately, *The Gestapo and German Society: Enforcing Racial Policy, 1933–45*. Oxford, 1990.

H. Graml, *et al, The German Resistance to Hitler*. London, 1987.

R. Grunberger, *A Social History of the Third Reich*. London, 1974. Often seen in second hand bookshops in paperback, this is a thematic study of the regime, and deals with the various sections of society in turn. Excellent and detailed.

Klaus Hildebrand, *The Third Reich*. London, 1984. This includes a review of the historiography. A readable general survey.

Klaus Hildebrand. *The Foreign Policy of the Third Reich*. London, 1973.

Ian Kershaw, *The Nazi Dictatorship: Problems and Perspectives of Interpretation*. London, 1989. This book reviews all the historians' approaches, and the fourth edition includes more recent debates. The definitive book on the historigraphy, but hard going unless you tackle it in small chunks.

Ian Kershaw, *The Hitler Myth*. Oxford, 1987. An excellent study of Hitler as simply the arch-propagandist and a mediocre leader.

Ian Kershaw, *Hitler* (2 vols). The brilliant and thorough grand survey of Hitler's life.

G. Martel, ed., *The 'Origins of the Second World War' Reconsidered*. London, 1986.

Tim Mason, *Social Policy in the Third Reich*. Oxford 1993.

F. Neumann, *Behemoth: The Structure and Practice of National Socialism*. London, 1967. A classic Marxist view.

Jeremy Noakes, 'Nazi Voters' in *History Today*, August 1980.

J. Noakes and G. Pridham, *Nazism, 1919–1945*, vols. 1–4 Exeter, 1983. A vivid and carefully selected documentary approach to the study of Nazism. Vol. 1 deals with the rise of the Nazis to 1934; vol. 2 covers the regime from 1933 to 1939, in the domestic sphere; vol. 3 is entitled Foreign Policy, War and Holocaust; vol. 4 deals with the home front during the war. New editions have indexes.

Richard Overy, *The Nazi Economic Recovery 1932–38*. London, 1982. An exposition of Overy's views on the supremacy of the economic approach to the study of Nazism. Excellent and authoritative.

W.L. Shirer, *The Rise and Fall of the Third Reich*. London, 1960.

A. Speer, *Inside the Third Reich*. London, 1970. Useful insights into the workings of the Third Reich in practice.

Peter Stachura, ed., *The Nazi Machtergreifung*. London, 1983. A series of studies on the Nazi seizure of power.

A .J. P. Taylor, *The Origins of the Second World War*. London, 1964.

Biographies

President von Hindenburg (1847–1934)

War veteran of the First World War, Paul von Hindenburg ran the German war effort as a dictatorship with his colleague von Ludendorff. He was elected President in 1925 and again in 1932. He tried to select conservative chancellors but was persuaded by his old friend von Papen to take on Hitler in January 1933 because of their reliance on emergency decrees.

Hindenburg

Franz von Papen

Papen served in the same regiment as von Hindenburg's son and fought in the

von Papen

First World War. He led the 1932 'cabinet of barons', a conservative and nationalist coalition, to undermine the left-wing parties of Germany. Having removed left wingers from the Prussian civil service, he tried to harness Hitler and the NSDAP to give his government popular backing. The only alternative seemed to be military dictatorship. He served as Hitler's deputy in 1933, before returning to a diplomatic career. He was sentenced to imprisonment in 1947 and released after two years.

General Kurt von Schleicher

Military officer in the First World War, he intrigued against his superior the Minister of the Interior when he was a defence advisor. He was the last Chancellor before Hitler, and murdered in the 1934 purge.

von Schleicher

Heinrich Himmler (1900–1945)

He was the most colourless personality of the inner circle. An agricultural graduate, he had been a poultry farmer in Bavaria before joining the NSDAP in

Himmler

1923. He had a weak and timid appearance, yet he dreamt of a master race of tall, blond, blue-eyed supermen personified by the early recruits for Hitler's personal bodyguard, the SS. He stressed a code of honour and of family pedigree and marriage. He believed in a master race – an Aryan *Herrenvolk*. Though he had taken part in the failed attempt to seize power in Munich in

1923, his career did not develop until after he became *Reichsführer* of the SS in 1935, the chief paramilitary elite group and Hitler's bodyguard. Under Himmler its membership grew from 500 to 50,000 and it created its own network of administration. In 1933 he became President of Police in Munich and established a model camp at Dachau. Under Himmler a system of terror was carried out with great efficiency by his deputies such as Eichmann and Hoess. From its base in Bavaria the SS extended its control as the political police of Germany. He controlled a substantial portion of the real power through the police state and as a result of the terror he achieved even greater psychological power. Real power visibly shifted towards him and the SS, which determined the future face and history of the Third Reich. Subsequent posts acquired by Himmler included Reich Minister of the Interior. Even in his lifetime there was a 'Himmler myth'. The basis of his evil reputation was his association with the SS state, the extermination camps and system of terror. Behind the myth was a man who was mediocre, undistinguished by any special character trait, a man described by Albert Speer as a 'half crank, half schoolmaster'.

Hermann Goering

He was the number two Nazi, Hitler's named successor and high military and economic leader of the Third Reich. Son of a colonial officer and a much decorated air ace, he joined the Nazi Party in 1923. He took part in the failed Nazi attempt to seize power in the Putsch and was injured in the groin. He took morphine for the pain and became an addict, which later accounted for his personal and professional decline. In 1932 he was elected Speaker of the *Reichstag* having convinced Hitler of his value as a 'high society Nazi'. He was very popular but resented for his ambition and greed for power. A man of great personal vanity, he loved to show off. He acquired wealth and works of art, much of which was plundered from Nazi victims. He was one of the richest men in Germany.

Goering

Some historians see him as the most evil of the Nazis since he was brutal and ruthlessly exploited others. He was concerned with his own pursuit of power rather than with any allegiance to Hitler or the Nazi Party. Goering's contributions to the State can be summed up in the various offices he amassed. He expanded his 'circle of duties' 1933–35 to include *Reichstag* President, Reich Minister of Aviation, Prussian Minister of the Interior, Head of the Gestapo, President of the Prussian State Council, Commander-in-Chief of the *Luftwaffe*, and in 1936 Commissioner of the Four Year Plan. 1936 marked the peak of his career when he was Hitler's heir apparent, but thereafter he was physically in decline. In 1937 he was denied the office of minister in charge of the army, despite being a part of the intrigue to topple the previous holder. He was probably at the peak of his popularity in 1939, but failures during the early years of the war cost him Hitler's approval; between 1939 and 1942 he was excluded by Hitler though he still remained in control of his high offices. By 1943 he ceased to be a part of the highest leadership. He was arrested, and sentenced to death at Nuremberg but committed suicide.

Dr Josef Goebbels

He obtained a Doctorate after the First World War, but had only clerical duties in the Great War. Initially he supported the party's left-leaning 'working group' but switched allegiance to Hitler and was rewarded as *Gauleiter* of Berlin in 1926, and director of propaganda in 1929. He became *Reichsminister* of Popular Enlightenment and Propaganda in 1933. He controlled media and

Goebbels

education. He was appointed plenipotentiary of Total War when he roused to party faithful to persuade Hitler to adopt a total war programme for the economy. He was always close to Hitler except when he had an affair with a Czech actress.

Rudolf Hess

Hess served in Hitler's Regiment in the First World War and was present at his side in Putsch. He wrote down *Mein Kampf* as Hitler dictated in prison. He was a harmless idealist, devoted to Hitler but regarded as no threat at all despite his post as Deputy *Führer*. He acted as a secretary in the party but defected in 1941 to the Western powers. He may have been trying to convince Britain to join the war against Russia. He was sentenced to life imprisonment in 1945.

Hess

Martin Bormann (1900–1945?)

A protégé of Rudolf Hess, Bormann's rise through the Party was more steady than spectacular. In 1933 he was elected to the *Reichstag* and, in 1938, became *Gauleiter* of Thuringia. His opportunity for advancement came in 1941 after Hess's flight to Britain when Bormann was appointed head of the Party Chancellery. Two years later he became the Führer's official

Bormann

secretary. Described by William Shirer as 'a mole-like man who preferred to burrow in the dark recesses of Party life to further his intrigue', he was a bureaucrat and workaholic. Known to his Party colleagues as 'the man of the shadows', he was a power seeker prepared to use his position to win maximum influence. He kept detailed records on each member of the Nazi hierarchy and prevented others from having access to the Führer. He constantly schemed to manipulate or outmanoeuvre his rivals. Although he worked reasonably well with Goebbels, Goering loathed him and Himmler had little respect for him. Always available to do Hitler's bidding, who referred to him as 'my most loyal Party comrade', Bormann was responsible for reorganising the Party. This involved him in conflict with Himmler as the leader of the SS, the organisation which became the Party's rival for supremacy for power in the State. Mystery surrounds Bormann's fate after he appeared during the final days of the war. Did he flee to South America, or was he blown up by a bomb during his escape?

Albert Speer (1905–1983)

He joined the Nazi party in 1931. He was regarded by Hitler as sympathetic and reliable. In 1933 Hitler appointed him as 'builder' of the Third Reich designing the monumental buildings in Nuremberg and Berlin. He was the inventor of the 'forest of flags' and lighted vaults which gave a solemn setting to the party's mass meetings. He

Speer   refused to associate himself with the horrors of the regime and rejected an honorary rank in the SS. In 1941 he was appointed the Minister of Armaments and Munitions. He reshaped his ministry and under his direction armament production increased impressively even though he had to accept the necessity to employ slave labour from the camps. He was sentenced to 20 years imprisonment at Nuremberg.

Dr Robert Ley

A First World War pilot and chemistry graduate, Ley joined the party in 1924 and became Reich Organisation Leader in 1932, then leader of the German Labour Front. He ran the Kdf programme.

Ley

Julius Streicher

Nick-named the Jew Baiter, this outspoken racist joined the Nazis in 1922. He advocated action against the Jews and helped frame the Nuremberg Laws. He was unpopular with leading Nazis and ousted from real power by 1940. He was tried and hanged in 1945.

Streicher

Reinhard Heydrich (1904–1942)

He was Deputy Chief of the Gestapo. He looked typically German, but was of Jewish blood. He has been described as 'a young evil god of death'; 'the blond beast' and *der Henker'* (the hangman). Unlike Himmler, he was very intelligent, even brilliant in many fields, including music, sport and languages. Heydrich aimed at nothing less than the actual leadership of the Third Reich, and was utterly selfish in this aim. He was superior to Himmler, and was more dangerous and indispensable. Heydrich was the originator of the plan to develop the police force of the Third Reich from the SS into a party security police. He realised that state security offered unrestricted power. He accumulated offices rapidly. In 1934 he became head of the political police, in 1936 of the criminal police and by 1936, at the age of 32, was one of the most powerful men in Germany. In 1939, he organised the Reich Central Security Office nominally subordinate to Himmler, but it became independent and a part of his offices and activities. He developed a system of surveillance throughout Germany and Europe. He was given responsibility for destroying opposition from the churches and from the Jews. He never shrank from any task, including herding the Jews out of Europe and sending them to their deaths. He devised the plan to make vast areas of the East available as an 'experimental field' for breeding. He devised the idea of forcing the Jewish communities to organise the Final Solution at its lowest levels, by causing the Jewish councils to choose the quota of Jews to be sent to the camps. In 1941 Heydrich was sent to Prague, after Himmler and Bormann had joined forces to remove him from the centre of power and curtail his rapid rise which they regarded as threatening. In January 1942 he chaired the meeting at Wannsee at which plans were made for the 'Final Solution' of the Jewish Question. Heydrich was assassinated in Prague on 27 May 1942 by agents sent from London. Hitler was outraged and ordered savage retribution. The entire male population of the Czech village of Lidice was shot and every house burned to the ground. In Prague a further 860 were executed, as well as 360 at Brno. Himmler was very relieved at Heydrich's death, but called him a 'master by birth and by behaviour'.

Heydrich

Rudolf Hoess

Commandant of Auschwitz, he prided himself on his own efficiency and moved his family into the camp headquarters. He was executed by the Polish authorities in 1947.

Hoess

Blomberg

General Werner von Blomberg
Appointed the Commander in Chief of the German Army in 1935, Blomberg opposed plans for war in 1937 and was shamed by his marriage to a former prostitute. Hitler took over his post.

Werner Freiherr von Fritsch
A senior officer of the German army, Fritsch opposed Hitler's war plans and the SS contrived to accuse him of homosexuality. He served at the front in the attack on Poland and was killed in action, a fate some say he sought deliberately.

Fritsch

von Stauffenberg

Claus Schenk Graf von Stauffenburg
An officer with experience in North African campaigns, Stauffenburg returned to Germany when wounded and joined a conspiracy to kill Hitler. They failed to get Allied backing because they refused to give up the territory gained if they successfully deposed Hitler. The plot failed, and all the plotters were executed after torture and show trials.

Index